THE EMPEROR TITUS

BRIAN W. JONES

CROOM HELM
London & Sydney

ST. MARTIN'S PRESS
New York

937. 070924
J71e
1 45776
Jan. 1989

©1984 B.W. Jones
Croom Helm Ltd, Provident House, Burrell Row,
Beckenham, Kent BR3 1AT

Croom Helm Australia Pty Ltd,First Floor, 139 King Street,
Sydney, NSW 2001, Australia

British Library Cataloguing in Publication Data

Jones, B.W.
  The Emperor Titus.
  1. Titus, *Emperor of Rome*
  2. Roman emperors—Biography
  I. Title
  937'.07'0924   DG290
  ISBN 0-7099-1430-X

Library of Congress Cataloging in Publication Data

Jones, Brian W.
  The Emperor Titus.

  Bibliography: p.
  Includes index.
  1. Titus, Emperor of Rome, 40-81.   2. Rome – History –
Titus, 79-81.   3. Roman emperors – Biography. I. Title.
DG290.J66   1984   937'.07'0924   [B]   83-40703
ISBN 0-312-24443-6

Printed and bound in Great Britain

CONTENTS

Contents

LIST OF TABLES

LIST OF MAPS

LIST OF ABBREVIATIONS

AAN	Atti della Accademia di Scienze morali e politiche della Società nazionale di Scienze, Napoli
AC	L'Antiquité Classique
AE	L'Année Epigraphique
AFLN	Annali della Facoltà di Lettere e Filosofia dell' Università di Napoli
Agr	Agricola (Tacitus)
AJ	Antiquitates Iudaicae (Josephus)
AJA	The American Journal of Archaeology
AJAH	The American Journal of Ancient History
AJPh	The American Journal of Philology
AJTh	The American Journal of Theology
AncW	The Ancient World
Ann	Annales (Tacitus)
ANRW	Aufstieg und Niedergang der Römischen Welt (W. de Gruyter, Berlin and New York, 1970 ff.)
ANSMusN	The American Numismatic Society Museum Notes
APAW	Abhandlungen der Preussischen Akademie der Wissenschaften
BCAR	Bulletino della Commissione Archeologica Communale in Roma
BICS	Bulletin of the Institute of Classical Studies of the University of London
BJ	Bellum Iudaicum (Josephus)
BLE	Bulletin de Littérature Ecclésiastique
BSFN	Bulletin de la Société française de Numismatique
CAH	The Cambridge Ancient History
CE	Chronique D'Egypte
CIL	Corpus Inscriptionum Latinarum
CJ	The Classical Journal
CPh	Classical Philology
CQ	Classical Quarterly
CR	Classical Review
CW	The Classical World
DE	Dizionario epigrafico di antichità romane
Dial	Dialogus de Oratoribus (Tacitus)

DUJ	Durham University Journal
ES	Epigraphische Studien
G & R	Greece and Rome
GRBS	Greek, Roman and Byzantine Studies
HSPh	Harvard Studies in Classical Philology
Hist	Historiae (Tacitus)
HT	History Teaching
HThR	Harvard Theological Review
ICS	Illinois Classical Studies
IEJ	Israel Exploration Journal
IGRR	Inscriptiones Graecae ad res Romanas pertinentes
ILS	Inscriptiones Latinae Selectae
IRT	The Inscriptions of Roman Tripolitania
JDAI	Jahrbuch des Deutschen Archäologischen Instituts
JÖAI	Jahreshefte des Österreichischen archäologischen Instituts
JQR	Jewish Quarterly Review
JRS	Journal of Roman Studies
JSS	Journal of Semitic Studies
JThS	Journal of Theological Studies
LEC	Les Études Classiques
LF	Listy Filologické
MAAR	Memoirs of the American Academy in Rome
MDAI(R)	Mitteilungen des Deutschen Archäologischen Instituts (Röm. Abt.)
MEFR	Mélanges d'Archéologie et d'Histoire de l'Ecole française de Rome
MH	Museum Helveticum
NAC	Numismatica e Antichità classische
NC	Numismatic Chronicle and Journal of the Numismatic Society
NCirc	Numismatic Circular
NTS	New Testament Studies
OCD	The Oxford Classical Dictionary
P & P	Past and Present
PBA	Proceedings of the British Academy
PBSR	Papers of the British School at Rome
PCPhS	Proceedings of the Cambridge Philological Society
PEQ	Palestine Exploration Quarterly
PIR[1]	Prosopographia Imperii Romani Saeculorum I, II, III (G. Reimer, Berlin, 1897/1898)
PIR[2]	Prosopographia Imperii Romani Saeculorum I, II, III (W. de Gruyter, Berlin and Leipzig, 1933 ff.)
PP	La Parola del Passato
QAL	Quaderni di Archeologia della Libia
QAP	Department of Antiquities in Palestine Quarterly
RA	Revue Archéologique
RBi	Revue Biblique
RBPh	Revue Belge de Philologie et d'Histoire
RD	Revue Historique de Droit français et étranger

RE	Real-Encyklopaedie der classischen Altertumwissenschaft
REA	Revue des Etudes Anciennes
REG	Revue des Etudes Grecques
REJ	Revue des Etudes Juives
REL	Revue des Etudes Latines
RFIC	Rivista di Filologia e di Istruzione Classica
RhM	Rheinisches Museum für Philologie
RIL	Rendiconti dell' Istituto Lombardo, Classe di Lettere, Scienze morali e storiche
RIN	Rivista Italiana di Numismatica e Scienze affini
RPAA	Rendiconti della Pontificia Accademia di Archeologia
RPh	Revue de Philologie, de Littérature, et d'Histoire ancienne
RSA	Rivista storica dell' Antichità
RSR	Revue des Sciences Religieuses
TAPhA	Transactions of the American Philological Association
TAPhS	Transactions of the American Philosophical Society
Titus	Diuus Titus (Suetonius)
Vesp	Diuus Vespasianus (Suetonius)
WS	Wiener Studien
YCS	Yale Classical Studies
ZPE	Zeitschrift für Papyrologie und Epigraphik

PREFACE

It has been said that history represents the propaganda of the victors; but, if so, contemporary or near contemporary accounts of the Roman emperors of the first century A.D. clearly give the lie to such a generalization. Tiberius, Gaius, Claudius, Nero and Domitian are hardly presented in favourable colours. The senatorially inclined sources resented the loss of their order's preeminence. It was the vanquished who provided the propaganda.

For a variety of reasons Titus' brief reign has suffered a different fate. Of some significance is its very brevity - yet that did not save Gaius' reputation. Then, too, the relevant books of Tacitus' *Historiae* have not survived, Suetonius' later *Lives*, for whatever the reason, are less satisfactory than the earlier ones, whilst Josephus' *Bellum Iudaicum*, limited in scope if not in extent, was intended to eulogize his protectors. Pliny was more concerned with what he saw as the tyranny of Domitian's reign and, presumably, was not unaffected by his uncle's close association with Titus. In any case, his references to him are brief but innocuous. Essentially, though, the senatorial tradition, consistently hostile to Domitian, sought to illuminate his alleged villainy by stressing his brother's virtues. So Philostratus, Dio and the writers of the fourth century (Aurelius Victor, the epitomator of the *De Caesaribus*, Eutropius, Ammianus Marcellinus and Asconius) are all highly eulogistic, as are the *Scriptores Historiae Augustae* and Joannes Lydus. Whoever, if not Suetonius, first applied to Titus the phrase "darling of mankind" (it was not original - see Cicero, *Phil.* 6.5.1) managed to set the official version of his character and therefore of his reign - not that it should be automatically rejected on that score.

The problem of the literary sources, then, is a serious one. Essentially, we have to rely on Suetonius, Josephus and the epitome of Dio Cassius made in Byzantine times, and they, apart from Josephus, are concerned mainly with the events of Rome and, to a lesser extent, those of Italy. The empire as a whole they regarded as of far less importance. Fortunately, modern scholarship has corrected the imbalance - or at least to some extent. Epigraphists, numismatists, papyrologists and archaeologists have provided abundant evidence for a broader view of Titus' principate.

Not all of this is readily available to those without Latin and Greek. In this regard, some explanation is required. I have tried to provide both text and translation of the more important inscriptions (as well as the literary evidence) relevant to Titus' reign. I regret that it has not been practicable to include the Greek texts, though that lacuna can be filled by consulting the readily available Loeb editions.

I am grateful to the University of Queensland for support during my recent periods of study leave when much of this book was written, to Mr Danny Sheehy of this University's Audio-Visual Services Department for preparing the maps, and to my colleagues in the Classics and Ancient History Department's Antiquities Museum for the Sestertius of Titus. In particular I am indebted to Mr Erik Estensen for his many valuable suggestions on an earlier draft of this book. Responsibility for the errors and misconceptions that remain is, of course, mine alone.

BWJ
Brisbane

Chapter One

EARLY CAREER

BACKGROUND

Titus was born at Rome on December 30, A.D. 39[1], in a small
room of a rather unpretentious house near the Septizonium[2].
His family, though certainly not of ancient or noble lineage,
had some claim to renown: Suetonius (*Vesp.* 1.2) was able to
trace its origin back to the civil war between Caesar and
Pompey. According to his account, Titus' great-grandfather,
Titus Flavius Petro, came from Reate (now Rieti), a town in
the Sabine territory on the Avens (Velino) at the point where
the Via Salaria crossed the river. In Cicero's time, it was a
prefecture, but had gained municipal status together with its
own magistrates by 27 B.C.[3] Petro served as a soldier in
Pompey's army, possibly holding the rank of centurion: his
military achievements seem to have been limited to fleeing
from the field of Pharsalus[4] (in Thessaly, 48 B.C.).
Ultimately, he was pardoned by Caesar, received an honourable
discharge and proceeded to conduct a successful banking
business: his descendants inherited at least his financial
acumen. We do not know whether he managed to achieve equestrian status, though it is reasonable to suppose that he had
the means to do so, for his wife Tertulla (*PIR*[1] T 87) was also
wealthy, owning estates at Cosa, a coastal town in Etruria
with an important harbour, the *portus Cosanus*.
    His son, Titus Flavius Sabinus (= Sabinus I: *PIR*[2] F 351),
had a not dissimilar career. There are three versions of his
military service: according to one account, he was a senior
centurion, in another he was forced to retire from command of
a cohort through ill-health, and in the third he avoided
service entirely. On the other hand, he did accumulate considerable wealth and gained equestrian rank. It seems that he
was in charge of the *quadragesima Asiae* (probably at the level
of *pro-magister*), supervising the collection of various import
duties with such aplomb that the grateful citizens of a number
of cities in Asia erected statues in memory of "An Honest Tax-
Gatherer" (*Vesp.* 1.2-3)[5]. Subsequently, he became a banker in

Switzerland. Through these various activities, he acquired
sufficient wealth to provide both his sons with the senatorial
census; at the same time, he saw the necessity of gaining
access to highly placed patrons, and, as will be seen, prospered in this venture also.

His wife, Vespasia Polla (*PIR*[1] V 300), was undoubtedly
the most eminent of Titus' grandparents. Her father,
Vespasius Pollio (*PIR*[1] V 299), had risen to the rank of
praefectus castrorum, a post held by experienced officers,
especially senior centurions, whilst her brother Vespasius
(*PIR*[1] V 298) had entered the senate (the first of Titus'
ancestors to achieve this honour), presumably during the reign
of Augustus, and had eventually held a praetorship. Suetonius
attests to her family's renown and antiquity, citing as
evidence the numerous tombs of the Vespasii at a place called
Vespasiae on the road from Nursia to Spoletum (*Vesp*. 1.4). Of
the three children born to Sabinus I and Vespasia Polla, two
survived. The elder was Titus' uncle, Titus Flavius Sabinus
(= Sabinus II: *PIR*[2] F 352), destined for a highly successful
administrative career culminating in a long tenure of the city
prefecture under Nero. His significance in Titus' career will
be considered later. The younger, Titus Flavius Vespasianus
(*PIR*[2] F 398), became emperor. These relationships are summarized in Table 1.

TABLE 1: TITUS' GRANDPARENTS AND GREAT-GRANDPARENTS

T. Flavius Petro m. Tertulla   Vespasius Pollio
          | ┌──────────┴────────┐
      Sabinus I m. Vespasia Polla Vespasius
     ┌─────────┴─────────┐
  Sabinus II   Vespasian

The brothers' immediate families merit examination. The
name of Sabinus II's wife has not survived, but the Flavia
Sabina (*PIR*[2] F 440) who married L. Caesennius Paetus (*PIR*[2] C
173) was probably his daughter[6]. Possible children of that
marriage are L. Junius Caesennius Paetus (*PIR*[2] C 174) and L.
Caesennius Sospes (*PIR*[1] S 567)[7]. Less easy to determine is
their relationship with A. Caesennius Gallus (*PIR*[2] C 170)[8].
For the moment it will be sufficient to note that these four
Caesennii were all eminent senators of consular rank, the
oldest of them gaining that honour under Nero[9]. Sabinus II's
son was probably the T. Flavius Sabinus (= Sabinus III: *PIR*[2]
F 353 and 354) who held two consulships and the curatorship of
public works under Vespasian and Titus. His sons were T.
Flavius Sabinus IV (*PIR*[2] F 355), who married Titus' daughter
Julia (*PIR*[2] F 426), and T. Flavius Clemens, whose wife was
Domitilla III (*PIR*[2] F 418), daughter of Titus' sister,
Domitilla II (*PIR*[2] F 417): both held ordinary consulships
under Domitian. For these relationships, see Tables 2 and 3.

TABLE 2: TITUS' COUSIN AND DESCENDANTS

Flavia Sabina m. L. Caesennius Paetus, *cos. ord.* 61

L. Junius Caesennius Paetus, /   L. Caesennius Sospes,
    cos. suff. 79   *cos. suff.* 114

A. Caesennius Gallus, *cos. suff.* by 81

TABLE 3: TITUS' UNCLE AND DESCENDANTS

Sabinus II

Flavia Sabina   Sabinus III, *cos. II suff.* 72

Sabinus IV,   T. Flavius Clemens
cos. ord. 82,   *cos. ord.* 95,
m. Julia   m. Domitilla III

Vespasian's wife was far less distinguished. A former slave, so it seems[10], Flavia Domitilla (*PIR*[2] F 416) was the daughter of a quaestor's clerk, Flavius Liberalis (*PIR*[2] F 302), and at one time the mistress of an equestrian, Statilius Capella, from Sabrata in Africa. Some connection between Flavius Liberalis and Sabinus I is of course possible, and similarly with the ancestors of that interesting pair, L. Flavius Silva Nonius Bassus (*PIR*[2] F 368), the conqueror of Masada, and C. Salvius Liberalis Nonius Bassus (*PIR*[1] S 105)[11]. Vespasian's daughter Domitilla II[12] seems to have married Q. Petillius Cerialis Caesius Rufus (*PIR*[1] P 191), who already had two sons, Q. Petillius Rufus (*PIR*[1] P 193) and C. Petillius Firmus (*PIR*[2] F 159): the father held two suffect consulships in Vespasian's reign, the eldest son held one suffect consulship then and a second, ordinary, in 83 whilst the younger son, a young man of great promise, seems to have died young[13]. These relationships are summarized in Table 4.

In later years, Vespasian was fond of parading his "obscure birth", which was in keeping with his unostentatious lifestyle (*Vesp.* 12.1). However, this was a deliberate ploy on his part, as he strove to distance himself and his family from the taint of upper-class corruption, and so from one feature of the latter part of the Julio-Claudian dynasty. If this was a matter of chosen policy, one is entitled to question the real standing of his family. Certainly, it could not boast a stemma similar to that of Republican *nobiles*, but such families died out rapidly in the empire and were all but extinct by the time of Nero's death. A new aristocracy began to grow to fill the void, and many of the new families, amongst them the Flavii, could not trace their origins beyond the civil war - or, if they could, did not advertise the fact.

Table 4: TITUS' IMMEDIATE FAMILY

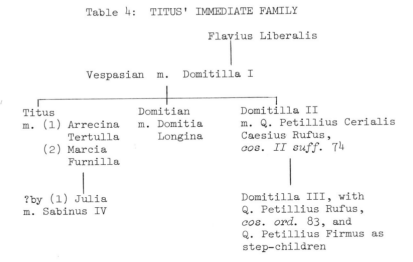

Flavius Liberalis

Vespasian m. Domitilla I

Titus	Domitian	Domitilla II
m. (1) Arrecina	m. Domitia	m. Q. Petillius Cerialis
Tertulla	Longina	Caesius Rufus,
(2) Marcia		*cos. II suff.* 74
Furnilla		

?by (1) Julia
m. Sabinus IV

Domitilla III, with
Q. Petillius Rufus,
cos. ord. 83, and
Q. Petillius Firmus as
step-children

This growth necessitated rapid advancement of comparative un-
knowns, who, as they became established, perpetuated their
families and their influence in the accustomed manner by
marriage ties and patronage. So significant sociological
changes were occurring during the first century of the empire,
as the rise to power of two of the emperors of 69, Vitellius
and Vespasian, clearly illustrates. The equestrian Publius
Vitellius had been one of Augustus' imperial procurators; his
four sons (Aulus, Quintus, Publius and Lucius) obtained
senatorial status - the eldest, Aulus, reaching the consulship
(suffect) in 32 and the youngest, Lucius, gaining the rare
honour of a third ordinary consulship in 47 as colleague of
the emperor Claudius. In the third generation, Lucius' son
became emperor. The criteria for advancement were many, and
included wealth, ability and access to patronage, but ambition
played a significant part, and in this quality the Flavians
were not lacking. At Titus' birth, the family could be placed
in the category of emergent - but his mother's status suggests
that the Flavians were still not sufficiently eminent to
attract marriage ties with leading families.

PATRONS

In the last years of Augustus' reign and the early years of
Tiberius', Sabinus I clearly prospered; he had acquired
wealth and, so it would seem, highly placed patrons, for his
two sons were offered the *latus clauus*[14]. Who his patrons
were cannot be determined with absolute certainty, but it is
not unlikely that he had managed to gain access to the circle
of Germanicus and, following his death, to that of his mother

Antonia; thereby his sons gained prominent patrons amongst
the closest associates of Germanicus' brother, the emperor
Claudius. These included representatives of four very powerful families, the Petronii, Pomponii, Plautii and Vitellii,
which were linked together by marriage ties, by their common
interests and by the patronage of Antonia's circle[15].
     One example of their marriage ties will suffice. Early
in Augustus' reign, Aulus Plautius, *cos. suff.* 1 B.C., married
a Vitellia; their daughter Plautia married Publius Petronius,
cos. suff. 19; whilst Petronia, the daughter of that marriage,
became the wife of Aulus Vitellius, the future emperor[16].
These four families did not constitute a permanent league in
any sense; but, as was the normal practice, they were prepared to promote the careers of men with promise, so long as it
advanced in some way their individual or collective interests
to do so. Nor was their influence constantly powerful. From
16 to 19, the year of Germanicus' death, members of the group
held four consulships, but only six during the remaining
eighteen years of Tiberius' reign[17]: no doubt Tiberius bore
in mind the attempts of Publius Vitellius to avenge the death
of Germanicus under whom he served on the Rhine and Danube
(*Ann.* 3.10 ff.). With the accession of Claudius, however, the
position quickly changed, and between 41 and 48 seven consulships were awarded to representatives of the group, i.e. in 41
(Q. Pomponius Secundus, *suff.*), 43 (L. Vitellius, *II ord.*), 44
(P. Calvisius Sabinus P. Pomponius Secundus, *suff.*), 45 (Ti.
Plautius Silvanus Aelianus, *suff.*), 47 (L. Vitellius, *III
ord.*), 48 (A. Vitellius, *ord.*; L. Vitellius, *suff.*)[18]. This
was the period of rapid advancement for Vespasian and Sabinus
II, as will be seen: Claudius and his advisors must have
known them well and trusted them. The part played by their
father Sabinus I in their ultimate success cannot be neglected; for too long the farsightedness and political dexterity
he possessed have not received the credit they merit.
     Another source of patronage was the contact Vespasian
himself secured with Antonia's court. Suetonius attests to
the influence wielded by Antonia Caenis, a trusted servant of
Germanicus' and Claudius' mother Antonia, and mistress of
Vespasian in both his youth and old age[19]. Through her, he
could well have become known to the household, one which had
very close connections with an oriental group that was to be
of immense help to him in the civil war. Their number
included M. Julius Agrippa who assisted the Flavians in
Judaea, and Ti. Julius Alexander who was prefect of Egypt in
69. No doubt Vespasian had inherited his father's political
acumen.
     The influence of these patrons should be kept in per-
spective. Until the reign of Claudius, the progress of the
brothers seems to have been unspectacular. Little is known of
the early career of Titus' uncle, Sabinus II[20]: understandably,
Vespasian's is better documented. It would appear that, after

5

spending his military tribunate in Thrace, he held the
quaestorship in 35, at the age of twenty-six or one year above
the legal minimum, though this delay may be explained by his
initial reluctance to follow his elder brother into a senatorial career[21]. At his first attempt to secure the aedileship
he was defeated, and, though managing to be elected in the
following year, he gained the lowest total of votes and thereby sixth and last place[22]. Gaius was apparently unimpressed
with his efficiency as aedile, if we are to believe Suetonius,
since he ordered him to be covered with mud for having
neglected his duty of keeping the streets clean (*Vesp.* 5.3).
So there was no rapid advancement here, no indication of
future preferment beyond the normal. For the brothers' early
careers[23], see Table 5.

TABLE 5: EARLY CAREER OF SABINUS II AND VESPASIAN

	SABINUS II		VESPASIAN
ca 3	Birth	9	Birth
ca.21	??*XXvir*	ca.28-29	?*XXvir*
ca.23 -26	?laticlave tribune	ca.30-33	laticlave tribune (Thrace: perhaps with *legio IV Scythica*)
ca.28	quaestor	ca.35	quaestor in Crete-Cyrene
ca.31	tribune of the people/ aedile		
ca.33	praetor		

Towards the end of Gaius' principate, Vespasian gained
the emperor's favour by some well-timed public flattery. In
39, the conspiracy of Lentulus Gaetulicus and Aemilius Lepidus
against the emperor was suppressed by Gaius himself at Mainz
shortly before the end of October[24]. Then, in 40, the emperor
moved against the Cannenefates, a German tribe on the North
Sea coast, where his subordinates were able to achieve some
success[25]. We are told by Suetonius that, in his praetorship,
Vespasian made a special effort to win Gaius' support, and he
cites his speech (or possibly speeches) in the senate asking
for extraordinary games to be held for the emperor's victory
in Germany and for Lentulus and Aemilius Lepidus to be "cast
out unburied". He also took the opportunity to thank Gaius
before the senate for the honour of an invitation to dinner[26].
Traditionally, it has been assumed that Vespasian held the

praetorship in 39, the year of Titus' birth. But this is unlikely, for, whilst ancient commentators remark on the coin-
cidence of Vespasian's consular year and the year of Domitian's
birth, nothing similar is said of his praetorship[27].
No less significant than his election as praetor *in
primis*[28] and his successful flattery of the emperor was his
relationship with Gaius' sister Agrippina. She had been
forced to return from Germany to Rome with the remains of her
lover Lepidus, and if she left Mainz immediately after the
cremation, she would probably have reached Rome early in 40[29].
If Vespasian's proposal to refuse burial to the conspirators
was deliberately timed to coincide with her arrival - he would
have assumed the office of praetor by that time - then the
subsequent deterioration in their relationship may have had
its origins in this incident.

With the accession of Claudius, the patronage secured by
Sabinus I bore fruit. Vespasian was advanced rapidly, com-
manding a legion in the invasion of Britain, receiving two
priesthoods (by 47 at the latest), and finally securing the
consulship in 51[30]. The role played by his patrons was
considerable. L. Vitellius held two ordinary consulships (in
43 and 47) and the censorship, on each occasion having the
emperor as his colleague. Aulus Plautius had the overall
command in Britain and was clearly the senior general of the
time[31]. Within the imperial household, virtual control lay in
the hands of Antonia's freedman Pallas, together with
Narcissus, who had been in Claudius' service before his
accession[32]. Vespasian had the advantage of the support of
them all: it was said that he was once a client of Vitellius
and that he received his post in Britain through the influence
of Narcissus[33].
Titus' uncle Sabinus II attained greater eminence. He
accompanied his younger brother to Britain and was awarded a
consulship in 44. Subsequently, he may have held a three-year
post (ca. 45-48) and was then appointed *legatus Augusti pro
pr. Moesiae*, a position he held at least until the end of
Claudius' reign[34].

EDUCATION

It was undoubtedly as a result of his uncle's and father's
achievements that Titus was granted the honour of a court
education (*Titus* 2). As far as the ancient sources indicate,
this was somewhat rare. Otho's grandfather had been reared in
the house of Livia (Suet., *Otho* 1) and Marcus Aurelius grew up
in Hadrian's court (HA *Marc. Anton.* 4.1). On the other hand,
the sons of foreign rulers were sometimes treated in this way -
witness Agrippa II who was educated at Claudius' court (*AJ*
19) - but this may not have been entirely an honour. At all
events, Titus was brought up with the son of Claudius and
Messallina who was appropriately named Britannicus, after the

victory in which Titus' uncle and father had played no small
part[35]. The boys, so we are told, shared the same teachers
and the same curriculum (*Titus* 2). Although Britannicus had a
number of tutors, the name of only one survives, that of
Sosibius, who was probably a freedman[36]. Titus enjoyed the
friendship of Britannicus and revered his memory. According
to Suetonius, "Titus set up a golden statue[37] of his friend in
the palace, and dedicated another equestrian statue of ivory
and attended it in the processions in the Circus, where it is
still carried to this day"[38]. Some scholars have also
suggested that it was then that Titus had a sestertius struck
in memory of his young friend, though this is somewhat unlikely, and the coin in question was probably issued by Claudius[39].
     So Titus spent his youth among the children of wealthy,
high-born and influential families, and emerged in no way as a
social outcast. Quite the contrary, for it may be inferred
from the sources that he won the esteem of his companions by
the charm of his personality, an attribute that Suetonius
(*Titus* 1) notes in him as either inborn, or cultivated, or else
the result of good luck[40]. In any case, it was to serve him
well in the years ahead. His early opportunities obviously
had a marked effect on his future prospects and the development of his character. A reasonably clear outline of these
years can be deduced by considering the normal educational
procedures adopted for boys of senatorial families[41], together with what is known specifically of Titus during this
period and with the talents he later displayed. In general,
it appears that the end product of the educational programme
was a highly cultured man. Titus wrote tragedies and poems in
Greek (Eutropius, 7.14) and also poems in Latin (*Titus* 3.2),
most of them, probably, before his accession to the throne[42].
     His early education was probably entrusted to a *paedagog-
us*, under whom he would have learned the elements of writing
in Latin and Greek; his mastery of both languages attests to
the success of this early training[43]. At the age of ten to
twelve, he would have begun instruction under a *grammaticus*,
studying classical literature with emphasis on appreciation,
analysis and paraphrase; he would also have learned to write
aphorisms, moral essays and character sketches[44]. The
curriculum included the study of geometry and athletics[45];
the latter must have been undertaken, for the ancient
authorities attest to his muscular physique, graceful and
dignified bearing, and expertise in riding and in handling
arms[46]. He was also taught music, an indication of a liberal
curriculum, for although Quintilian, Seneca and Cicero
realized the educational value of music, it never became an
integral part of education in Rome[47]. Titus responded well to
his musical training - he sang pleasantly and enjoyed playing
the *cithara* (*Titus* 3.2).
     When a boy had made sufficient progress under the
grammaticus, he was then placed in the care of a *rhetor* who

taught him the art of declamation. Even in ancient times, opinions varied as to the terminal date of studies with the *grammaticus*[48], and, with Titus, the position is complicated further because of the uncertain political situation in which the family had become involved. Military training was not neglected. Whilst Britannicus and Titus were not educated with Nero, even after he had come to live on the Palatine, it is likely that military exercises were conducted together, under the eye of the praetorian prefects Geta and Crispinus, and subsequently Burrus[49]. It is interesting to note that Titus seems to have maintained close links with the praetorians. His first wife, Arrecina Tertulla, was the daughter of Gaius' praetorian prefect, Arrecinus Clemens; her brother, also Arrecinus Clemens[50], became the first senator to hold the praetorian command (*Hist.* 4.68; *Titus* 6); Titus' cousin, Sabinus III, married, so it seems, another Arrecina, sister of Tertulla and Clemens[51]; and finally Titus himself served as prefect for most of Vespasian's reign.

By the time Titus had reached the age of twelve, his father's popularity with the regime had declined. The lacuna in Tacitus' *Annales* (Books *VII* to *X*) severely inhibits any attempt to reconstruct the political dissensions which resulted in the disintegration of the group supporting the Flavians, but their influence seems to have reached its zenith ca. 47/48 and then to have waned, not long after the disposal of the illustrious Valerius Asiaticus. Accused of treason by Publius Suillius[52], a known supporter of Messallina and Sosibius, he was hastily arrested and tried in Claudius' chamber in the presence of Messallina; at her instigation, Vitellius subtly persuaded the emperor to pass the death sentence and Asiaticus was compelled to take his own life (*Ann.* 11.1-3). Sosibius' role had been to arouse the emperor's suspicions of Asiaticus' wealth and power: he was duly rewarded with one million sesterces. Officially, the award was for "giving Britannicus the benefit of his teaching and Claudius that of his advice" (11.4). Subsequently came the group's decline. With the death of Messallina in 48, Claudius sought assistance in the appointment of a replacement: Vitellius and Pallas supported Agrippina, whilst Narcissus favoured Aelia Paetina. As a result, Narcissus and Agrippina became bitter enemies; the group behind the Flavians lost unity and influence. It was not a sudden occurrence but rather became more and more obvious as Claudius' reign came to an end and Nero's began. The Vitellii and Petronii supported Nero and were rewarded: Petronius Turpilianus was ordinary consul in 61. But they did not support each other, as the divorce of Petronia and Aulus Vitellius publicly indicated[53]. The Plautii, with the possible exception of Ti. Plautius Silvanus Aelianus, suffered most, with at least two of them being either executed or asked to commit suicide[54]. But the most significant factor was the death of Lucius Vitellius ca. 51, which meant that

there was no one influential enough to hold the group together.
The extent of the Flavians' decline is not easily measur-
ed or assessed. The brothers displayed typical Flavian
sagacity by splitting their support between the two contending
parties, Sabinus II either siding with Vitellius or else
remaining neutral, whilst Vespasian, in view of his attitude
to Agrippina in 41, together with his debt to Narcissus for
having advanced his career, inevitably followed the latter's
lead. In support of such a stand, it should be noted that in
49 it was by no means certain that Agrippina would emerge
triumphant: Claudius' freedmen had removed one of his wives
before. Sabinus chose correctly, as it turned out: witness
his subsequent continual employment by both Claudius and Nero.
For a summary of the brothers' careers from 40 to 70[55], see
Table 6.

TABLE 6: LATER CAREER OF SABINUS II AND VESPASIAN

	SABINUS II		VESPASIAN
42-43	with Vespasian in Britain	40	praetor
		ca.43 -47	*legatus legionis II* in Britain
44	consul	44	*ornamental triumphalia* and two priesthoods
ca.45 -48	?unknown office for three years		
ca.50 -56	*legatus Augusti pro pr. Moesiae*	51	consul
ca.56 -58	*praefectus urbi I*		
61	*curator census Gallici designatus*		
61-68	?*praefectus urbi II*	ca.63	*proconsul Africae; comes Neronis*
69	?*praefectus urbi III*	67-69	*legatus Augusti pro pr. exercitus in Judaea*

At first glance, Vespasian seems to have suffered a major set-
back: one scholar has suggested that he was actually forced
to withdraw from public life[56], but there is no positive

evidence that this was so. As a senator and priest, he had
duties to perform in Rome[57]. Now some senators known to be
imperial favourites were often retained in Rome, close to the
emperor. Consider the career of M. Ulpius Traianus, the
future emperor. A loyal supporter of Domitian at the time of
Saturninus' revolt against the emperor in 89, he held no
official post for the rest of the reign, as far as our literary and epigraphic sources indicate[58]. This lacuna does not
prove loss of influence - it could just as well suggest that
he was retained at the seat of power, where his support was
considered to be more useful. Whilst Vespasian's career from
51 to the death of Agrippina was, at best, unimpressive, it
does not prove banishment from public life. If one were to
suggest that it did, then a good many senators at every period
of the empire must have suffered a similar fate, for compar-
able gaps exist in a high proportion of known senatorial
careers. Each case must be considered on its merits. With
Trajan, the likeliest interpretation is that the emperor
preferred to have him in Rome where he could be consulted;
Vespasian, on the other hand, was probably no longer welcome
at court. He was banished from intimacy with the emperor but
not from his senatorial duties.

Titus remained with Britannicus, but, as Nero's prospects
were advanced, those of Britannicus suffered: he received
neither honour nor care and those who were devoted to him were
either removed or killed by Agrippina[59]. It would seem that
after 51 the political significance of Titus' education at
court was minimal[60]. Yet he must have learned much from two
masters of intrigue, Narcissus and Sosibius: their influence
on the future emperor was profound. He remained with
Britannicus throughout Claudius' reign and, indeed, until the
very end of the unfortunate prince's life: he was said to
have been next to him at the time of his death (*Titus* 2) and
to have risked his life by draining the cup in sympathy for
his friend[61].

Titus' education involved a liberal curriculum presided
over by a tutor with close access to the most influential
group in the imperial circle and on whose advice the emperor
relied. His military training was conducted by the praetorian
prefects. Even in Claudius' last years, the quality of his
formal education was surely maintained and one suspects that
Titus was better able than Britannicus to handle the atmos-
phere of that time. He had developed friendships with some of
the most influential families and no doubt impressed many by
his manner. Our sources all attest to his skill in diplomacy,
a skill that his father was subsequently to rely on heavily,
and this was no doubt one of the products of his early years
at court.

EARLY POLITICAL AND MILITARY CAREER

With a father and uncle of consular status, Titus could well
have been expected to undertake the senatorial *cursus*. His
first ten years had coincided with Vespasian's sudden rise to
prominence in the forties after an inglorious career in the
preceding decade, but his adolescence was marked by his
father's fall from favour after holding the consulship in 51.
Leading the opposition was the formidable Agrippina, who
"hated any friend of Narcissus even after Narcissus' death"
(*Vesp.* 4.2). Her forceful personality and hostility towards
Narcissus' friends were as significant for Titus' career as
for his father's. The years immediately following his sixteenth birthday (Dec. 30, 55) were critical, for Claudius and
Britannicus had been removed, and Titus was of an age to take
the first steps in what could be a senatorial career. But his
patrons[62] were now virtually ineffective and represented no
bulwark against Agrippina.

As the son of a senator, he presumably held the *latus
clauus* automatically on assuming the *toga uirilis*[63]. Thus,
like all young *laticlauii* from the time of Augustus, he would
have been encouraged to attend meetings of the senate, become
familiar with the proceedings, and thereby develop contacts
with those of influence and experience[64]. This he no doubt
did: possibly he was able to follow up relationships he had
already established from his earlier years at the court of
Claudius. But these advantages did not guarantee a successful
career.

First of all came the vigintivirate: it seems to have
been a "necessary preliminary to a senatorial career"[65] for
those aspirants whose fathers were senators. According to Dio,
it was made obligatory shortly before 13 B.C.[66] Now this
cannot be accepted without qualification[67]. Some senators of
equestrian origin omitted it, or rather, it is not recorded on
their career inscriptions[68]; on the other hand, Germanicus'
son had to seek permission to avoid it, a concession that was
refused to the prospective sons-in-law of Claudius[69]. In
other words, omission of the vigintivirate probably indicates
non-senatorial origins. For Titus, then, the post was
essential.

A potential senator was required to serve a year at Rome
in this office. It consisted of four colleges whose members
were graded, possibly according to social status, influential
connections and/or the emperor's view of his potential. Any
attempt to specify to which of the four Titus belonged is
admittedly speculative, but this does not preclude a brief
investigation. Two were of higher social standing, the
tresuiri monetales[70] and the *decemuiri stlitibus iudicandis*.
The former was reserved in the first instance for patricians,
whilst other vacancies went to plebeians with powerful patrons
and obvious potential for future command. It has been

suggested that Vespasian had been adlected *inter patricios* in 47/48 through the influence of Vitellius[71]. If this is so, and it cannot be proved, then Titus was qualified for this college on these grounds alone; on the other hand, the military record of his father and brother may well have marked him out as a possible commander. The second college, the *decemuiri stlitibus iudicandis*, seems to have been for those intending to pursue a career in the courts[72]. Perhaps in view of Suetonius' assertion that Titus did not intend to make court work his career (*Titus* 4.2) and was unenthusiastic about it, this college may be rejected. Of the two of lower status, the *quattuoruiri uiarum curandarum*, like the *tresuiri monetales*, tended to be reserved for future military commanders, whilst an analysis of the careers of senators who began as *tresuiri capitales* shows that only a very small percentage ever attained distinction[73], and these may be regarded as abnormal, for they can all be explained by exceptional circumstances[74]. We may be justified then in excluding this college, thus leaving two possible choices, the *tresuiri monetales* and the *quottuoruiri uiarum curandarum*. The former may well be more likely in view of Titus' family connections and background. It is pointless to speculate further, but the possibility that he began his career as one of the *quattuoruiri uiarum curandarum* cannot be completely rejected[75].

The completed seventeenth year was required for entry into one of these offices[76], but there is no evidence whatsoever that men always served at the earliest date. It is generally assumed that Titus did in fact enter the office at this time, even though Agrippina was then at the height of her power[77]. The assumption is unwarranted. Indeed, it is likely that many aspiring senators were well over seventeen years of age when they held their vigintivirate office: there were twenty such posts available each year but only half as many military tribunates[78], and until their completed twenty-fourth year, no other office was open to them. The earlier this preliminary office was held, the greater the backlog of anxious quaestorian aspirants. Again, the responsibilities of a *tresuir monetalis* or of a *decemuir stlitibus iudicandis*, for example, were probably more than merely nominal, more than could reasonably be expected of any seventeen-year-old.

There is no reason to assume that it was regular or somehow obligatory for senatorial offices to be held at the legal minimum age. Consider the consulship. Most of the consuls of Domitian's reign[79] whose ages can be determined with some sort of accuracy held the *fasces* when they were beyond the legal minimum age for that post, and not all of them were in disfavour[80]. C. Antius A. Julius Quadratus was in almost continual employment from the time of his praetorship in 73/74 until his consulship in 94 when he would presumably have been at least five years above the legal minimum age for the post[81]. He must have been trusted, since he commanded a military province at the time of Saturninus' revolt[82]. No one could hold a post in the vigintivirate before completing his seventeenth year; equally it was not obligatory to hold it then and only then. Now it seems that the significant honour of an imperial commendation for the quaestorship went primarily to those who, in their vigintivirate office, had been either *tresuiri monetales* or *quattuoruiri uiarum curandarum* rather than *decemuiri stlitibus iudicandis* or *tresuiri capitales*[83]; according to Birley[84], the first two offices also provided the bulk of those senators who went on to high military commands in the imperial service. Therefore, he argues, at the very beginning of the senatorial career, the emperor made a selection of those on whom he would particularly depend, and so drafted the abler candidates into the imperial service. In such circumstances, there would be no point in coming to an early decision. It could easily be postponed until, for instance, the candidate's nineteenth or twentieth year, still leaving him adequate time for up to three years' service as military tribune[85] before being eligible for the quaestorship.

Vespasian and a number of his relatives prospered after the death of Agrippina. His own proconsular year (in Africa) could well have been 61/62, though some scholars place it as late as 64/65[86]. L. Caesennius Paetus, almost certainly the husband of Titus' cousin Flavia Sabina, became ordinary consul in 61[87]; his colleague was P. Petronius Turpilianus whose father, P. Petronius, was a prominent member of a group that favoured Vespasian and his brother in earlier days[88]. Q. Petillius Cerialis Caesius Rufus, very probably Titus' brother-in-law, could well have been appointed to the command of a legion then, for it is in 60 that he is first attested as *leg. leg. IX Hispanae*[89]. Plautius Silvanus, for many years one of Vespasian's supporters, was to receive a long-overdue military command, Moesia, at this time[90]. The only exception was Vespasian's brother, T. Flavius Sabinus, whose career continued on uninterrupted through the fifties and sixties[91]. But if he could not overcome Agrippina's hostility and have Vespasian brought out of his *otium secessusque* (*Vesp.* 4.2), there is no reason to assume that he would have been of any help to Vespasian's son. In all, whilst there is no evidence for the precise date of Titus' vigintivirate, it would seem that the likeliest year is 60, when the tide began to turn once again in the Flavians' favour.

From the vigintivirate, Titus advanced to the military tribunate. As *trib. mil.*, he is attested as serving in the same provinces as had his father whilst *leg. leg. II Augustae* - Upper Germany and Britain (*Titus* 4.1). It would seem that he served the first part of his term in Upper Germany, and, if Tacitus' version of Mucianus' comments to Vespasian in 69 can be accepted literally, then Titus remained in Germany for more than one year before proceeding to Britain[92]. His total period of service in the military tribunate would not have exceeded three years.

The date of commencement is not recorded; the earliest date suggested by scholars is 56[93], the latest 64[94]. The argument for 56 or thereabouts is based on the elder Pliny's reference to his *contubernium*[95] with Titus, for which two possibilities exist, Titus' military tribunate or his Judaean campaign in 70. The former is more acceptable. It is not likely that Pliny, whose name does not appear amongst the leading officers during the campaign of 70 (*BJ* 6.237), would have been a *contubernalis* of the commander: the word is suited to men of similar rank. Furthermore, Pliny would surely have made more than passing reference to his service with Titus had he been part of the Judaean campaign. The details of Pliny's career, then, are of some relevance[96]. Syme argues for 56 as the earliest date for the *contubernium* and for 59 as the latest[97]. In posing the earlier date, Syme notes Pliny's reference (*NH* 33.143) to a silver plate used by Pompeius Paullinus in camp[98]; he had governed Upper Germany in 56/57[99], and Pliny's use of the word *scimus* can perhaps be interpreted as indicating that he personally witnessed the custom to which he refers. But dating on these grounds is not without difficulties. *Scimus* does not show that he was physically present; again, the reference occurs in a list of examples illustrating the value of silver plate, few or none of which Pliny would have seen. The suggestion of 56/57 as the early limit for the *contubernium* should be regarded warily. The date proposed for the upper limit, 59, is also problematical. Pliny (*NH* 2.180) reports the details of an eclipse seen in Campania on April 30, 59 with such precision that he possibly witnessed the event in person[100]. Comparing the accuracy of these arguments poses problems, but it is more likely that he was in Italy in 59 than that he was in Germany in 56/57: neither is certain[101]. Yet even if he was in Italy in 59, this need not mark his return from Germany but rather could be the latest date before his service there; he could well have been in Germany after 60. No posts are attested for him in the sixties[102]. So his *contubernium* with Titus may well have occurred after 59, a date that would accord with the suggestion that the death of Agrippina removed the final barrier to Titus' advancement as well as allow sufficient time for his vigintivirate office. Titus, then, probably began his military tribunate in 61.

Confirmation may be possible. Mucianus' words to Vespasian in 69, as reported by Tacitus (*Hist.* 2.77), praise Titus' early military achievements in Germany but neglect to mention Britain. The omission may well be a subtle indication that nothing laudable was achieved there. If this is so, then it is not likely that Titus' service coincided with that of the energetic and skilful Suetonius Paullinus[103]. But he was followed by Petronius Turpilianus who, so we are told, spent time in more leisurely pursuits[104]. It is even less likely

that he could have served under Paullinus' predecessor[105], for
this would place his tribunate in Britain in 57/58. Since
Titus had already served in Germany for more than one year, he
would then have begun his tribunate in 56 at the latest, at
the age of sixteen, leaving no time for the requisite preliminary year as *uigintiuir*. The most acceptable date for his
military service in Britain falls within the period 61 to 63,
having been preceded by a term in Germany. Whatever his
defects as *legatus Augusti*, Petronius Turpilianus was a member
of a family that had long supported the Flavians and was himself favoured by Nero, returning from Britain (perhaps with
Titus) in 63 to be appointed *curator aquarum* and receiving the
insignia triumphalia in 65[106]. His father and uncle, Publius
and Gaius Petronius, had been patrons of Vespasian and
Sabinus[107]; his father was a *uetus conuictor* of the emperor
Claudius[108]; and his mother Plautia was a sister of the Aulus
Plautius who governed Britain during Vespasian's legateship
there[109], who consistently supported Vespasian, and who became
yet another member of that influential group centred on
Lucius Vitellius, whose son, the future emperor, married
Petronia, a sister of Petronius Turpilianus[110]. Now many
uigintiuiri were unable to receive appointments as military
tribunes, for there were not enough posts to go around, and
since the tribunate was commonly regarded as the gift of the
army commander, to be awarded to relatives and close
friends[111], it could well be that Titus' post in Britain was a
gift of Turpilianus himself.

Titus' achievements as military tribune have sometimes
been exaggerated. Mucianus praised him as "having won
distinction in the eyes of the very armies of Germany in the
first years of his military career" (*Hist.* 2.77); but the
context was a speech to Vespasian calling on him to assume the
position of emperor (*Hist.* 2.76) and urging him "not to fear
what might seem mere flattery". But there is no hint of the
exploit that brought him this renown at a time when the Rhine
frontier was abnormally peaceful[112]. One view is that he
received the title of *Germanicus* for his successes at this
time[113]. This is simply wrong: the legend *imp. Caes. T.
Vesp. Aug. Germ.* does appear on a coin but it is a "coin of
Trajan altered" according to Mattingly[114]; again, Tacitus
attributes the title to a son of Vitellius, not to Titus[115].

Whilst serving in Britain, he is supposed to have saved
Vespasian's life:-

> In Britain Vespasian had on a certain occassion been
> hemmed in by the barbarians and been in danger of
> destruction, but his son Titus, becoming alarmed for his
> father, managed by unusual daring to break through their
> enclosing lines and then pursued and destroyed the fleeing
> enemy (Dio, 61.30.1).

The story is erroneous: Titus was no more than eight years
old at that time. There must be a fault in the narrative,

presumably due to a misunderstanding on the part of Dio's epitomator Xiphilinus[116]. Boissevain is probably correct in suggesting that Dio had inserted at this point an incident that occurred much later when father and son were fighting in the Judaean campaign[117]. Consider Josephus' account of the siege of Jotapata: when Vespasian was wounded,

> The first on the spot was Titus, with grave fears for his father, so that the troops were doubly agitated, both by their affection for their chief and by the sight of his son's anguish. However, Vespasian found little diffi-culty in allaying both the fears of his son and the tumult of the army (*BJ* 3.236-239).

Again, when Vespasian was trapped in Gamala and had to fight his way out, Josephus explains why Titus was not there to assist his father: he had just been sent to Mucianus in Syria (*BJ* 4.32). But why should Xiphilinus have placed in Britain the account of Titus' bravery? It could be that Dio had recorded some of Vespasian's exploits in Britain, using Judaea as a parallel; Xiphilinus, in drafting his epitome, may have confused the provinces, since father and son had served in both. The stories have similar elements: the father in danger, the son rushing to his rescue. Later historians were fond of exaggerating Titus' qualities[118] and achievements, as indeed was Suetonius (*Titus* 4.1) who refers to the numerous busts and statues in Germany and Britain commemorating Titus' achievements. No doubt these were erected after the Flavian accession. All this was *post euentum*.

With the death of Agrippina, Titus entered on a senator-ial career. Like many of the family's supporters and relatives - Vespasian himself, L. Caesennius Paetus, Q. Petillius Cerialis Caelius Rufus, P. Petronius Turpilianus and Plautius Silvanus - Titus emerged in the early sixties, holding one of the posts in the vigintivirate (60) and serving as *tribunus laticlauius* in Germany and Britain from 61 to 62 or 63.

MARRIAGES

No later than the first months of 64, after some three years of military service, Titus returned to Rome to practise law. During this period, his father had received the proconsulship of Africa and returned with a reputation for severity and parsimony[119]. The art of advancing one's reputation through the law was not uncommon, and indeed, amongst the cases a lawyer should undertake, Pliny mentions those which "bring fame and recognition, for there is no reason why a speaker should not sometimes act for his honour and reputation's sake and so plead his own case"[120]. Suetonius included Titus in this category (*Titus* 4.2), describing his activity in the courts as *honestam magis quam assiduam* - it was a means to fame, he did not intend to pursue a legal career. His measure of success may only be surmised, but it is most probable that Titus managed to achieve the prominence he sought.

Titus was now in his middle twenties, an age when an ambitious senator should consider a suitable marriage. In the early sixties[121], he married Arrecina Tertulla, daughter of M. Arrecinus Clemens[122]. Little is known of the family's background[123], and it is therefore difficult to estimate the reasons for the alliance. It has been suggested that connections between the two families may have existed for some generations[124], but the evidence is slight. Vespasian's grandmother bore the cognomen Tertulla[125], but the name is reasonably common. Beyond this, there is no evidence, and the suggestion of long-held family ties as a reason for the marriage must remain speculative. Arrecina's brother, also M. Arrecinus Clemens, was possibly adlected into the senate[126], but the family was of equestrian status. Suetonius seems to suggest that such connections were not highly esteemed[127], but they could be politically and practically advantageous, particularly if the members of the equestrian family were wealthy or held key positions. The elder Clemens had been prefect of the praetorian guard under Gaius in 41[128], not only the highest position open to a man of equestrian status, but also a source of political power almost as great as the highest senatorial office[129]. There may have been further advantages in the connection with the Arrecini. Suetonius (*Vesp.* 4.3) records the grave financial difficulties suffered by Titus' family after his father's proconsulship in Africa. The date, though uncertain, corresponds with this period. The situation appears to have been critical. Vespasian was obliged to mortgage all his property to his brother Sabinus and to engage in trading mules: his home town of Reate was famous for them, according to the elder Pliny (*NH* 8.167), and it is possible that he made use of his connections in that town to supply Nero's court with its famous asses and mules. Even if this proved financially rewarding, marriage into a wealthy family would still have been most desirable and possibly necessary. If the younger Pliny's attitude was typical, Roman aristocrats certainly had a businesslike attitude to marriage. In his recommendation of Minicius Acilianus to Junius Mauricus as a suitable husband for the latter's niece, he merely listed the prospective groom's political offices but carefully explained his financial status:-

> He has held the offices of quaestor, tribune and praetor, thus sparing you the necessity of canvassing on his behalf... I am wondering whether to add that his father has ample means, ... but, in view of the prevailing habits of the day and the laws of the country which judge a man's income to be of primary importance, perhaps after all it is something which should not be omitted. Certainly if one thinks of the children of the marriage, the question of money must be taken into account as a factor

influencing our choice[130].

Not long after the marriage, Arrecina died, and Titus once more sought an advantageous alliance, marrying Marcia Furnilla, daughter of Q. Marcius Barea Sura and Antonia Furnilla[131]. Again, there may have been connections between the two families prior to the marriage. Barea Soranus, in all probability the brother of Barea Sura, was a friend of Vespasian, according to Tacitus[132]. Marriage with Marcia Furnilla represented a notable social success for the Flavians: Marcia was *splendidi generis* (*Titus* 4.2), for her paternal grandfather, Q. Marcius Barea, had been proconsul of Africa in 41/42 - 42/43[133], with Barea Soranus proconsul of Asia ca. 51/62[134].

In keeping with Roman sentiment, Titus must have looked forward to the birth of a child and he was not to be disappointed, for he became the father of a daughter, Julia[135]. Until recently, it was accepted without comment that her mother was Marcia Furnilla. Evidence for this conclusion was Suetonius' statement that Titus "divorced Marcia after acknowledging his daughter" (*Titus* 4.2). But he does not give the girl's name and Philostratus (*Vit. Apoll.* 7.7) indicates that Titus had more than one daughter. So it is possible that Julia was not Marcia's daughter[136]. Now the fact that no other Julia is known in the Flavian family led to the conclusion that, following the divorce of Marcia, his daughter was brought up in the household of his former wife, with, as foster mother, a supposed Julia, sister of Julius Lupus (*trib. praet.* 41) and also wife of the elder Clemens[137]. On the other hand, it has also been suggested that Arrecina Tertulla, Titus' first wife, was Julia's mother[138]. This theory has the merit of providing a Julia in the family line and is much more probable than the alternative. Her subsequent history is dismal[139]. She was offered in marriage to her uncle, the future emperor Domitian, who refused her; subsequently she married her cousin, Flavius Sabinus (grandson of Sabinus II). After Domitian executed him (*Dom.* 10.4), Julia lived with the emperor for a time and finally died from an abortion he forced on her, according to Suetonius (*Dom.* 22). The exact date of her death is not known, but must have been in the period 87-90, when she would have been no more than twenty-five[140].

The marriage with Marcia Furnilla was brief and ended in divorce, as has been indicated, for her family had come into official disfavour. Soranus, her uncle, was accused of fostering sedition and of hindering Nero's agents during his proconsulship of Asia, whilst her cousin, Soranus' daughter Servilia, was implicated by her marriage to Annius Pollio, recently exiled for alleged complicity in the Pisonian conspiracy[141]. Pollio's brother was the Annius Vinicianus[142] whose execution was also ordered by Nero. The Annii had been implicated in conspiracies before. L. Annius Vinicianus, father of Annius Pollio and Annius Vinicianus, had been involved with Arruntius Scribonianus, Caecina Paetus and others in a revolt against Claudius[143], whilst their grand-father, Annius Pollio[144], had been charged with treason during Tiberius' reign[145]. The Annius Vinicianus who was executed by Nero was married to one of the daughters of Corbulo[146], Nero's general and victim (Titus' brother was later to marry the other daughter). These relationships are illustrated in Table 7.

It was the Pisonian Conspiracy that caused the Flavians to reassess the marriage. Nero, alarmed at the weight of opposition, turned the conspiracy to advantage by disposing not only of those directly involved, but also those whose opposition was an embarrassment to the regime and whom he saw as a danger to his supremacy. But the conspiracy was less a concerted attempt to remove Nero than the outcome of a loose confederation of various groups mutually dissatisfied with his rule, either because of personal grievances or through adher-ence to Stoic or Republican ideas[147]. As a means of protest against the regime, Thrasea Paetus had adopted a policy of abstention from senatorial life; his actions gained him notoriety, and although there was no intention to overthrow the regime, his abstention was interpreted as treason. Thrasea himself was condemned to death and his son-in-law Helvidius Priscus was exiled[148]. Vespasian had to act, for he was a friend of both Soranus and Thrasea (*Hist.* 4.7). When this connection was severed is not known, but it was done in time to save the family's reputation with Nero. So the Flavians moved rapidly. Sabinus II (who for some years had held the prestigious post of city prefect), Sabinus III (his son, who was probably designated ordinary consul for 69 by Nero)[149], Vespasian (recently returned from the proconsulate of Africa and a consul of some fifteen years' standing) and Titus himself had too much to lose: they could not afford to be seen as associates of such people. On the other hand, it could well be that the divorce was accompanied by not a little disappointment amongst the Flavians, for some members of the family had not performed well in recent years. L. Caesennius Paetus' fiasco in the east was still very fresh in men's minds (Dio, 62.21.2) and the recent "achievements" in Britain of Q. Petillius Cerialis Caesius Rufus could at best be assessed as mediocre[150]. But, whilst the brilliant marriage might well have enhanced the family's reputation, it had to be severed, albeit with regret, when it threatened their very survival.

Little is known of Titus' political career after his return from Britain. Probably, he held the quaestorship at the legal minimum age, his twenty-fourth year (Dec. 63 - Dec. 64)[151]. According to the normal rules of procedure, he would not have been eligible for a praetorship until his twenty-ninth year - with the proviso that a year's reduction was allowed for each child[152]. In the interval, the tribunate of the people or an aedileship had to be held, except in the case

TABLE 7: TITUS' CONNECTIONS WITH THE OPPOSITION

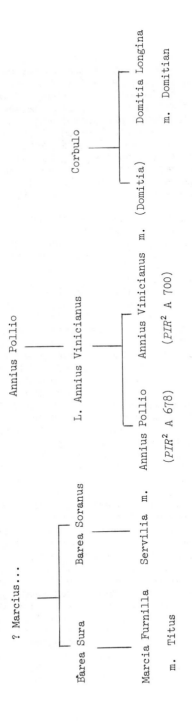

of a patrician, who omitted this stage entirely. Titus is not recorded as holding any of these. It has been suggested that the omission is to be explained by the adlection of his father to patrician status in 47, through the influence of Vitellius[153]. But whilst such a promotion would not be surprising, there is no evidence whatsoever that it occurred. Perhaps the explanation is less complicated - nothing noteworthy may have happened during either of these posts. If he held the quaestorship in 64, he possibly became tribune or aedile in 66, allowing for the *biennium*, the clear interval of at least one year that had to be left between each office, unless one had special exemption[154], and there is no hint of this for Titus.

By the age of twenty-seven, then, Titus had had a normal, if not particularly distinguished, career as a senator: his initial posts may have been slightly delayed, but there is no hint of retardation in his quaestorship or (if he ever held it) his tribunate. The most remarkable feature, though, was the nature of his education - or, with the advantage of hindsight, of his preparation for the principate; compare his brother's early education and subsequent performance as emperor. Titus had, of course, gained full advantage of his grandfather's foresight, political awareness and common sense; his father and uncle had built on the foundations he had laid and had strengthened them. Contact with the powerful group surrounding L. Vitellius had greatly increased the family's status to Titus' advantage and he was accepted into the imperial court. There need be no doubt about the soundness of the general education he received there. His personality and natural talents were developed fully - note Vespasian's readiness to use him subsequently to conduct extremely delicate negotiations with Galba (*Hist.* 2.1) and with Mucianus (*Hist.* 2.5.2), tasks in which his role was far more than nominal. The manoeuvres of Narcissus and Sosibius, with whom his relationship was very close, provided excellent lessons in practical politics and no doubt their successes and eventual failures taught him a great deal. In addition, the training provided by the praetorian prefects stood him in good stead, and particularly so when he assumed the post himself. But he must have learned more than this from these instructors. Even though his practical military experience had been normal for a senator in his late twenties, it could still be fairly described as minimal, and his natural rashness had to be carefully supervised once the Judaean campaign was underway. Yet he had learned the necessity of winning and maintaining his troops' absolute support. One has to allow for the exaggerations of Josephus, but, nonetheless, his account of Titus' behaviour in the first year's sieges in Judaea does indicate that he was able to win and hold the soldiers' full loyalty: his reappearance after a visit to Mucianus immediately restored their spirits; he was a commander who, like his father, led the fighting, and his men, like those of Julius Caesar, would do anything for him.

NOTES

1. On the date, see Philocalus in *CIL* 1 p. 356 (for the alternative, Dec. 28, *PIR*² F 399) and also Suetonius (*Titus* 1), who assigns the birth to the year of Gaius' assassination (Jan. 24, 41) but later contradicts this statement (*Titus* 11), claiming that Titus died at the age of forty-one (i.e. on Sept. 13, 81). Dio is more accurate, giving his age on accession (June 24, 79) as thirty-nine years, five months and twenty-five days (66.18.4). Possibly, Suetonius has in mind the birth of Britannicus in 41. Fortina, 1955a: p. 19, sensibly concludes that Suetonius would more easily have confused the dates in a general statement (as in *Titus* 1), but later, when referring specifically to the length in years, months and days (as he usually does) of Titus' rule, he would presumably be more accurate. See also McGuire, 1980: pp. 24-25 (for an attempt to reconcile *Titus* 1 and 11); Martinet, 1981: pp. 6-7.

2. On the Septizonium, see Price, 1919: p. 5; Mooney, 1930: pp. 467-468; McGuire, 1980: pp. 25-27 (for a conjecture that Suetonius' Septizonium may be identified with the Pantheon in the Campus Martius built by M. Agrippa in 27-25 B.C.); Martinet, 1981: pp. 7-8. All that we can say with confidence is that there must have been an older Septizonium before the Septizonium Severi built in 203.

3. *CIL* 9.4677.

4. The relationship between the Flavii and the Plautii may date from this period. A. Plautius, praetor in 51 B.C. and probably great-grandfather of A. Plautius, *cos. suff.* 29 (Taylor, 1956: pp. 13, 26), was one of Pompey's officers at Pharsalus. The patronage of the Plautii and others was of considerable assistance to Titus' father and uncle in their rise under Claudius and may possibly date from this early period.

5. For his post, see De Laet, 1949: p. 377.

6. On the relationship between Flavia Sabina and L. Caesennius Paetus, see the discussion of *ILS* 995 (*Flauiae T.f. Sabinae Caesenni Paeti*) by Townend, 1961: p. 56. Paetus' career has been the subject of many studies, the most important being those of Houston, 1971: pp. 38-41; Syme, 1977: pp. 38 ff. and 1981: p. 133; Nicols, 1978: pp. 30-31. It is now known that Paetus' full name was L. Junius Caesennius Paetus (*AE* 1973, 141); however, the older, briefer form of his name has been retained in the text to avoid confusion between Paetus and his son, the suffect consul of 79 (see Table 2).

7. Their careers are discussed by Syme, 1977: pp. 38-49; for the former, see also Houston, 1971: pp. 41-42.

8. On him, see Houston, 1971: pp. 37-38. According to Syme, 1981: p. 135, he may have governed Syria in Domitian's reign, i.e. after his tenure of Cappadocia-Galatia. He also suggests that he may be polyonymous, noting a later inscription linking Gallus to Fabricius Veiento whose second consulship was awarded by Titus in 80 (and his third by Domitian, probably in 83). The inscription, *CIL* 14.354, refers to an equestrian named L. Fabricius L. f. Pal. Caesennius Gallus: on this, see Syme, 1980: p. 73.

9. L. Caesennius Paetus was *cos. ord.* in 61, his eldest son *cos. suff.* in 79 and the younger in 114; Gallus was *cos. suff.* before 81.

10. See Ritter, 1972: pp. 759-761, together with the sensible comments of Evans, 1979: p. 201 with n. 2. They reject the older view (e.g. of Braithwaite, 1927: p. 25) that she was freeborn.

11. Their background and careers are discussed in detail by McDermott, 1973b: pp. 335-351.

12. Townend, 1961: p. 62, suggests that Flavia Domitilla was born around 45. But such a date would involve an early return from Britain or else the presence of Vespasian's wife in the war zone, both of which are unlikely. In addition, such a conjecture would require that Suetonius' chronological order of the births of Vespasian's children be disturbed - Titus, Domitian and Domitilla. Domitian was born in 51 and Domitilla soon afterwards, since she had died before Vespasian came to the throne but had produced a daughter.

13. The careers of the Petillii have been much discussed, most recently by Bosworth, 1980: pp. 267-277, who also provides a list of previous work on them. Bosworth's reconstruction of their careers has been adopted in the text.

14. But see Chastagnol, 1976: pp. 253-256.

15. Nicols, 1978: pp. 20-21; according to Syme, 1970: p. 39, P. Petronius (*cos. suff.* 19) was part of "an influential group and nexus at the core of which stands the great L. Vitellius".

16. For a table indicating some of these relationships, see Nicols, 1978: pp. 13-14.

17. For the details of these Tiberian consulars, *ibid.*, pp. 15-16.

18. For the details, see Gallivan, 1978: pp. 407-426.

19. On Caenis, see *PIR*[2] A 888; Braithwaite, 1927: p. 26; Mooney, 1930: p. 386; McGuire, 1980: pp. 190-191. Her influence in Vespasian's reign is outlined by Dio, 66.14.1-3.

20. The most recent discussions of his career are those of Nicols, 1978: pp. 26-30; Griffin, 1976: pp. 456-457.

21. For his quaestorship and military tribunate, see Braithwaite, 1927: p. 24; Mooney, 1930: p. 381; Graf, 1937: pp. 12, 114 n. 58; Homo, 1949: pp. 18-20; Nicols, 1978: p. 3.

22. For his aedileship, see Braithwaite, 1927: p. 24; Mooney, 1930: p. 381; Graf, 1937: pp. 12-14; Homo, 1949: p.

21;   Nicols, 1978: pp. 3-4.
   23.   The dates suggested are those of Nicols, 1978.
   24.   Lepidus was Gaius' nominated successor (Dio, 59.22.
6);   on him see *PIR*² A 371, and, for Gaetulicus, *PIR*² C 1390.
The details of the conspiracy are outlined by Balsdon, 1934a:
pp. 72-75.   Lepidus and Gaetulicus were executed before Oct.
24 - see the minutes of the Arval Brethren for 39 (Smallwood,
1967: No. 9).
   25.   For the details of this campaign, see Bicknell,
1968: pp. 502-504.   He convincingly argues that this was the
victory to which Vespasian was referring in his speech (*Vesp.*
2.3:   see following note).
   26.   *praetor infensum senatui Gaium ne quo non genere
demereretur, ludos extraordinarios pro uictoria eius Germanica
depoposcit poenaeque coniuratorum addendum censuit, ut
insepulti proicerentur.   egit et gratias ei apud amplissimum
ordinem, quod se honore cenae dignatus esset*:   Vesp. 2.3.
   27.   For the traditional date, see the first five
authorities cited in note 29.   Nicols, 1978: pp. 4-7, on the
other hand, argues persuasively for 40.
   28.   Balsdon, 1934a: p. 74 and 1934b: pp. 16 ff.
   29.   For his praetorship, see Braithwaite, 1927: p. 24;
Mooney, 1930: pp. 381-382;   Graf, 1937: pp. 14, 115 n. 75;
Homo, 1949: p. 21;   Morris, 1964: p. 319;   Nicols, 1978: pp.
4-7.
   30.   For Vespasian's position and achievements as *leg.*
leg. II Augustae, see Braithwaite, 1927: p. 27;   Mooney,
1930: pp. 386-387;   Graf, 1937: p. 16;   Homo, 1949: p. 22;
Nicols, 1978: p. 8.   According to Eichholz, 1972: pp. 149-163,
there is no evidence to show that Vespasian left Britain in 44
to attend Claudius' triumph.   For his two priesthoods, see
Mooney, 1930: p. 388;   Nicols, 1978: p. 9, and, for his
consulship, Gallivan, 1978: p. 413.
   31.   For him, see *PIR*¹ P 344;   A.R. Birley, 1967: pp. 64-
65;   note 109 below.
   32.   The activities of these prominent freedmen are outlined in *PIR*² A 858 (Antonius Pallas) and *PIR*¹ N 18 (Narcissus).   The most recent account is that of Griffin, 1976.
   33.   *Vitellii cliens, cum Vitellius collega Claudio
foret*: Hist. 3.66 and *Claudio principe Narcissi gratia
legatus legionis in Germaniam missus est*: Vesp. 4.1.
   34.   See note 20.
   35.   Ti. Claudius Caesar Britannicus, son of Claudius
and his third wife Messallina (*PIR*² C 820; *RE* 3.2685.92;
Suet., *Claud.* 27; *Ann.* 11.32, 34) was probably born on Feb.
12, 41 (Suet., *Claud.* 27; *Ann.* 13.15).   He was first called
Ti. Claudius Germanicus, but the senate decreed that the title
Britannicus be awarded him after the victories in 43 (Suet.,
Claud. 27; Dio, 60.22).   After his mother's death and
Claudius' marriage to his niece Agrippina in 49, he gradually
lost status: her son L. Domitius Ahenobarbus was adopted in

the following year and named Nero Claudius Caesar Drusus
Germanicus (Suet., *Nero* 6; *Ann.* 12.26.1); subsequently, he
received greater honours. Not long after Nero's accession to
the throne in 54, Britannicus was poisoned: see McGuire,
1980: pp. 35-37; Martinet, 1981: pp. 12-13.
   36. *PIR*[1] S 552.
   37. For the significance of the statues, see Scott,
1931: p. 118; Pekáry, 1968: pp. 144-148; Martinet, 1981: pp.
14-15.
   38. *statuam ei auream in Palatio posuit et alteram ex
ebore equestrem, quae circensi pompa hodieque praefertur,
dedicauit prosecutusque est*: *Titus* 2.
   39. Mattingly, 1930: p. lxxviii, argues that it was
"very probable" that the coin was issued in 80; for the
contrary view, see Griffin, 1976: p. 242 n. 3.
   40. The ancient authorities attest to his charm:
frequently, the phrase *amor et deliciae generis humani* is
applied to him, e.g. by Suetonius, *Titus* 1; Eutropius, 7.21;
Aurelius Victor, *Caes.* 10.6; Pacatus, *Pan. in Theod.* 11. The
elder Pliny calls him *iucundissimus* (*NH Praef.* 1), Eutropius
(7.21) *facundissimus, bellicosissimus, moderatissimus* and
Augustine *suauissimus* (*Ciu. Dei* 5.21). Ausonius is even more
enthusiastic: *felix imperio, felix breuitate regendi, expers
ciuilis sanguinis, orbis amor* (*Caes.* 11). Dio also comments
on his *fortuna*: "It is maintained that Augustus would never
have been loved had he lived a shorter time, nor Titus had he
lived longer... If Titus had lived a long time, it might have
been shown that he owes his present fame more to good fortune
than to merit" (66.18.5). For a discussion of his *fortuna*,
see Luck, 1964: pp. 72-73; McGuire, 1980: pp. 21-23; Martinet, 1981: pp. 4-5.
   41. For this, see Parker, 1946: pp. 29-50.
   42. The elder Pliny, who died in 79, refers to the
latter - *NH* 2.25.89, *Praef.* 5; for a discussion of his
cultural achievements, see Bardon, 1968: pp. 274 ff.;
McGuire, 1980: pp. 43-44.
   43. Mooney, 1930: pp. 471-472; Martinet, 1981: pp. 20-
21.
   44. The role of the *grammaticus* is described by Cicero,
De Oratore 1.42 (187), and by Quintilian, *Inst.* 1.9.1 ff.;
for the subjects studied, see *ibid.*, 1.9.2, 3.
   45. *ibid.*, 1.10.34 ff. (geometry); 1.11.15 ff.
(athletics).
   46. *Titus* 3.2; Dio, 65.15.2.
   47. Quintilian, *Inst.* 1.10.1-33; Seneca, *Ep.* 88;
Cicero, *De Oratore* 3.87; but according to Nepos (*Epam.* 1),
music was unseemly for a man of eminence.
   48. Quintilian, *Inst.* 2.1.7. For a suggestion that the
rhetor was Cn. Domitius Afer, see McGuire, 1980: p. 31.
   49. For L. Lusius Geta, Rufrius Crispinus and Sex.
Afranius Burrus, see *PIR*[2] L 435, *PIR*[1] R 121 and *PIR*[2] A.441;

note also Passerini, 1939: pp. 280-281, and, more recently, Griffin, 1976.
50. The careers of Gaius' prefect and his children are discussed in *PIR*² A 1072-1074. See also B.W. Jones and R. Develin, 1976: pp. 79-83; McGuire, 1980: pp. 51-52.
51. This is the suggestion of Townend, 1961: p. 62.
52. *PIR*¹ S 700; according to Morford, 1968: p. 66 n. 33, "The skill and power of this sinister person are indicated by his surviving the convulsions of 48-51 and, as an old man, avoiding the death penalty in 58". For an account of the fall of Asiaticus, see Scramuzza, 1940: p. 74.
53. Nicols, 1978: p. 21 n. 32.
54. Soon after 59, A. Plautius (*PIR*¹ P 345) was killed by Nero for allegedly aspiring to the empire with the help of Agrippina (Suet., *Nero* 35.4): see the discussion by Bradley, 1978: pp. 214-215. In 65, Q. Plautius Lateranus (*PIR*¹ P 354), the nephew of Claudius' legate, died because of his involvement in the Pisonian Conspiracy (*Ann.* 15.60.1).
55. The dates suggested are those of Nicols, 1978.
56. Braithwaite, 1927: p. 29.
57. Augustus had established two regular senate meetings per month at which attendance was obligatory, with fines levied on absentees (Dio, 55.3.1).
58. Eck, 1970: pp. 146-148, for instance, assigns him (with hesitation) to Upper Moesia during the years 95/96 and 96/97; however, a recently discovered diploma of July 12, 96 indicates that the governor at that time was Gnaeus Aemilius Cicatricula Pompeius Longinus - see Dusanic and Vasic, 1977: pp. 291-304; Roxan, 1978: pp. 36-37. Subsequently, Eck has suggested (1982: pp. 326-328) that he served in Upper Germany during the period 96/97-97/98.
59. "While Nero was being advanced, Britannicus received neither honour nor care. On the contrary, Agrippina removed or even put to death those who were devoted to him; Sosibius, who had been entrusted with his rearing and education, she slew on the pretext that he was plotting against Nero. After that she handed Britannicus over to those who suited her purpose and did him all the harm she could. She would not let him be with his father nor appear in public, but kept him in a kind of imprisonment, though without bonds" (Dio, 61.32.5).
60. Morford, 1968: p. 66.
61. On Britannicus' death, see Suet., *Nero* 33.2-3; *Ann.* 13.15-17; Dio, 61.7.4; *AJ* 20.153; Eutropius, 7.14.3; Herodian, *Hist.* 4.5,6. There are comprehensive accounts by Bishop, 1964: pp. 27-33; Warmington, 1969: pp. 10-20; Bradley, 1978: pp. 198-200; McGuire 1980: pp. 35-37 (who doubts that Titus was present when Britannicus was poisoned); Martinet, 1981: pp. 12-13.
62. The rise of Sabinus and Vespasian early in Claudius' reign was greatly assisted by the group that centred on L. Vitellius; its influence had now been dissipated, but it was

to regain strength after 59 (see notes 107-110).
    63. Dio, 59.9.5. For the senatorial *latus clauus*, see Mommsen, 1887-1888: I 410; III 1 219, 470; III 2 887-888. In the case of *noui homines*, the *latus clauus* was actually presented (*Dial.* 7; Pliny, *Ep.* 2.9, 8.23), but there seems to be no clear example for the sons of senators, and it is not certain whether they held it by right of descent or whether it was presented to them by the emperor.
    64. Suet., *Aug.* 38; Pliny, *Ep.* 8.14; Millar, 1964: p. 14. Although cultural and similar interests were factors in such associations (Pflaum, 1964: pp. 544-560), it is clear that the major aim was political advancement (Pliny, *Ep.* 1.14, 2.13, 3.2, 4.4).
    65. E. Birley, 1953: p. 199.
    66. Dio, 54.26.5.
    67. McAlindon, 1957a: pp. 191-195.
    68. *ibid.*, p. 191, for seven examples.
    69. *Ann.* 3.29 (Germanicus' son); Dio, 60.5.8 (Claudius).
    70. On the early background to this college, see Hamilton, 1969: pp. 181-199. For its significance, see E. Birley, 1953: p. 203; J.R. Jones, 1970: pp. 70-78.
    71. Nicols, 1978: p. 32.
    72. The *cursus* of the younger Pliny may be regarded as a good example of the type of career that began with this post. Here, his duties involved presiding over the Centumviral Court, and even his later service with a legion in Syria was restricted to administration, for he saw no active service (*Ep.* 7.31, 8.14). His later career followed along similar lines: see Sherwin-White, 1966: pp. 72-82.
    73. See A.R. Birley, 1981: pp. 6-7, for the *IV uiri* as future military commanders, and, for the *III uiri capitales*, see E. Birley, 1953: p. 205.
    74. For a discussion of those few senators who achieved eminence after holding this initial post, see A.R. Birley, 1981: pp. 5-6 n. 10.
    75. C. Dillius Vocula (*PIR*[2] D 90), who held this vigintivirate post, later commanded the Upper German forces in 69.
    76. Mommsen, 1887-1888: I 506 n. 2, 546, 573.
    77. As far as can be determined, no scholar specifically mentions a date for his vigintivirate office. However the year(s) they assign to his military tribunate suggests the period 55-56 for the post. Sherwin-White, 1966: p. 221; Fortina, 1955a: p. 21 n. 13; Syme, 1969: p. 206; McGuire, 1980: p. 47; Martinet, 1981: p. 25 give the following dates for the tribunate - ca. 56 (Sherwin-White), 57 (Fortina and McGuire), "56, more likely 57 or 58" (Syme), and 58 (Martinet). Griffin, 1976: p. 242, suggests a similar period: "When Agrippina died, Titus was already doing his military service". A.R. Birley, 1981: p. 269, argues that he was tribune ca. 60 (and, presumably, *uigintiuir* before Agrippina's death). McGuire, 1980: p. 47, assigns the tribunate to the period

57/58 - 60/61 when L. Duvius Avitus was governor (of Lower Germany).   She argues that, since Duvius owed both his consulship and his German command to the influence of Burrus, "Titus' former instructor in military exercises, Titus' appointment may have been requested by L. Duvius Avitus at the recommendation of Burrus" (*ibid.*). The argument seems somewhat tenuous.
    78.   E. Birley, 1953: p. 200. Morris, 1965: p. 25, points out that "there were no more than 23 to 29 laticlave tribunates, and [that] the annual appointments can hardly have been more than ten or twelve".
    79.   The most recent discussions of Domitian's consuls are those of Eck, 1980: pp. 51-60 and Gallivan, 1981: pp. 215-218.
    80.   For a discussion of ten senators of the reign whose consulships must have been awarded well after they had reached the minimum legal age for the post, see Eck, 1970: pp. 65-67. Two more names can be added to his list. Both P. Herennius Pollio and his son M. Annius Herennius P.f...Pollio received suffect consulships in 85 (Modugno *et al.*, 1973: pp. 87-108 and especially p. 96): presumably, the father was over 60. C. Cilnius Proculus and his son of the same name were suffect consuls in 87 and 100 respectively (see B.W. Jones, 1976b: pp. 256-257): again, the father must have been well over the legal minimum age.
    81.   *PIR*² J 507, and, most recently, Halfmann, 1979: pp. 112-115, for the career of Julius Quadratus.
    82.   Syme, 1980: p. 27.
    83.   Brassloff, 1905: pp. 60-70.
    84.   E. Birley, 1953: pp. 203-204.
    85.   There is some dispute as to the length of service that was required for the legionary tribunate. Mommsen, 1887-1888: I 545, puts the general period at a year and is followed by Sherwin-White, 1966: p. 73 ("usually only for a single season") and by Syme, 1958a: p. 22 ("brief"). E. Birley, however, 1953: p. 200, refers to "the legend of a single year's service" and argues convincingly that "the period of service will have been nearer three years than one". This would be particularly true of Titus who saw service in more than one legion. See also A.R. Birley, 1981: p. 9 n. 19.
    86.   For the various possibilities, see Alföldy, 1967: p. 5; Griffin, 1976: p. 453; Nicols, 1978: p. 10.
    87.   See note 6.
    88.   Nicols, 1978: pp. 15-16, with the table on p. 13. On Turpilianus, see note 104.
    89.   For Cerialis, see A.R. Birley, 1973: pp. 179-190 and especially p. 181 n. 16 for the date of his legionary command.
    90.   Griffin, 1976: pp. 244-245.
    91.   Nicols, 1978: pp. 26-30 but cf. Griffin, 1976: pp. 456-457.
    92.   *(Titus) capax iam imperii...et primis militiae annis*

apud Germanicos quoque exercitus clarus: *Hist*. 2.77. According to Martinet, 1981: pp. 24-25, Titus served in both Upper and Lower Germany and then in Britain. McGuire, 1980: p. 47, on the other hand, assigns him to Lower Germany for the entire period (see note 77).
  93. See note 77.
  94. Mooney, 1930: p. 473.
  95. *et nobis quidem qualis in contubernio*: *NH Praef*. 3.
  96. Ziegler, *RE* 12.273 ff., and especially 279, assigns the *contubernium* to 70 on the basis of *NH* 5.70-73 and 12.111-113, but his argument is not convincing. The major discussions of the elder Pliny's career are those of Ziegler, *RE* 12.271-285; Münzer, 1899: pp. 67-111; Syme, 1958a: pp. 60-63, 291-293 and 1969: pp. 201-236; Pflaum, 1960: pp. 105 ff.; Sherwin-White, 1966: pp. 219 ff.
  97. Syme, 1969: p. 206.
  98. *PIR*[1] P 419.
  99. Houston, 1971: p. 471.
  100. Syme, 1969: p. 206.
  101. A.R. Birley, 1975: p. 149 n. 17, believes that "Pliny need not necessarily have been in Campania in person on 30 April 59".
  102. The accepted view is that he was "in retirement" in this decade: thus Syme, 1969: p. 209; Griffin, 1976: p. 437.
  103. On him, see A.R. Birley, 1981: pp. 54-57.
  104. *is (Turpilianus) non inritato hoste neque lacessitus honestum pacis nomen segni otio imposuit*: *Ann*. 14.39. For his career, see A.R. Birley, 1981: pp. 57-58; *PIR*[1] P 233.
  105. On Paullinus' predecessor, Q. Veranius, see A.R. Birley, 1981: pp. 50-54.
  106. Frontinus, *De Aq*. 102; *Ann*. 15.72. For a discussion of the curators of the water supply, see Rodgers, 1982: p. 173.
  107. The father, Publius (*PIR*[1] P 198), was suffect consul in 19 and governed Syria from 39 to 41. The uncle, Gaius (P 197), was suffect consul in 25, with a son, C. Petronius Pontius Nigrinus, ordinary consul in 37 (P 218: adopted, according to Dessau) and another who became governor of Galatia ca. 54/55 (Q. Petronius Umbrinus, P 238). The latter's son held a suffect consulship in 81, at the time of Titus' death in September: for this man, M. Petronius Umbrinus, see P 237 and Gallivan, 1981: p. 215. Turpilianus' father was a prominent member of the group centred on L. Vitellius: see Syme, 1970: p. 38.
  108. Seneca, *Apoc*. 3.49.
  109. Plautia has no entry in *PIR*[1]; she is discussed by Syme, 1970: p. 38 with n. 1. For Aulus Plautius, see *PIR*[1] P 344; A.R. Birley, 1981: pp. 37-40. He was connected with the Pomponii (also members of the group that centred on L. Vitellius: see note 107) through his wife, Pomponia Graecina (P 579), whose father (Pomponius Graecinus, *cos. suff*. 16: P

540) and uncle (Pomponius Flaccus, *cos. ord.* 17) were, together with P. Petronius (*cos. suff.* 19: see note 107), granted special favour by Germanicus. Associated with these three consulars was P. Vitellius (V 502), the older brother of the illustrious Lucius, and "Germanicus' most trusted lieutenant on the Rhine and in Syria" (Nicols, 1978: p. 17).

110. For the elder Vitellius, see *PIR*[1] V 500, and Nicols, 1978: pp. 13 ff. for his influence. For the emperor, see V 499, and P 241 for his wife.

111. L. Caesennius Paetus, when he went to the Cappadocian command as consular legate in 62, was accompanied by his son (presumably L. Junius Caesennius Paetus, *cos. suff.* 79) as military tribune, according to *Ann.* 15.28.2: see Syme, 1977: pp. 44 ff. For sixteen instances of tribunes serving under close relatives, see A.R. Birley, 1981: p. 11, and, for a general discussion of the point, pp. 9-12.

112. Chilver, 1979, p. 236.

113. *RE* 6.2697.

114. Mattingly, 1930: p. 268.

115. *nec tantam Vespasiano superbiam ut priuatum Vitellium pateretur, ne uictos quidem laturos: ita periculum ex misericordia. ipsum sane senem et prosperis aduersisque satiatum, sed quod nomen, quem statum filio eius Germanico fore?*: *Hist.* 3.66.

116. On Ioannes Xiphilinus, see Millar, 1964: pp. 2-3, 125-126.

117. Boissevain, 1901: p. 3: • *Dio uel Xiphilinus hic errauerit necesse est: fortasse res a Vespasiano fortiter gestas enarrans, tanquam in transcursu memorauerat in Judaea eum quondam a filio e periculo ereptum fuisse.*

118. See note 38.

119. The comments of Suetonius (*Vesp.* 4.3: *integerrime*) and Tacitus (*Hist.* 2.97: *famosum inuisumque*) on his proconsulship are contradictory. His unpopularity was probably due not to *auaritia* but rather to his parsimony: see Braithwaite, 1927: p. 29; Mooney, 1930: pp. 389-390; Graf, 1937: pp. 19-20; Homo, 1949: p. 26; Nicols, 1978: p. 10.

120. Pliny, *Ep.* 6.29.3: see Sherwin-White, 1966: p. 389.

121. If the dates assigned above to his post in the vigintivirate and military tribunate are correct, then he would not have had time to marry Tertulla before 64 - unless one cares to postulate two years' service in Britain and Germany rather than three: perhaps *Hist.* 2.77 (*annis*) need not be taken literally. On the other hand, the traditional dates for these posts enable the first marriage to be assigned to 63 rather more easily.

122. See note 50.

123. Passerini, 1940: pp. 145-163, discusses the family and argues (pp. 147-148) that they came from Pisaurum in Umbria. His argument rests on the fact that the inscription

listing M. Arrecinus Clemens' legateship of Spain was set up there (*AE* 1947, 40): perhaps the fact that it also seems to indicate his tenure of the city prefecture (thus B.W. Jones and R. Develin, 1976: p. 80) strengthens his case. See also note 124. The Arrecini had close links with the military, since both father and son held the post of praetorian prefect (under Gaius and Vespasian respectively).

124. Townend points out that "Suetonius (*Vesp.* 1.4) knew of a belief that Flavius Petro came *e regione Transpadana* and had dealings in Umbria and the Sabine Country. Pisaurum could well have been his base for collecting labourers to work further south, and the connection with the Arrecini could date from that period, a daughter or some other relation of Petro's wife Tertulla (herself from Reate) marrying the father of the elder Clemens": 1961: p. 57.

125. *PIR*[1] T 87.

126. He may, of course, have been offered the *latus clauus* during Claudius' reign (Townend, 1961: p. 62, suggests that he was born ca. 33); on the other hand, his connection with the Flavians may have prompted his adlection into the senate at a later date. He was certainly *senatorii ordinis* in 69 (*Hist.* 4.68).

127. Suetonius (*Titus* 4.2), in referring to Gaius' prefect, comments: *patre eq. R. sed praefecto quondam praetorianarum cohortium*. Price, 1919: p. 19, compares Suet., *Jul.* 1.1: *quae familia equestri, sed admodum diues* (referring to a proposed marriage into a wealthy equestrian family) and points out that, "in each case, *sed* implies 'only' with the preceding phrase, e.g. 'the daughter of a man who was only a Roman knight, but once prefect of the praetorian guards'".

128. For the details, see *PIR*[2] A 1073.

129. See the discussion of Durry, 1968: pp. 367-376.

130. *quaesturam tribunatum praeturam honestissime percucurrit, ac iam pro se tibi necessitatem ambiendi remisit...nescio an adiciam esse patri eius amplas facultates. ..cum publicos mores atque etiam leges ciuitatis intueor, quae uel in primis census hominum spectandos arbitrantur, ne id quidem praetereundum uidetur. et sane de posteris et his pluribus cogitanti, hic quoque in condicionibus deligendis ponendus est calculus*: *Ep.* 1.14.7-9.

131. For Barea Sura, see *PIR*[1] M 161 and *RE* 14.1549.38; for Antonia Furnilla, *PIR*[2] A 890, and *CIL* 6.31766:- *Antonia A.f. Furnilla Q. Marcii Q. f.C.n., C. et Gemini Artori pronepotis, Bareae Surae*. Note also Table 7.

132. For Barea Soranus and the suggested relationship, see *PIR*[2] B 55. In *Hist.* 4.7, Helvidius Priscus comments that *fuisse Vespasiano amicitiam cum Thrasea, Sorano, Sentio*: on this, see B.W. Jones, 1973a: pp. 85-86.

133. *PIR*[1] M 160; *RE* 14.1549.37. He was *cos. suff.* in 34 with T. Rustius Nummius Gallus (*PIR*[1] R 164): Degrassi, 1952: p. 10. For his post in Africa, see *CIL* 8.11002, 19492;

AE 1935, 32; 1951, 85; Thomasson, 1960: pp. 31-32.
    134. *PIR*² B 55; he was *cos. suff.* in 52: Gallivan, 1978a: p. 425. See also Magie, 1950: p. 1422.
    135. Titus took Jerusalem on his daughter's birthday (*Titus* 5.2).
    136. Stein (*RE* 6.2732 ff.) suggests that the Flavia Domitilla who is referred to in inscriptions (e.g. *ILS* 1839) as *diui Vespasiani neptis* may be a daughter of Titus; his suggestion is rejected, rightly, by Townend, 1961: p. 58 n. 15. For a review of the arguments, see Martinet, 1981: pp. 28-33.
    137. Townend, 1961: p. 57.
    138. Castritius, 1969: pp. 492-502, especially pp. 492-494.
    139. *PIR*² F 426 (but cf. *PIR*¹ F 281); Mooney, 1930: p. 475.
    140. Her name appeared in the vows of the Arval Brethren for the safety of the imperial family taken on Jan. 3, 87 but was omitted from those of Jan. 3, 90. See McCrum and Woodhead, 1966: Nos. 14 (87) and 16 (90).
    141. For the details, see *Ann.* 16.21-23, 30 ff. and Dio, 62.26.1-3; for Servilia, see *PIR*¹ S 432, and, for Pollio, *PIR*² A 678.
    142. *PIR*² A 700.
    143. On these individuals, see *PIR*² A 701 (father of the two Annii), A 1140 (Scribonianus); C 103 (Paetus).
    144. *PIR*² A 677.
    145. These relationships are discussed in detail by B.W. Jones, 1973a: pp. 86-88.
    146. Her name has not survived; see *PIR*² D 172.
    147. Modern literature on this conspiracy is extensive; note, in particular, Bishop, 1964: p. 90-113; Warmington, 1969: pp. 135-154; and the works cited by Bradley, 1978: p. 220.
    148. The death of Thrasea and the downfall of his associates have been discussed at length on a number of occasions. See Bishop, 1964: pp. 153-157; Warmington, 1969: pp. 142-154; Bradley, 1978: p. 224.
    149. Townend, 1962: p. 114.
    150. See the pertinent comments of A.R. Birley, 1973: p. 182.
    151. Morris, 1964: p. 317.
    152. Sherwin-White, 1966: p. 74.
    153. Nicols, 1978: p. 32.
    154. Sherwin-White, 1966: p. 74.

Chapter Two

JUDAEA

THE CAMPAIGNS OF 67 AND 68

In 66, Vespasian was given a special command in the east with the task of settling the revolt in Judaea[1]. Deeply ingrained and long-felt grievances, intense national pride and hatred of Roman domination were aggravated by social and economic unrest, as the poorer classes, oppressed by the conditions imposed on them, resented the alliance between the wealthy landowners and the foreign rulers. Apart from this, the country suffered from the friction between the various mutually hostile religious groups. Under the procuratorship of Felix (52-60), violent outbursts by the Zealots (*BJ* 2.253) and then by the *sicarii* (*BJ* 2.254-257) together with rioting between the Jews and the Greeks in Caesarea (*BJ* 2.266-268) produced increasing unrest, and the discontent was not quelled, for subsequent procurators were less concerned with peace than with increasing their own wealth. Finally, during the term of Gessius Florus (64-66), matters reached a head[2]. The immediate cause of the war was rioting at Caesarea and Jerusalem, leading in the latter city to the slaughter of Jewish leaders and Roman soldiers. Attempts by Cestius Gallus[3], governor of Syria, to suppress the rebellion were unsuccessful. The fanaticism of the war parties who had now tasted success required sterner measures from Rome, and so Vespasian was sent to deal with the problem.

The reasons for his appointment have been disputed[4], but probably a number of factors influenced Nero. Vespasian was a commander of "tried energy" and his family's reputation was not a matter for concern or fear (*Vesp.* 4.5). More importantly, he was on the spot. Immediate action was essential, for over 6,000 Roman soldiers had perished, and the time of year, mid-winter 66/67, meant that, unless someone suitable could be found amidst the emperor's entourage in Greece, Nero would have to send word to Rome and wait for the *legatus* to arrive from Italy, if, of course, a satisfactory candidate was on hand there. Vespasian was at least available, if in "exile"

(*Vesp.* 4.4). Finally, he could well have been recommended to Nero by two very powerful pro-Roman Jews, Ti. Julius Alexander, prefect of Egypt since 66, and M. Julius Agrippa II[5]. Through their fathers[6], they were both connected with Antonia's circle, and Agrippa had been educated in Claudius' court (though it should be noted that he was some ten years older than Titus). Again, Ti. Julius Alexander had already served as procurator of Judaea (46-48). As both he and Agrippa were presumably well aware of Vespasian's ability and of his connections with Antonia, they could have urged Nero to appoint him.

The precise nature of the appointment is important, since it was to have some bearing on Vespasian's relationship with Licinius Mucianus[7]. According to Josephus (*BJ* 3.7), Vespasian was sent "to take command of the army in Syria", i.e. presumably, as *legatus Augusti pro praetore ad exercitum qui est in Syria*, but this has been disputed. Some scholars insist that Josephus must have meant that Vespasian commanded only that part of the Syrian army that was destined for Judaea (i.e. legions V, X and XV)[8] and cite Tacitus' statement that "Licinius Mucianus governed Syria with four legions..., the conduct of the Jewish War, with the command of three legions, lay in the hands of...Vespasian"[9]. But he was describing the situation of early 69, not mid-winter 66/67. Furthermore, Tacitus refers to Vespasian as the direct successor of Cestius (*Hist.* 5.10.1). Vespasian, then, had effective control of the entire area, including Syria, until Mucianus arrived in Aug./Sept. 67. For this reason, he had no hesitation in basing his forces for some time in Syria - in the city of Ptolemais: after all, most of Judaea was in open revolt. It could well be, then, that the conflict Tacitus mentions between Mucianus and Vespasian had its origins in this period of overlapping jurisdiction[10].

Titus was given command of the *legio XV Apollinaris*[11]. It was most unusual for the commander's son to receive such an appointment: perhaps Nero regarded the prudent and timely divorce of Marcia as establishing his reliability[12]. But there was another anomaly. He had not yet held the praetorship and it was usual, but not obligatory, for legionary legates to be appointed from the ranks of ex-praetors[13]. Such rapid advancement can hardly have resulted from his performance as military tribune: despite Mucianus' comments (*Hist.* 2.77), it was not so outstanding. The promotion, recommended by Vespasian and perhaps supported by Agrippa and Alexander, did clearly indicate that, for Nero, the Flavians represented no threat to his supremacy; after all, he could hardly have imagined that a *nouus homo* would ultimately replace the illustrious Julio-Claudians. It was not until the troops of Verginius Rufus urged him to assume the purple that it was evident to everyone that the imperial position need not necessarily be the preserve of the most noble section of the

aristocracy. The gap between a new senatorial family and one
such as the Claudii or Sulpicii was immense; once Verginius'
troops closed it, the position was far different, but not
until then. Nero always thought that the east was safe and
secure for him, even when the west obviously was not[14]. So
Titus' promotion, as well as Vespasian's appointment to
command the seven legions in Syria, is definite proof of their
reliability in Nero's eyes.

Vespasian left Greece and travelled over the Hellespont
towards Syria during the winter of 66/67, and, in February 67,
reached Antioch (*BJ* 3.8, 29), where he met two legions (*V
Macedonica* and *X Fretensis*) and their respective commanders
Sex. Vettulenus Cerialis and M. Ulpius Traianus (subsequently
referred to as Traianus to distinguish him from his son, the
future emperor Trajan)[15]. After a brief stay to assess the
situation and make preliminary plans, they proceeded to Syria,
where a base camp was established at Ptolemais (*BJ* 3.29).
Titus, meanwhile, had brought the *XV Apollinaris* from
Alexandria[16] (*BJ* 3.64-65). Apparently, Vespasian had no
intention of assigning the best legion to his son, for even
Titus' ardent admirer Josephus, in describing the arrival of
legio XV at Ptolemais, refers to the other two legions as "the
most outstanding"(*BJ* 3.65). Further troops were supplied by
Malachus II of the Nabataeans, C. Julius Antiochus IV (king of
Commagene in 69), C. Julius Sohaemus of Emesa, and M. Julius
Agrippa II: in all, the force numbered 60,000 (*BJ* 3.66-69)[17].

It seems that Vespasian's plan was first to gain control
of Galilee and, with a secure rear, to cut off Jerusalem from
all sides. At the beginning of May, the Roman army left
Ptolemais (*BJ* 3.115) and marched to the borders of Galilee
where an initial display of military strength[18] was made to
deter opposition. The first major Jewish stronghold to be
laid under siege was Jotapata (*BJ* 3.142 ff.), the chief centre
of resistance and regarded as the strongest in Galilee through
its natural and artificial fortifications (*BJ* 3.158-160).
Josephus, the commander of the insurgent forces of Galilee,
had assumed control of the city, which was able to withstand
the Roman attack for forty-seven days. It was during this
period that Vespasian himself was wounded (*BJ* 3.236). Meanwhile, inspired by the apparent success of Jotapata's
resistance in face of the Roman siege, one of the neighbouring
towns, Japha (*BJ* 3.289), also revolted. It was some ten miles
to the south of Jotapata (and two miles south-west of Nazar-
eth). Traianus, *legatus* of the *X Fretensis*, was sent to
subdue it. Due to the military inexperience and confusion of
the townsfolk, the majority of Japha's fighting force was
destroyed in the first onslaught. Assuming that the town was
capable of no further resistance, Traianus invited "Vespasian
to send his son Titus to complete the victory" (*BJ* 3.298). He
assumed command for the final assault and the town was taken
with little difficulty on June 25[19]. Titus' colleague, Sex.

Judaea

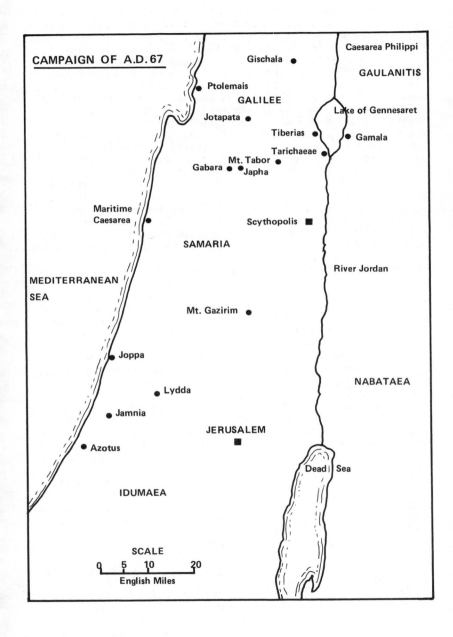

CAMPAIGN OF A.D. 67

Gischala ●

Caesarea Philippi

GAULANITIS

● Ptolemais

GALILEE

Lake of Gennesaret

Jotapata ●

Tiberias ●   ● Gamala

Tarichaeae

Mt. Tabor ●

Gabara ● ● Japha

Maritime
Caesarea ●

Scythopolis ■

SAMARIA

River Jordan

MEDITERRANEAN
SEA

Mt. Gazirim ●

● Joppa

NABATAEA

● Lydda

● Jamnia

JERUSALEM
■

● Azotus

Dead | Sea

IDUMAEA

SCALE

0   5   10   20

English Miles

37

Vettulenus Cerialis, had meanwhile been sent into Samaria and crushed the rebels assembled on Mt Garizim (*BJ* 3.315: June 27). At Jotapata, the end was at hand; once again, Titus was assigned a part in the final victory. Together with Domitius Sabinus and a small number of men from his legion, Titus scaled the walls in a surprise attack by night, and by morning the Romans were victorious (*BJ* 3.339: July 1). According to Josephus, 40,000 perished during the siege, all the remaining men were then killed by the Romans (the number was not indicated) and 1,200 women and children were sold into slavery. Josephus himself was brought before Vespasian (*BJ* 3.392 ff.), but, thanks to the arguments put forward by Titus[20], was allowed to live; then, in a second interview, he predicted[21] that soon Vespasian would be Caesar and emperor.

On July 4, the army returned to Ptolemais. The resistance at Jotapata and at Japha had shown that the suppression of the revolt would be a lengthy business and would require another season's campaigning at least. To rest his troops before continuing operations, Vespasian established permanent bases for the legions in non-Jewish cities, stationing legions V and X at Maritime Caesarea, whilst XV, with Titus, was assigned to Scythopolis, a city thirty-five miles to the east and also outside the province (*BJ* 3.412).

The most urgent task was to restore sea communications. In July, the prevailing winds rendered direct navigation between Alexandria and Rome impossible, and westbound ships had to travel via the coasts of Palestine, Syria, Asia Minor and across the Aegean. But Jewish rebels had occupied Joppa and were using it as a base for piracy, endangering Vespasian's links with Greece and Italy and threatening Rome's corn supply. By the end of July, it had been captured by a small Roman force (*BJ* 3.428).

Vespasian then set out for Agrippa's capital, Caesarea Philippi, arriving in early August. There he remained for twenty days to rest his army. But two of Agrippa's cities on the Lake of Gennesaret were in revolt (*BJ* 3.445) and Vespasian decided to subdue them. With his three legions he marched on Tiberias which opened its gates at the mere threat of force and welcomed the Romans as saviours and benefactors, whilst the rebels fled to Tarichaeae (*BJ* 3.461). There the occupants drew up their forces on the plain outside the town. Titus was sent against them with six hundred cavalrymen, but finding himself seriously outnumbered and detecting signs of alarm in his troops, sent a request to his father for reinforcements. Meanwhile, he fired his men with such enthusiasm that, when Traianus arrived with the reinforcements, Titus' troops were disappointed that a shared victory would bring them less credit. If reliable, Josephus' version of Titus' address to his forces (*BJ* 3.472-484) is a significant comment on Titus' ability to influence an audience: Josephus records the reaction as one of supernatural frenzy. At the first onset, the forces from Tarichaeae were routed and fled back to the city, fomenting political unrest amongst the townspeople. The fall of Tarichaeae (*BJ* 3.542: September 8) and the capture of Jotapata meant that all of Galilee except the rebel bastions of Mt Tabor and Gischala had been reduced. But, before tackling them, Vespasian moved into Agrippa's territory of Gaulanitis to subdue the fortress of Gamala which the king's troops had been besieging in vain for seven months. The fierce resistance displayed by the rebels together with the natural strength of Gamala forced Vespasian to use all three legions in the siege, which lasted almost as long as that of Jotapata, from August 24 until October 23 (*BJ* 4.17 ff.). It was during this siege that Titus was sent to Syria to visit Mucianus (*BJ* 4.32)[22]; he returned in time to lead the success-ful attack on the town.

During this period, Placidus led the capture of Mt Tabor (*BJ* 4.54-61). Gischala, the last of the unsubdued towns of Galilee, was at first inclined to peace, but the inhabitants were persuaded to fight by the redoubtable John, son of Levi (*BJ* 4.84-120); once he realized that the town was incapable of holding out against a siege, he begged Titus to defer to the Jewish law according to which the use of arms and even the signing of peace treaties were forbidden on the Sabbath (*BJ* 4.99-101). Titus, who was in sole command of an operation for the first time, was deceived by the stratagem, and John fled to Jerusalem. Nevertheless, Gischala was soon secured without loss[23] and those of its inhabitants who fled with John were captured and killed. Finally, Vespasian moved quickly to the south of Galilee and captured Lydda, Jamnia and Azotus (*BJ* 4.130, 444). With the year's operations at an end, Vespasian sent legion X under Traianus to Scythopolis and returned to Maritime Caesarea with legions V and XV, enabling Titus' legion to enjoy the amenities of that city instead of spending the winter in Scythopolis, where it had been assigned in August (*BJ* 3.412).

During the winter, Vespasian and his *legati* began to examine the problems involved in an attack on the capital. They urged (*BJ* 4.366) taking advantage of the city's internal problems[24] and attacking at once; Vespasian preferred to allow the rebels to continue fighting amongst themselves rather than risk the prospect of their reunification in face of an immediate attack on the city. So it was decided to isolate Jerusalem by subduing the rest of the province. Early in the following year (68), Vespasian emerged from Maritime Caesarea and moved on Gadara, capital of Peraea; its wealthy governing class quickly surrendered the city to avoid the risk of damage, but the rebels fled to be subdued ultimately by the efficient Placidus (*BJ* 4.419). Vespasian entered Gadara on March 4. He then returned the one hundred miles to Caesarea where he heard of Vindex' revolt (*BJ* 4.440): he would presumably not have arrived there before March 11[25].

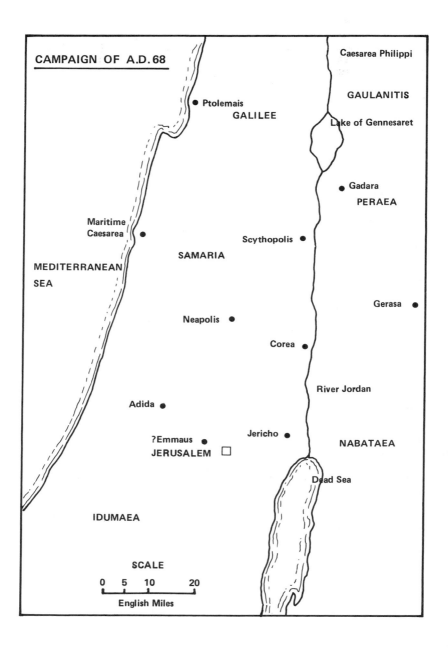

CAMPAIGN OF A.D. 68

Caesarea Philippi

GAULANITIS

Ptolemais
GALILEE

Lake of Gennesaret

Gadara
PERAEA

Maritime
Caesarea

Scythopolis

SAMARIA

MEDITERRANEAN
SEA

Gerasa

Neapolis

Corea

River Jordan

Adida

?Emmaus
JERUSALEM

Jericho

NABATAEA

Dead Sea

IDUMAEA

SCALE

0   5   10   20

English Miles

With the onset of spring, Vespasian moved south, in line with his intention to isolate the capital. Leaving *legio V* outside Emmaus to secure his rear, he marched along the coastal plain, systematically devastating the countryside; Idumaea was subjugated without undue delay (*BJ* 4.448). He then turned back northwards by way of Emmaus, through Samaria to Neapolis and camped at Corea on June 2 (*BJ* 4.449). To complete the encirclement of Jerusalem, garrisons were established at Jericho and Adida (*BJ* 4.486). Gerasa, north-east of the capital, was also taken, thus preventing exit from the city on every side. With encirclement complete, Vespasian returned to Maritime Caesarea, where he heard, not immediately, of Nero's death. The emperor had died on June 9 and the news would have reached Caesarea before the end of the month[26]. For a summary of the campaigns of 67 and 68, see Table 8.

Assessment of Titus' military ability as revealed in these campaigns is difficult, but one starting point is Table 8, listing thirteen towns subjugated during the first two years of the war. On this admittedly arbitrary criterion, Titus figured prominently in the conquest of five rebel centres, an impressive number of appearances for a quaestorian legionary legate. But no town was wholly subdued by Titus, with the exception of Gischala, and it lacked defences: it was largely a farming community: the subjugation consisted in accepting a surrender, in killing a number of refugees who were fleeing under the leadership of John, and involved no complex military strategy or manoeuvre. Titus' other conquests are similarly superficial when stripped of Josephus' embellishments. He could not disguise Titus' purely nominal role in the capture of Japha. Some modern historians[27] argue that the Romans' numerical inferiority at this time compelled Traianus to send for reinforcements and that therefore he needed Titus to achieve, rather than complete, the victory. But Josephus (*BJ* 3.298) has Traianus sending his message to Vespasian immediately after informing his readers that 12,000 had perished within Japha: if the Jews retained numerical superiority even then, it would have redounded to Titus' credit and Josephus would have had no reason not to mention it. Titus' role, then, was nominal, as it was in the siege of Jotapata, where he was conspicuously absent until his sudden appearance in the final chapter. In the siege of Tarichaeae, he again emerges in Josephus' narrative as a true hero. Yet the leaders managed to escape in boats on the lake and Vespasian was obliged to send after them on rafts: his success in capturing them was commemorated on a coin[28], and this was the only battle to be given such prominence. Thus the victory was Vespasian's, and Titus' inexperience only too apparent. Titus' appearance at Gamala was also dramatically presented: he had gone to visit Mucianus in Syria and, on his return, "was indignant at the reverse which the Romans had sustained in his absence...(but when) the guards were

TABLE 8:   SIEGES OF A.D. 67 AND A.D. 68

STRONGHOLD	JOSEPHUS, *BJ*	COMMANDER	DATE
Jotapata	3.142,316-408	Vespasian (and Titus)	July 1, 67
Japha	3.289 ff.	Traianus (and Titus)	June 25, 67
Mt Gazirim	3.307 ff.	Cerialis	June 27, 67
Joppa	3.414 ff.	None recorded	ca. July 67
Tiberias	3.453	Vespasian	Aug. 67
Tarichaeae	3.462-542	Vespasian (and Titus, Traianus and Antonius Silo)	Sept. 8, 67
Gamala	4.11	Vespasian (and Titus)	Aug. 24/ Sept. 23, 67
Mt Tabor	4.54-61	Placidus	ca. Oct. 67
Gischala	4.84 ff.	Titus	ca. Oct. 67
Lydda, Jamnia, Azotus	4.130 ff.	Vespasian	ca. Oct. 67
Gadara	4.419-439	Vespasian	March 4, 68
Jericho	4.450 ff.	Traianus	June 3, 68
Gerasa	4.480	Lucius Annius	ca. June 68

informed of his entry, they flew with shouts to arms, and those (of the enemy) who faced Titus were incessantly dropping" (*BJ* **4.70-71**).

In general, the tasks assigned to Titus were efficiently performed, and whilst his competence was beyond doubt, they were all relatively easy to accomplish and intended to show him as a daring and successful leader. On the other hand, he was the son of the supreme commander, and it could be expected that he would be granted more eminence than his experience warranted. Again, it may be that he made some contribution to the planning of strategy at Vespasian's councils of war. Josephus' account discloses no trace of this, as he avoids any mention of strategy and Roman politics generally.

Now an assessment of Titus' military ability during the first two seasons (67 and 68) is complicated by the fact that he does not appear in the battle records of 68: Josephus' silence is significant. During the siege of Gamala he had gone to Syria, presumably to welcome Mucianus to his new command (*BJ* 4.32: Aug./Sept. 67). After that, he could well have had duties of a similar but more personal and delicate nature. It is fairly certain that Vespasian knew of Vindex's revolt before it was officially proclaimed in Gaul, i.e. on his return to Caesarea from Gadara (March 11, 68)[29]. Prudence demanded that he should be aware of the attitude of his colleague in Syria; after all, Vindex had sent letters to various provincial *legati*[30]. In such delicate negotiations, Titus must have been invaluable[31]. But there were other problems, in particular that of overlapping jurisdiction. Vespasian had not hesitated to operate from Syria, as he was almost certainly entitled to do; but the arrival of a governor of that province demanded that the position be explained and any problems solved. It would seem that some were fairly difficult, and hence Titus was obliged to maintain fairly frequent contact with Mucianus during the first half of 68. Now it has been argued that Vespasian's imperial aspirations can be dated to October 67, the time of Titus' first visit to Mucianus and of Josephus' astonishing predictions[32]. But Mucianus can hardly have reached Syria before late summer 67, which would not allow time for the quarrel between him and Vespasian to break out and then be solved by October. Our ancient sources stress that the two governors resolved their differences at around the time of Nero's death (*Hist.* 2.5; *Vesp.* 5.1; Dio 66.8.3), which implies a date nearer June 68 than October 67. Thus the meeting of 67 must have been restricted to an exchange of diplomatic niceties between neighbouring *legati*: but relations cooled once Mucianus became aware of Vespasian's "encroachment" into his territory and further meetings in the first months of 68 became essential. As Tacitus notes:

> As governors of Syria and Judaea respectively, Mucianus and Vespasian had been divided by the jealousy which is typical of the administration of neighbouring provinces. It was Nero's death that finally healed the breach and led to close collaboration, initially at staff level. Then Titus did much to inspire confidence. He managed to remove petty friction by an appeal to their common interests, and in him a nice mixture of frankness and diplomacy was able to fascinate even the sophisticated Mucianus[33].

Tacitus clearly believes that the dispute between them was still of significance during the early months of 68, and that therefore Vespasian's (and Titus') imperial ambitions had to be assigned to 69 rather than to 67. He also pays tribute to Titus' undoubted ability as a mediator, perhaps an unexpected role for a senator who was not yet thirty.

NERO'S DEATH: PROCLAMATION OF VESPASIAN

By the end of June 68, news of Nero's death had reached Vespasian at Caesarea. The uncertainty of events in Rome and the attitude of the new emperor demanded that he consult neighbouring *legati* about problems of mutual safety and common policy; for this, Titus was his agent. Furthermore, Nero's death was followed by a period of inactivity in Judaea and, in fact, during the next twelve months[34], all efforts were directed towards the civil war (*Hist.* 5.10), culminating in Vespasian's proclamation as emperor by Ti. Julius Alexander on July 1, 69 (*Hist.* 2.79). In these events, Titus' role was not inconsiderable.

He continued acting as his father's representative in negotiations with Mucianus in order, no doubt, to determine a common policy in face of the new emperor's intentions, but, in effect, all that could be done was to recognize Galba and await his reaction. It was negative. His failure to confirm Vespasian's command was typical of his attitude to those he distrusted, and other incidents would have done little to reassure Vespasian: a slow[35], bloody march to Rome had been followed by widespread executions (*Hist.* 1.6) and Sabinus II was dismissed from his post as city prefect. A meeting with the new emperor was essential and, once again, responsibility was thrust on Titus.

His visit to Galba was subsequently used by Flavian propagandists to enhance the dynasty's image and legalize the usurpation of power. Ti. Julius Alexander's proclamation in Egypt, together with the well-attested support of oriental kings, savoured not a little of the east, and it was hoped to remedy this by proposing a novel explanation for the voyage from Palestine to Rome in the middle of winter: Galba wanted to adopt Titus as his successor[36]. Another implausible reason, offered subsequently, was Titus' desire to stand for the praetorship (*Hist.* 2.1); but even though he was of the appropriate age, it was far too late for him to offer himself as a candidate, since the elections for 69 had already been conducted[37]. The trip must have been undertaken at that time of the year, mid-winter, for more substantial reasons - the deaths of prominent officials (*Hist.* 1.7), the dismissal of Vespasian's brother and the possible continued failure to confirm the Judaean command[38]. Titus, Agrippa II and some *amici* were sent to Rome, presumably in the hope of arranging a *modus uiuendi* with Galba in the light of these problems. But, on reaching Corinth, probably towards the end of January, Titus heard that "Galba was dead and that Vitellius was arming for war" (*Hist.* 2.1).

At a meeting of the members of the Roman delegation,

Titus argued that it would be foolish for him to continue on
to Rome and become a hostage in the hands of either Otho or
Vitellius; on the other hand, to return to Judaea might be
interpreted by the new emperor as an insult, one that would
probably be forgiven so long as his father joined the winner's
side. But if Vespasian claimed the principate (*sin Vespasianus rem publicam susciperet*), any insults would be forgotten
(*Hist.* 2.1). It would seem that Titus was the first of the
Flavian group to consider seizing the empire and he did so in
February 69, at the Corinth meeting[39].

It was decided that Agrippa should continue on to Rome
whilst Titus rejoined his father. Despite the attractions of
Berenice (*Hist.* 2.2), he seems to have been in no hurry to
return but, on the contrary, consulted the oracle at Paphos
(*Hist.* 2.2-4), and rejoined Vespasian at Maritime Caesarea,
presumably no earlier than the middle of February, after first
passing through Syria[40]; his arrival restored the troops'
confidence (*Hist.* 2.4). Furthermore, it was on his return
that Vespasian and Mucianus realized the inevitability of
civil war and began to prepare for it (*Hist.* 2.6-7). Suetonius (*Vesp.* 5) and Dio (65.8.3) confirm the date[41]: only
Josephus, in an effort to be consistent with Flavian propaganda, prefers a later period.

In fact, Josephus' version is particularly interesting.
In his account of the aftermath of Galba's death (*BJ* 4.498
ff.), mention is made of Titus' voyage, of his rapid return
through fear, of the suspense into which the murder of Galba
threw the Flavian leaders and of Vespasian's decision to post-
pone action in the war against the Jews. There is no hint of
Titus' attitude at Corinth nor of the suggestion that his
father might claim the principate; the visit to Paphos is
omitted as is the reaction of the soldiers on his return.

Consistent with this is his account of the Judaean
campaign of 69, and, in particular, the commencement of it,
which is assigned (*BJ* 4.550) to 5 Daisios, i.e. June 5, 14 or
23, depending on which calendar Josephus used[42]. Yet the
general context suggests that it began at the usual time,
around the last week of March. Essentially, Vespasian aimed
at re-establishing control of the approaches to Jerusalem, and
Josephus' account of his actions begins immediately after his
notice of Otho's death (*BJ* 4.548: April 16). Vespasian moved
from Maritime Caesarea into Judaea, whilst Cerialis concentrated on the area of Idumaea (*BJ* 4.550 ff.). There follows a
description of Jerusalem's internal problems (*BJ* 4.577, which
he dates to April/May 69), of the condition of Italy under the
victorious Vitellian armies and of the return of Vespasian to
Caesarea where he learned that Vitellius was emperor (*BJ* 4.585
ff.). The chronology of the campaign has long been in dispute.
One scholar[43] simply assigns the events of 69 to 68, whilst
another[44] argues that "5 Daisios" refers, not to the commencement, but rather to the conclusion of the campaign, a solution

45

that does considerable violence to the rest of the text. It has also been suggested that "Daisios" be amended to read "Dystros" (March). On the other hand, Josephus may well have deliberately (but inconsistently) altered the chronology so as to be more in line with the official version of Vespasian's proclamation, the spontaneous acclamation by the soldiers of Judaea (not Egypt, for that would seem too "oriental"), as they returned victorious against Rome's enemies and heard of Vitellius' attacks on Italy and on Rome herself[45].

The February meeting at Corinth was of some significance, for it was then that Titus considered the possibility of seizing the empire, and he made his attitude known to his associates. He provided the stimulus, and, on his return, the Flavians began organizing and preparing for civil war, as all the ancient sources except Josephus indicate. Yet in a sense his attitude confirms that the Flavians started planning early in 69: his omission of significant facts concerning Titus' Corinth meeting and his rearrangement, or inaccurace presentation, of others (the "hasty" return to Judaea through "fear", the reaction of the Flavians on hearing of Galba's death, Vespasian's postponement to June of the campaign against the Jews and the acclamation by the Judaean legions before those of Egypt), all suggest a deliberate effort by Josephus to conceal something significant.

From February to June, whilst preparations were being made for civil war, little is heard of Titus, but considerable use must have been made of his diplomatic talents in dealings with Mucianus in Syria, Agrippa and Berenice in Caesarea Philippi, and Ti. Julius Alexander in Egypt. Perhaps there is a hint of Titus' activities in Mucianus' comment (at the time when the oath to Vitellius was being administered, presumably by the end of May) that, whilst he was not unfriendly towards Vespasian, he was still more attached to Titus (*Hist*. 2.74); just as suggestive is the fact that Ti. Julius Alexander was promoted from Egypt to be Titus' chief of staff in the Judaean war. His relationship with both of these was close and obviously a significant factor in the Flavian organization.

After the death of Otho and the recognition of Vitellius, first by the senate on April 19 and later by the legions, Vespasian either hesitated[46] or else played a waiting game until about the middle of June when he, Mucianus and their legates and friends met, possibly at Mount Carmel (*Hist*. 2.74 ff.). Presumably, a decision to act was taken and a date may even have been fixed; but after returning to Maritime Caesarea, Vespasian sent Titus back to Mucianus, presumably to finalize their arrangements (*Hist*. 2.79). The culmination came on July 1 when the legions of Egypt declared for Vespasian; Judaea followed two days later and all of Syria by the 15th (*Hist*. 2.79-81). Before the end of the month a conference was held at Berytus, where it was decided that Mucianus should lead the forces against Vitellius, that

Vespasian should move to Egypt with the aim of gaining control
of the grain shipments in case it was necessary to starve
Italy into surrender, and that Titus should assume control of
the Judaean war (*Hist.* 2.82).

During the remaining months of 69, Vespasian and Titus
spent two to three months in Syria and Palestine arranging
matters to their satisfaction. It would appear that Titus was
given overall control of both Judaea and Syria; Mucianus had
left in the middle of August and L. Caesennius Paetus did not
arrive to take up his appointment as *legatus* until late in
70[47], and so, in the interim, the legate of the legion *IV
Scythica*, Gnaeus Pompeius Collega, probably had the responsibility for only the civil administration of Syria[48]. By the
end of 69, Vespasian and Titus were in Alexandria, planning a
blockade of Rome and an invasion of Africa by land and sea to
gain complete control of the grain supply (*Hist.* 3.48).

Despite the official propaganda, the Flavian attack was
well organized. Preparations had been made early in 69 and
Titus' role, both in the initial stages and, subsequently, in
the vital negotiations with Mucianus and Ti. Julius Alexander,
was particularly significant but not pre-eminent. The
evidence does not suggest that anyone other than Vespasian was
in charge. He alone knew when to act and when to wait, a
quality conspicuously lacking in Titus. His recklessness had
been evident in the first year's campaigns and was to be even
more apparent during the siege, despite the presence of
Alexander.

SIEGE OF JERUSALEM

Titus' siege of Jerusalem is undoubtedly the exploit for which
he is most remembered[49], for almost every author who discusses
Titus or the history of the city itself acclaims him as its
conqueror[50]. Details of the siege, however, are far less
widely recorded, the only substantial account surviving being
that of Josephus, recently examined by Schürer and Smallwood[51].
Titus' achievement can to some extent be assessed by considering the minutiae of the siege, so carefully documented by
Josephus, and also by examining the factors which influenced
its outcome. Thus the situation in Jerusalem, her internal
politics, her contemporary social problems and her fortifications should be compared with the experience of Titus' army,
the competence of his generals and the previous Roman
victories in Judaea - all of which suggest that Rome's success
was in fact inevitable. This is not to denigrate Titus'
achievement: it was the deserved result of his persistence
and efficiency, qualities which Vespasian had earlier shown in
the campaign against Judaea, and which Titus, as his father's
legate, must have learned to appreciate.

The political scene in Jerusalem at the outset of the
siege has been variously interpreted. Josephus' bias against

his rival, John of Gischala, and his anti-Zealot feelings have unfortunately dominated his account, and, in the absence of further literary evidence, this bias is highly detrimental to any balanced understanding of the factional strife[52] within the city. The arrival in Jerusalem of John of Gischala and his followers together with various other extremists towards the end of 67 strengthened the hands of the war party (*BJ* 4.121 ff.). The country population around the capital had for some time been in a state of dissension between the advocates of war and the more moderate element who desired peace, headed by Ananus, the high priest. As the Zealots were in a minority, they sought the assistance of the Idumaeans, whom they admitted into the city by night. The Idumaeans, incensed by the Zealots against the moderate party, fell upon Ananus and his followers. Ananus was killed and, with him, many of his supporters (*BJ* 4.305-317). The Idumaeans then withdrew from Jerusalem. The situation was still further complicated by the factions within the Zealot party, for John was not the only Zealot leader. Eleazar, son of Simon, also had a considerable following; he established his base in the Temple, which was garrisoned as a fortress. A temporary alliance between these two groups of extremists soon collapsed (*BJ* 4.31), and the situation worsened when the moderate party invited yet a third Zealot leader into the capital with the intention of weakening the others. The new arrival was Simon, son of Giora, whose entry into Jerusalem can be assigned to April 69 (*BJ* 4.538 ff.).

Thus there existed three extremist factions within the city, each violently opposed to the others. Eleazar, with about 2,400 followers, held the inner court of the Temple; John, with 6,000, controlled the outer court and part of the Lower City, whilst Simon, with 15,000, was in control of the rest of the Lower City and most of the Upper (*BJ* 4.577-584; 5.239, 248-252). A three-cornered struggle followed in which a substantial amount of the city's grain stock was destroyed; before the next harvest was gathered in April/May 70, the siege had begun.

Torn by internal strife, the city was further burdened by the arrival of the faithful who had come to celebrate the Passover. Many of the city's inhabitants at the time of the siege were thus not prepared for a prolonged stay, and the drain on resources clearly took its toll early. Famine and disease were rife. On the Roman side, Titus was not loath to take advantage of the city's distress: walls were erected to prevent egress from the city, and every precaution taken to stop her food supply. On the other hand, the city's fortifications, both natural and artificial, were a decided advantage[53]. Jerusalem was built on two hills, a high western one and a smaller one to the east, divided by a north-south ravine, the Tyropoeon. North of the smaller hill was the site of the Temple and adjoining it lay the Antonia fortress. Both hills

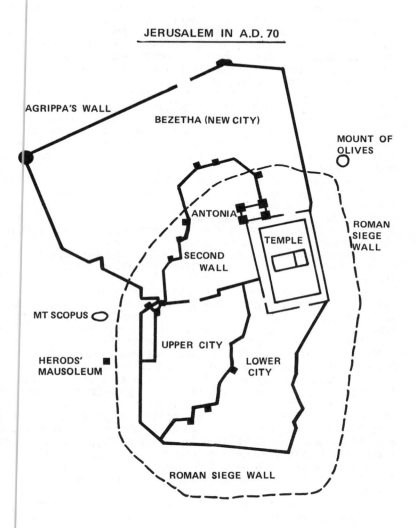

JERUSALEM IN A.D. 70

AGRIPPA'S WALL

BEZETHA (NEW CITY)

MOUNT OF OLIVES

ANTONIA

ROMAN SIEGE WALL

TEMPLE

SECOND WALL

MT SCOPUS

UPPER CITY

HERODS' MAUSOLEUM

LOWER CITY

ROMAN SIEGE WALL

were enclosed by a common wall, another one ran along the Tyropoeon, and the site of the Temple had substantial walls on all sides. To the west, south and east, the outer wall was built on high precipices, and hence the city had to be attacked from the fairly level north. On that side, three walls existed, the outer one being Agrippa's wall. The solidity of her fortifications represented Jerusalem's sole advantage, but this was severely outweighed by the disadvantages of internecine strife, overpopulation,together with limited resources, fighting men and knowledge of warfare. Moreover, with few minor exceptions, the whole of Judaea had already succumbed to the Romans. Thus, despite her strength, it could be only a matter of time before the endurance of the besiegers would overwhelm her.

Vespasian remained in Alexandria until the summer of 70, whilst Titus, who had been assigned overall command of the Jewish War at Berytus, had proceeded to Palestine[54]. He had four legions at his disposal, the legion *XII Fulminata* from Syria having been added to the Judaean force, and also 2,000 men from the two legions of Egypt (*III Cyrenaica* and *XXII Deiotariana*) who were intended to replace the soldiers taken by Mucianus for the campaign against Vitellius. The auxiliary forces remained as before, but the client kings increased their forces, with Agrippa and Sohaemus leading theirs in person. The commanders of the legions were Sextus Vettulenus Cerialis (V), A. Larcius Lepidus Sulpicianus (X) and M. Tittius Frugi (XV); the *legatus* of legion XII is not named by Josephus. In charge of the forces from Alexandria was C. Aeternius Fronto[55], whilst the procurator of Judaea, M. Antonius Julianus, was also on the staff[56].

The most interesting appointment was that of Ti. Julius Alexander[57] as chief of staff to Titus; apparently, Vespasian felt that his son lacked the experience to be in sole command of the army. Alexander was a man of considerable talent. His Jewish background, administrative ability (he had been procurator of Judaea from 46 to 48 and prefect of Egypt twenty years later) and military experience with Corbulo made him an excellent choice - and he and Vespasian were old friends. Josephus comments on Vespasian's choice of Alexander as follows:-

> With them was the most tried of all his friends for loyalty and sagacity, Tiberius Alexander, formerly in charge of Egypt in the interests of Titus and his father, and now considered worthy to assume command of these armies, because he had been the first to welcome the arising dynasty, and, with splendid faith, had attached himself to its fortunes while they were as yet uncertain. Through his age and experience, he was pre-eminent in the exigencies of war... (*BJ* 5.45-46).

Alexander's services were soon needed. Whilst part of the army had been ordered to meet him outside Jerusalem, Titus

himself set off from Caesarea with the main force (*BJ* 5.40)
and reached his destination a few days before the Passover;
but he had hurried on ahead with six hundred cavalrymen and
was fortunate not to have been taken by the Jews (*BJ* 5.47-66).
Finally, the army was assembled near Jerusalem: legion X
established a base on the Mount of Olives, whilst the other
three were camped on Mt Scopus.

Following an unsuccessful attempt to persuade the Jews to
accept terms - concern for Jerusalem was not in Titus' mind:
surrender would have been less costly - Titus began an assault
on Agrippa's wall which enclosed the so-called New City or
suburb of Bezetha. After fifteen days, the Roman siege-
engines breached the wall; all of Bezetha fell into their
hands, a long section of Agrippa's wall was demolished, and,
more importantly, they were much closer to the Antonia (*BJ*
5.302: May 5). The attack was continued immediately. Titus
advanced his camp inside Agrippa's wall just out of bowshot
from the second wall, which provided the city with more
effective defence than had Agrippa's. It was flanked at each
end by a fortress and further reinforced by a great tower
almost midway between two flanking towers. This was now the
Romans' chief target. Within five days, the second wall was
captured only to be regained by the Jews: their triumph was
brief, however, for, after four days, the Romans had recaptur-
ed it. The entire wall, apart from its western section, was
then demolished (*BJ* 5.347: May 14).

Titus now faced the most difficult part of the siege, the
capture of the first wall and the Temple, which, apart from
being a double fortress in itself, was also protected by the
Antonia. The defenders were now learning how to utilize their
artillery and to dig mines; consequently, the Romans' first
attacks were thwarted. It was then decided to construct two
platforms against the wall and two against the Antonia[58].
This operation took seventeen days, only to be undermined by
the ingenuity of John and Simon(*BJ* 5.466-485). Whilst this
was in progress, Titus again tried to persuade the Jews to
surrender. Josephus himself, from a safe distance, urged the
defenders to give in whilst there was still hope of mercy, but
his lengthy appeal fell on deaf ears (*BJ* 5.362-419). A more
powerful argument, however, was famine, for food was already
short. Those who sought relief in flight were cut down by the
Jews themselves; or else, if captured by the Romans, were
crucified in full view of those within the walls or sent back
with mutilated limbs (*BJ* 5.459).

As a result of these failures, a different plan of attack
had to be devised. A council of war (*BJ* 5.491) was summoned
in which the six leading officers discussed and accepted
Titus' plan of building a wall around the city. It extended
from the Roman camp inside Agrippa's wall to the Mount of
Olives where *legio X* was camped, then continued south and west,
turned north past the Herods' mausoleum and back to the

starting point. It had thirteen towers, each two hundred feet
in circumference (*BJ* 5.504-507), allowing the Romans to keep
the Jews under strict surveillance. Its construction - in
three days, so we are informed (*BJ* 5.509) - surprised even so
ardent an admirer of Titus as Josephus himself, but, however
long it took, the circumvallation had the desired effect of
increasing starvation. Josephus has numerous gruesome stories
of the results, which, even if exaggerated, are horrible
enough (*BJ* 5.512, 548; 6.193). In June, Titus built new
platforms opposite the Antonia, and, as the surrounding
district was now thoroughly stripped of timber, he had to have
it brought from nine miles away (*BJ* 5.224). After twenty-one
days' labour, all was completed; the Jews, led by John, again
attempted an attack but were easily beaten back (*BJ* 6.22: July
1). Soon after, the wall of the Antonia subsided, partly
because of the tunnel John's men had driven under it in May to
undermine the Roman platforms (*BJ* 6.28); but the storming
operation was still difficult, since John had already erected
a second wall behind it. On July 3, after a rousing speech by
Titus, a Syrian soldier named Sabinus with eleven others tried
to scale this wall, but was killed in the attempt as were
three of his companions (*BJ* 6.67). Two days later, the Romans
were more successful, and even managed to drive the Jews back
to the Temple zone, but the forces of John and Simon, combined
for once, drove them back; the Antonia, however, was in Roman
hands and was razed to the ground, providing access to the
Temple on a wider front.

In spite of war and famine, the Jews had continued to
offer the daily morning and evening sacrifices, but, on the
day on which the demolition of the Antonia began,these had to be
suspended (*BJ* 6.94: July 17), not because of famine but rather
from lack of men. The suspension had a detrimental effect on
Jewish morale, but not so much as to cause them to succumb to
a further call to surrender (*BJ* 6.97-113). It soon became
clear that a full-scale attack on the walls of the Temple was
essential. It formed a fairly regular square surrounded by
substantial walls, inside of which was the inner forecourt,
also protected on all sides by strong walls. So Titus ahd
first to gain control of the outer defences. Again, all four
legions were set to the task of erecting platforms (*BJ* 6.149-
151) which were virtually completed by August 8. But, instead
of using the battering-rams, Titus had his men attempt to
scale the wall; when they were driven back with heavy losses,
he ordered the wooden gates to be fired and thus opened a way
to the outer Temple court (*BJ* 6.228: August 8).

The following day, a council of war[59] was held to determine the fate of the Temple and, according to Josephus, the
Romans decided to spare it (*BJ* 6.237-243). On the 10th[60],
however, the Jews mounted two attacks from the inner court,
and in repelling the second of these, one of Titus' soldiers
threw a firebrand (*BJ* 6.252) into the antechamber of the

Temple proper. Before the flames spread, Titus and his staff were able to enter the Holy of Holies without opposition (*BJ* 6.260), for the Jews respected its sanctity even at such a time. The Romans removed the golden furniture, the trumpets, the Table of the Shewbread and the seven-branched candelabrum, whilst the area was deliberately set on fire. Titus is said to have ordered the blaze extinguished, but the soldiers repeatedly ignored his orders (*BJ* 6.266): the accuracy of Josephus' statement is examined below. All who fell into the Romans' hands were butchered, though John managed to escape to the Upper City. The same evening, the Romans celebrated their victory by hailing Titus as *imperator*[61] and offering sacrifice in the outer court to their standards, the final desecration of the Temple.

Ultimate success against such a heavily fortified city as Jerusalem can be regarded as a clear indication of military proficiency, but whether credit belongs to Titus personally or to the efficiency of the Roman military machine is less easy to determine. The tactics employed throughout the siege reveal him as a commander in the traditional Roman mould, adhering closely to the standard manoeuvres for attacking a city - the defence wall designed to prevent the besieged from receiving supplies or reinforcements, the use of towers, catapults and battering-rams[62]. Again, the role played by extraneous factors should not be ignored: Josephus himself dated the fall of Jerusalem to the day when Ananus, the high priest, was murdered and factional strife overtook the city (*BJ* 4.318). The achievement of Titus was not so much the result of personal genius, despite the tone of Josephus' account. On the other hand, there is no need to deny him credit justly due. He was a relatively young man conducting a siege that would have taxed the skills of any experienced commander, and Jerusalem's defences were formidable. His immaturity was evident on a number of occasions in the campaign. His courageous but reckless intervention in the initial stages of the siege, despite the pleas and blunt advice (*BJ* 5.88) of his associates to remember his position as commander, could well have jeopardized the campaign at the outset. He once displayed an unfortunate naivety which directly caused the loss of the second wall and must have cost the Romans dearly in morale and manpower (*BJ* 5.332-339). On another eight occasions, he intervened in battles in a manner that indicated to Josephus his undoubted personal bravery, but, to a less biased observer, seem to be mere foolhardiness[63]. On one of these missions, he was wounded in the shoulder to such an extent that his arm was always weaker: it is perhaps not surprising that only Dio reports that incident (66.5.1). These flaws, more the result of inexperience and impetuosity rather than professional incompetence, were countered by his unfailing energy in the field of battle, and his ability to inspire the loyalty and cooperation of his troops. He seems to have lost control of them on one

occasion only, when, duped into thinking that the city was on
the point of surrender, they disregarded standing orders in
their eagerness for combat (*BJ* 5.109 ff.). His lack of tact-
ical imagination was probably of more serious consequence[64].
In spite of these reservations, his ability to use traditional
methods to overcome a stubborn, if divided, foe leaves little
doubt that, if he had continued to pursue a military career,
he could well have become one of the leading generals of his
day. He would never have been a Scipio, though.

During the confusion of her last days, so vividly portrayed by Josephus, Jerusalem's Temple was razed to the
ground, and historians have long been concerned with the
problem of establishing a culprit. According to Josephus (*BJ*
6.241, 254-260), the Temple was set on fire contrary to the
orders of Titus who had decided to overrule his staff and
spare the building: he made unavailing efforts to save it but
was thwarted by his men's refusal to heed his orders. Elsewhere, his fervent admiration for the Flavians leads him to
portray Vespasian and Titus in a more favourable light than
was justified, and, not surprisingly, historians both ancient
and modern have regarded his version with considerable suspicion. In the account of Sulpicius Severus, a Christian writer
of the fourth century, Titus is said to have supported those
of his officers who wanted the Temple destroyed:-

> Titus is said to have first summoned a council and
> deliberated whether or not he should destroy such a
> mighty temple, for some thought that a consecrated shrine,
> which was famous beyond all other works of men, ought not
> to be razed to the ground. Their argument was that to
> preserve it would bear witness to the moderation of Rome,
> while its destruction would forever brand her as cruel.
> Others, however, including Titus himself, opposed this
> view and said that the destruction of the Temple was a
> prime necessity in order to wipe out more completely the
> religion of the Jews and the Christians; for they urged
> that these religions, although hostile to each other,
> nevertheless sprang from the same sources; the
> Christians had grown out of the Jews: if the root were
> destroyed, the stock would easily perish[65].

Now, whilst it might seem hazardous to reject contemporary
evidence, it should be noted that Sulpicius Severus' source
was probably Tacitus, or perhaps M. Antonius Julianus, procurator of Judaea in 70 and one of those present at the council[66]:
Josephus did not have first-hand knowledge of the discussions
that took place at the meeting, although it is clear that he
was at imperial headquarters at the time. The suggestion that
Christianity motivated Titus is hardly likely: Tacitus seems
to have avoided all mention of the new religion in his
Histories[67]. No doubt Sulpicius Severus introduced it some
centuries later, after consulting and making substantial use
of Tacitus' version of Titus' deliberations.

Some have argued that Titus hoped to spare the building if it was at all possible and to destroy it only in case of military necessity: Josephus would then be guilty of only a partial lie[68]. That argument does not seem particularly convincing: the Romans had no intention of repeating the experience of the past few years. On the other hand, the view that Titus' natural brutality - compare the slaughter of thousands of Jews at the games (*BJ* 7.23-24) - motivated the decision is, at best, of limited value, in view of the general military and political considerations. The Temple was the symbol of Jewish resistance, dominating Jerusalem physically and spiritually. Note, for instance, the comment from the Talmud (B[e]ra*k*ot 33b) on the significance of the destruction: "An iron wall intervened between Israel and its Father in Heaven". Vespasian's policy had been to allow the enemy to flee into the capital rather than to deal with groups of fanatics spread over the countryside. Once he had them there, he meant to kill them and then destroy the symbol of their resistance. There were sound strategic and political reasons to limit the possibility of future rebellions. The Temple had to be destroyed[69].

The destruction of the Temple did not mean that the conquest was completed. The Upper City remained in the hands of John and Simon for about a month. They slaughtered the civilian refugees to make room for themselves, whilst the Lower City was left to the Romans to loot and burn at will. Finally, earthworks were begun on August 20 and finished on September 7. Success was immediate and the Jews fled, abandoning the Upper City to the Romans who spent the rest of the day, September 8, in indiscriminate massacring, looting and burning (*BJ* 6.407).

The inhabitants who had not died of famine or the sword were executed, sent to the mines or reserved for gladiatorial combat. Seven hundred of the tallest and most handsome of the young men were reserved for Titus' triumph. John and Simon both survived; the former surrendered, but Simon was caught after some effort. Their lives were spared so as to enable them to walk through Rome to grace Titus' triumph. The city was razed to the ground with the exception of one of the towers of Herod's palace and a part of the wall. The victory, achieved after a siege of five months, was celebrated by Titus with a long speech of praise for the army's valour, with rewards for outstanding acts of bravery and with a festive banquet (*BJ* 7.1-17). With the capture of Jerusalem, Titus felt that the war was virtually won and that the reduction of the fortresses of Herodium, Machaerus and Masada could safely be left to another commander with a smaller force: the first two were taken by Lucilius Bassus and Masada by L. Flavius Silva Nonius Bassus[70].

TITUS IN THE EAST

As it was October and, so it would seem, too late for a voyage
to Italy[71], Titus decided to spend the winter at Agrippa's
palace at Caesarea Philippi: *legio XII* was sent to Melitene,
X was left to garrison the province, whilst *V* and *XV* guarded
the prisoners and booty deposited at Maritime Caesarea (*BJ*
7.17-19). In Agrippa's capital, he arranged displays in which
the prisoners played leading roles, being thrown to wild
beasts or compelled to fight each other in battles staged for
the enjoyment of the spectators (*BJ* 7.23). At Maritime
Caesarea, over 2,500 perished at the games for the celebration
of Domitian's birthday (*BJ* 7.36: October 24). Titus then
moved to Berytus where he celebrated his father's birthday
with even more elaborate scenes of butchery (*BJ* 7.39-40:
November 17). After spending some time there, he moved on to
Antioch (*BJ* 7.96, 100-104) where the welcome was particularly
enthusiastic. He was urged to order the expulsion of the Jews
from the city but refused and immediately left, proceeding to
Zeugma on the Euphrates (*BJ* 7.105), where envoys from the
Parthian king, Vologaeses, presented him with a golden crown,
congratulating him for his victory over the Jews. The incident is not without interest. The Parthians were worried, and
with reason. In 69 they had offered Vespasian the use of
40,000 cavalry (*Vesp.* 6.4; *Hist.* 4.51): he told them that he
was flattered, but that they should send envoys to the senate,
and conclude a formal peace treaty (*Hist.* 4.51). In fact, he
had no intention of being seen as a dependant of a Parthian
king and, besides, the war was virtually won. It would seem
that the Parthians followed his advice, for Suetonius refers
to Vologaeses' envoys seeking to renew the *societas*[72] with
Rome (*Nero* 57.2). Despite this superficially cordial relationship with Vespasian, Vologaeses had good cause to worry in 70
when, at the conquest of Jerusalem, Titus captured several
sons of king Izates of Adiabene and of his successor and half-
brother Monobazus (*BJ* 6.356). Izates had been nominally a
Parthian vassal and Monobazus himself commanded (Dio, 62.20.2)
the auxiliaries sent to aid the Parthians in their invasion of
Armenia (*Ann.* 15.1); in addition, both Izates and Monobazus
were Jewish converts (*AJ* 20.92) and the latter's relatives are
attested as having fought well against the Romans (*BJ* 2.520)[73].
Vologaeses no doubt regarded with some embarrassment the
prospect of these associates of his being paraded as prisoners
through the streets of Rome; indeed their mere presence with
the Jewish forces may have prompted his offer to Vespasian.
    There were other reasons for him to be concerned. Titus
had recently sent the legion *XII Fulminata* to Melitene in
Cappadocia (*BJ* 7.18), a province that had no legions during
the Jewish war (*Hist.* 2.81). This may well have prompted the
Parthian embassy to Zeugma. In addition, it was at this time
that Titus' uncle (by marriage), L. Caesennius Paetus, was

sent to govern Syria[74]. Vologaeses would have regarded such an appointment as ominous, for it indicated that Vespasian expected confrontation with Parthia: Paetus would want revenge for his previous debacle at Rhandeia (Dio, 62.21.1). It is also possible, but not certain, that Vespasian had already begun the reorganization of the Cappadocia-Galatia complex; if so, the *XVI Flauia Firma* would have followed the *XII Fulminata* and been stationed at Satala[75]. But, even without that, Vologaeses had good cause to suspect Vespasian's and Titus' motives; their early actions were indeed threatening.

The meeting at Zeugma was of some significance. Titus was not acting on his own initiative, nor was he trying to distance himself from Vespasian. Nothing was done contrary to his father's wishes. His task was simply to reassure the Parthians and, at the same time, allow the new eastern policy to continue without disturbance. This he achieved, for the Parthians were entertained and sent home with their complaints noted. As far as can be determined, no other embassy was sent to Rome. Titus emerged with public recognition of his status and diplomatic ability: Vespasian and Mucianus were not the only ones aware of his attributes.

He returned once more to Antioch, and was again pressed to expel the Jews or at least limit their rights. With the briefest of replies, he departed for Egypt, leaving the position of the Jews exactly as it was (*BJ* 7.106-111). Before reaching Egypt, however, he visited Jerusalem to view its desolation (*BJ* 7.112-115), and stopped at Memphis where he attended a sacred ritual of Apis wearing a diadem (*Titus* 5.3). Once at Alexandria, he sent back to their former stations the two legions that had accompanied him on his triumphal journey (*BJ* 7.116-119) and hurriedly returned to Rome[76].

The journey had taken some seven months and was charact-erized by elaborate displays and games, and by frequent rapturous welcomes in the cities of the east; it must have been an enormously costly exercise, for the legionaries alone would have numbered over 10,000. Its purpose was presumably to provide a public display of Flavian military might and, by the punishment meted out to the Jewish prisoners, to demonst-rate the futility of rebellion against the new emperor. In addition, Vespasian may well have instructed his son not to return before 71, in case too much attention was drawn early in the reign to the eastern origin of the Flavians' seizure of power; at the same time, he would have done little to dis-courage rumours that Galba had proposed to adopt Titus, rumours that were no doubt current at this very time. By the middle of 71, their usurpation of the throne would be more widely recognized and accepted, and the more vocal opposition muted. If this was Vespasian's intention, then Titus' lengthy and expensive tour around the east, his huge entourage and his occasionally unwise behaviour must have caused not a little annoyance and concern. Apparently, Titus became aware of his father's attitude by the time he reached Alexandria or soon afterwards, for, in stark contrast to his leisurely progress through the east with a splendid retinue, he hastened from Rhegium to Puteoli in a commercial vessel and abandoned his chance of a triumphal progress overland from Brundisium in an effort to reassure Vespasian[77].

Suetonius' comments (*Titus* 5.3) and the persistent *concordia* legend on the coinage from 71 to 73[78] suggest that rumours concerning his behaviour had reached Rome. Two separate incidents probably provoked them. The first occurred after the fall of Jerusalem, when the victorious soldiers hailed Titus as *imperator* (*Titus* 5.2; *BJ* 6.316; Orosius, 7.9), as was the fashion in the days of the Republic when it was the soldiers' privilege to bestow this title on their general after a victory[79]. Augustus, however, had reserved the award for the emperor himself or an heir who held an extraordinary command; usually, too, the title had to be confirmed by the senate[80]. But, since the case of Germanicus under Tiberius, no heir to the throne had been of the appropriate age to hold an extraordinary command, so it would not surprise if the precise details of procedure had been forgotten. Furthermore, a salutation need not automatically indicate a grant of secondary proconsular *imperium* of the sort bestowed by Augustus on Agrippa and Tiberius. By itself, then, the soldiers' salutation was comprehensible in the excitement of the moment, after a long siege, but Titus' reaction to it, together with his behaviour immediately afterwards, gave rise to adverse comment.

His addresses to the soldiers could have been interpreted as indicating that he was trying to incite them to rebel against Vespasian[81], but the details are provided by Josephus who would surely, despite his lack of familiarity with Roman politics, have edited out anything even hinting at illegal activity or unconstitutional behaviour on the part of his. hero. Titus was indiscreet and reckless in battle - even Ti. Julius Alexander could not always restrain him - and in a speech of congratulation to thousands of soldiers after a long siege, similar behaviour could be expected. The malicious[82] could interpret such indiscreet language as treason, but it is highly unlikely that such was Titus' intention. That he regarded himself as co-ruler is quite possible[83], and he may even have hinted at it in the enthusiasm of the moment. But he was not planning rebellion. He was still his father's *legatus*, the salutation did not imply some special grant of *imperium*, nor could he have received anything similar before the siege, at the time of his appointment, since it was a Vitellian senate. Again, the official inscription[84], dated to Titus' own reign, refers to his victory in Judaea as being "under the precepts, advice and auspices of his father". But rumour could have been fired when he rewarded or promoted soldiers and moved legions to new destinations (which he would have done *auspiciis patris*).

The second incident that provoked comment was his wearing of a diadem when attending the sacred ritual of Apis at Memphis (*Titus* 5.3). Such behaviour was not viewed similarly in Rome and in the east. Augustus had refused to pay hommage to Apis (Suet., *Aug.* 93) and no doubt this precedent was quoted to Vespasian. Again, the diadem had regal connotations that Titus should not have disregarded. According to Suetonius, Claudius Rursus in 249 B.C. "set up his own statue with a crown on its head (*statua didemata*) and tried to take possession of Italy" (*Tib.* 2.2); Julius Caesar refused to accept the *diadema* from Antony at the Lupercalia (*Jul.* 79.2); Gaius came close to accepting the *diadema* and thereby "changing the semblance of the principate into the form of monarchy" (*Gaius* 22.1). But Titus was always the diplomat. He was no doubt well aware of these precedents, but could see no harm in acting as he did. Diplomatic courtesy dictated his behaviour. After all, at Zeugma, in his self-appointed role as Vespasian's representative, he had already accepted a golden crown. Added to this was a natural tendency to reject caution and take a risk, characteristics that had occasionally been to the disadvantage of his military reputation.

Despite the rumours, Titus was not co-ruler; during the Judaean campaign, he had the status of his father's legate and did not possess proconsular *imperium*. He was well aware of these realities but had acted unwisely, particularly in the pomp and splendour of his tour and the incident with the diadem, but he was not planning to usurp his father's power, and there is no evidence of antipathy between him and Vespasian. It is not consistent with what is known of Titus' character to suppose that he would jeopardize his chances for empire by opposing his father, who had now established himself in Rome. He had publicly indicated his standing within the regime and enhanced his reputation as a diplomat by his actions at Zeugma; on the other hand, the excessive cruelty shown to his prisoners (*BJ* 7.38-39) could be regarded as indicative of a less pleasant side of his character, one that was to cause comment during the next ten years.

AGRIPPA AND BERENICE

The Flavians had been aided in their Judaean campaign and their usurpation of power by a number of oriental kings, amongst them Agrippa II. Marcus Julius Agrippa, the eldest of the four children of Agrippa I and Cypros[85], was educated in Rome, as were most of the Herods, and consistently used his Roman name[86]. His ancestors had carefully maintained personal relations with members of the imperial family: cordial friendships are attested between Augustus[87] and Herod the Great (*AJ* 15.357, 362; Dio, 54.9) and between Livia and Salome (*AJ* 17.10). Agrippa's grandmother Berenice was a friend of Antonia, mother

of Claudius and Germanicus[88], whilst Agrippa I, inheriting
this friendship, became an intimate friend of Drusus, son of
Tiberius (*AJ* 18.143). He was also on good terms with Gaius
(*AJ* 18.167 ff.)[89] and knew Claudius from his days at Antonia's
court, assisting in his accession[90]. Likewise, his son
Agrippa II was closely associated with Claudius (*AJ* 20.137)
and secured his personal friendship. It is not surprising
that under both Claudius and Nero his kingdom was extended:
the latter granted him, *inter alia*, the cities of Tiberias
and Tarichaeae (*AJ* 20.159)[91]. Cities were named (or renamed)
in honour of the imperial family - Caesarea, Livias, Julias,
Tiberias, Neronias etc. - and both Agrippa I and II bore the
same grandiloquent title, "Great king, friend of Caesar,
pious, friend of Rome"[92]. In these circumstances, Agrippa II
naturally sided with the Romans in suppressing the Jewish
rebellion.

When it broke out in the spring of 66, he was at
Alexandria, paying his respects to his former brother-in-law,
Ti. Julius Alexander (*BJ* 2.309 ff.). He hastened back, but
was unable to avert the storm. His forces sided with those
desiring peace and were defeated; his palace and that of
Berenice, his sister, were destroyed (*BJ* 2.426). But in 67
came the appointment of Vespasian with whom he could well have
had a long-standing friendship dating back to the days at
Antonia's court. Agrippa's assistance was immediate: as well
as sending auxiliaries, he played an active role in the campaigns and was even wounded at the siege of Gamala (*BJ* 4.14).
There were additional reasons for supporting Vespasian later
in the civil war: he and Berenice thought that the Flavians
would win, and, in any case, it was sound policy in such
circumstances to side with the geographically nearest candidate, for, even if he were to lose, the argument would be
advanced that support had been given only under duress.

Vespasian saw Agrippa at Antioch in 67 (*BJ* 3.68) and many
other meetings are attested (e.g. *BJ* 3.540; 4.14..; *Vita* 342,
352, 407...); he helped him when Tiberias and Tarichaeae
revolted (*BJ* 3.445 ff.); he and Titus were lavishly entertained at Caesarea Philippi (*BJ* 3.443); Agrippa accompanied Titus
to Achaea in the winter of 68 and continued on from Corinth to
their intended destination, Rome, whilst Titus returned to his
father (*BJ* 4.498 ff.; *Hist.* 2.1.1-2); from the beginning of
the siege of Jerusalem, he was in Titus' company, and was
almost certainly present at the magnificent games sponsored by
Titus in Caesarea Philippi to celebrate the city's conquest
(*BJ* 7.23). For his services he received considerable territorial increments, though their extent is not known[93].

Agrippa had remained in Rome during the first part of 69
and returned to Palestine only after Vespasian was hailed by
the Egyptian and Syrian legions: he was hastily summoned by
Berenice[94] (*Hist.* 2.81). Whilst he was presumably acting as
Vespasian's agent in the capital (though Sabinus II was city

prefect for most of this period[95]), his capable sister, Titus'
mistress since 67[96] (*Hist.* 2.2; *Titus* 7.1), must have been in
charge of the negotiations with Vespasian and also distributing the money[97]. By birth, she was a descendant of the
Hasmoneans and the Herods, both Jewish royal families[98]. She
had been married three times before she met Titus, firstly to
Marcus Julius Alexander, son of the wealthy and influential
Alexander the Alabarch (*AJ* 19.276)[99]. On his death, she
married Herod of Chalcis[100], her uncle, by whom she had two
sons, Berenicianus and Hyrcanus (*AJ* 19.277; *BJ* 2.217, 221);
she would have been about twenty when he also died in 48.
Claudius decided to reduce Chalcis to provincial status and
appointed procurators (*AJ* 20.204); Berenice, consequently,
returned to her brother Agrippa[101].

She must have developed intellectually and politically
during this second marriage. Her brother recognized her
ability and she occupied the position of joint-ruler with him:
she is called "Great Queen" on an inscription from Athens,
Josephus regards them as joint sovereigns (*Vita* 49.180-181)
and Tacitus twice refers to her as *regina* (*Hist.* 2.2.1, 81.2)[102].
However, public scandal and notoriety over alleged incest with
her brother (*AJ* 20.145; Juvenal, 6.156-158) caused her to
seek yet another husband[103]. Polemo of Cilicia succumbed to
the charms and the wealth (*AJ* 20.146) of this thirty-seven-
year-old queen and even consented to be circumcised[104]; but
the marriage did not endure and Berenice returned once again
to Agrippa.

It appears that her honours were not merely titular, for
her wealth, influence and involvement in political affairs are
well attested. In 66, she had not hesitated to send her
cavalry commanders and bodyguards to Gessius Florus to ask him
to desist from his slaughter of the townsfolk (*BJ* 2.310);
later she wrote to Cestius Gallus, governor of Syria, complain-
ing of Florus' brutality (*BJ* 2.333); and when Agrippa
delivered his speech to the Jews urging peace, she stood with
him on the roof of the Hasmonean palace (*BJ* 2.344). Moreover,
there are frequent references to her wealth[105], her men and
arms (*BJ* 2.312), her influence and her association with her
brother Agrippa (*BJ* 2.310). When Titus met Berenice she was a
powerful, wealthy and experienced woman in her late thirties.

The lack of a detailed source indicating her activities
in the east and later, in Rome, is to be regretted. Tacitus,
Suetonius, Cassius Dio and Aurelius Victor refer to her
briefly, but Josephus, the principal source for the years of
the war in Palestine, consistently avoids mention of her
relationship with Titus[106]. Yet, despite the paucity of
literary evidence, some conclusions can be drawn. She may
have first met Titus early in 67 when he and Vespasian
assembled their forces at Ptolemais in preparation for the
campaign in Judaea[107]. Naturally enough, Josephus makes no
mention of her on this occasion, merely stating that Titus

reached Ptolemais where he found his father and the assembled
Roman forces, including Agrippa's contingent (*BJ* 3.68). They
had certainly met by the summer of the same year[108], for
Josephus records that Vespasian and Titus, after quartering
the legions at Caesarea and Scythopolis, continued to Caesarea
Philippi, Agrippa's capital, where they were lavishly entertained (*BJ* 3.412-413, 443).

Tacitus suggests that one possible explanation of Titus'
decision to discontinue his journey to Rome in the winter of
68 was his passion for queen Berenice (*Hist*. 2.2.1). Now,
whilst the reason is implausible, it would seem that the
affair between them was well known and of some duration; but,
though there can be no doubt that Titus was attracted by her,
it is very unlikely that marriage was mooted at this stage.
Certainly, as far as she was concerned, another union was
desirable, for the rumours of incest with her brother had not
been silenced by her brief marriage to Polemo. For Titus, too,
marriage had much to offer: the raising of children was highly
regarded and considered one of the first duties of a citizen[109].
Furthermore, it extended the range of one's political associates. His two previous marriages had been contracted with an
eye to political advantage and the same considerations would
presumably prevail in selecting a third wife. But though
wealthy and influential in the east, Berenice was probably not
within the range of his present aspirations, for, in 68, he
aimed at a successful senatorial career and, no doubt, a
prominent position in the imperial service; despite the
prestige of her lineage, she could not provide the necessary
political ties. Added to this was the bias against orient-
als[110] which had long characterized Roman political thinking.
Prejudice against them cannot have abated during the principate of Nero, and this attitude would probably have been
sufficient deterrent to a marriage which offered few political
advantages.

The liaison between them posed problems enough for an
ambitious senator; for a father desirous of seizing the
imperial throne, an overt connection with eastern royalty
would be disastrous. A movement starting from Egypt with the
backing of Serapis (*Hist*. 4.81-82) did not require the support
of a "Kleopatra im kleinen"[111]: it would have the appearance
of reversing the decision of Actium. This may well be why
Josephus reversed the order of Vespasian's proclamation[112] and
why Titus was kept discreetly from Rome. Again, the visit to
Galba, made before the decision to seize power, was subsequently interpreted (in the official propaganda) as a summons
to Rome to be adopted as Galba's heir (*Titus* 5.1). His
distinguished pedigree was intended to counteract the unsatis-
factory eastern image of the new regime's origins; the
supposed adoption would confer legality on the usurpation, as
was to happen half a century later when Trajan suddenly died.
Galba, of course, would never have considered a quaestorian

legionary legate with equestrian ancestors as an heir: Titus was no match for L. Calpurnius Piso Licinius Frugi Licinian-us[113], a descendant of Pompey the Great. With the accession of Vespasian, however, there was no one to deny the accuracy of the "popular rumour". Indeed, for the next decade, Galba's image appeared frequently on the reverse of the Flavians' coins[114]. It is clear that the Flavians had to distance themselves in their propaganda from the movement's real origins[115]. In such circumstances, Titus' liaison was an embarrassment and marriage an impossibility.

NOTES

1. Nicols, 1978: pp. 24-25. Schürer, 1973: p. 484, provides a comprehensive bibliography on the campaign.
2. For the causes of the rebellion, see Schürer, 1973: pp. 485 ff. and Smallwood, 1976: pp. 293 ff.; for Felix, see *PIR*[2] A 828 and Schürer, 1973: pp. 459-466; for Florus, *PIR*[2] G 170 and Schürer, 1973: p. 470.
3. For Cestius Gallus, see *PIR*[2] C 691; Mooney, 1930: p. 394; Brandon, 1970: pp. 38-46; Syme, 1981: p. 132.
4. Homo, 1949: pp. 28-35; Nicols, 1978: pp. 24-25.
5. Schürer, 1973: pp. 471-483 and below.
6. For Alexander (Lysimachus) the Alabarch, see *PIR*[2] A 510; Turner, 1954: p. 54; and, for Agrippa I, *PIR*[2] A 131; Schürer, 1973: pp. 442-454.
7. For Mucianus, see *PIR*[2] L 216; Crook, 1951: pp. 162-165; Fortina, 1955b; Houston, 1971: pp. 144-147; Nicols, 1978: p. 185; Rogers, 1980: pp. 86-95.
8. Weber, 1921: p. 113, Mooney, 1930: p. 395, Homo, 1949: p. 30 and Warmington, 1969: p. 105 reject the view that Vespasian had command of the entire Syrian army; for a convincing refutation, see Nicols, 1978: pp. 113-114.
9. *Syriam et quattuor legiones obtinebat Licinius Mucianus...bellum Iudaicum Flauius Vespasianus...tribus legionibus administrabat*: *Hist.* 1.10.
10. The Flavians, then, could not have contemplated the idea of seizing the empire in 67 as Drexler, 1956: p. 523, and Weber, 1921: p. 154, assert. It should also be noted that the administration of Syria posed further problems. During the period following Mucianus' departure in 69 until the arrival of L. Caesennius Paetus in 71, the civil administration was probably in the hands of Gnaeus Pompeius Collega (*RE* 21.2269. 74; Eck, 1982: p. 287 with n. 25), whilst responsibility for military matters was presumably assigned to Titus: i.e. the ultimate control of both Judaea and Syria became his and was so decided at Berytus in July 69. For a survey of the province of Syria, including Ptolemais, see A.H.M. Jones, 1971: pp. 226 ff. with Map No. 5; the status of Ptolemais (in Syria) is also disucssed by Avi-Yonah, 1975: p. 174 and Bietenhard, 1977: p. 224 (map).

11. *Vesp.* 4.6; *Titus* 4.3; *BJ* 3.64; Orosius, 7.8.
12. A.R. Birley, 1975: p. 151.
13. Only two similar cases are known from the year 70 onwards, that of A. Larcius Lepidus Sulpicianus who came straight from the quaestorship to become *legatus legionis* in 70 (*ILS* 987), and that of his son who was similarly promoted in 96 or 97 (*ILS* 1055). Their promotions are discussed by Syme, 1936: pp. 238-245 and by Morris, 1953: pp. 79-80. Compare the earlier appointment by Corbulo of his son-in-law Annius Vinicianus:- *nondum senatoria aetate et pro legato quintae legioni impositus*: *Ann.* 15.28.4.
14. Suet., *Nero* 47.2.
15. For Sextus Vettulenus Cerialis, see *PIR*[1] V 351; Houston, 1971: pp. 263-266; Isaac and Roll, 1976: p. 18 n. 30; Roxan, 1978: pp. 30-31 (military diploma dated April 28, 75). He may have come from Reate (*RE* 12.1582), Vespasian's home town, and enjoyed the latter's support, since he held a suffect consulship fairly early in the reign (certainly before April 75, unless he received it that year *in absentia*). He was left in command of Judaea after the siege of Jerusalem (*BJ* 7.163) and subsequently governed Moesia. He was not the only member of his family to support Vespasian. His brother-in-law A. Lusius Gallus (*PIR*[2] L 434, brother of his wife, Lusia Paullina, *PIR*[2] L 445) was an equestrian officer in the legion *XXII Deiotariana*, one of Ti. Julius Alexander's legions, the first to declare for Vespasian. Sextus' brother, Gaius Vettulenus Civica Cerialis (*PIR*[1] V 352), also had a distinguished career under the Flavians, governing Moesia (? immediately: see Eck, 1982: pp. 305 ff.) after his brother and later moving to the proconsulship of Asia. The brothers may even have been adlected to the patriciate in 73/74. For Traianus, see *PIR*[1] V 574; Grosso, 1957: pp. 318-342; Houston, 1971: pp. 273-279; Isaac and Roll, 1976: pp. 15-19; Schieber, 1976: pp. 69-71, pp. 221-223 notes 57-67. He was born in Spain and must have been a senior praetorian in 66/67 if he held a suffect consulship in 70 (but this is not certain: see Bosworth, 1976: p. 67 n. 28). He probably served under Corbulo, for Vespasian needed at least one legate with experience in the east, and Traianus was later prominent in the reorganization of the eastern frontier. Obviously, he won Vespasian's confidence, since he was adlected to the patriciate in 73/74, appointed to govern Syria and then became proconsul of Asia. The theory that he accompanied Vespasian to Alexandria in 69 has to be discarded as he is now known to have been in Judaea during the latter half of that year: Isaac and Roll, 1976: pp. 15-19.
16. Fortina, 1955a: pp. 39-41, questions the location of this Alexandria, since either the Egyptian or Syrian city is possible. Until Vespasian's reorganization of the Asia Minor provinces ca. 72, Cilicia Campestris (in which Alexandria ad Issum was situated) was almost certainly under the aegis of the *legatus* of Syria: see Macro, 1980: p. 665;

Judaea

Mitford, 1980: pp. 1240-1241. Weber, 1921: pp. 114 ff.,
follows Mommsen's preference for Alexandria in Syria, though
most modern scholars either avoid the point (e.g. Schürer,
1973: p. 492) or else assume that Egypt was meant (Homo, 1949:
p. 34). The *XV Apollinaris* was brought to Syria from Pannonia
in 63 (*Ann.* 15.25) and no further movements are recorded until
66/67(*RE* 12.1750). For the arguments in favour of the Syrian
city, see B.W. Jones, "Which Alexandria?" *Athenaeum* (forthcoming).

    17. For Malachus II, see *PIR*[1] M 85; *RE* 14.857.4;
Schürer, 1973: p. 583: he is a very shadowy figure not
mentioned anywhere else. It is thought that he died in 71.
For Antiochus IV, see *PIR*[2] J 149; Magie, 1950: p. 573;
Sullivan, 1977c: pp. 785-794: he had had a long friendship
with the Roman authorities, dating from the time of Gaius, and
had aided Corbulo in Armenia. He was not the only member of
his family to assist Vespasian: his son, Epiphanes, had been
wounded fighting for Otho against Vitellius and had then
accompanied his father when he provided aid to Titus. The
subsequent history of Antiochus and his dynasty is related by
Josephus, *BJ* 7.219 ff.; Magie, 1950: p. 574; Sullivan,
1977c: pp. 732-798. Sohaemus (*PIR* J 582; Barrett, 1977: pp.
153-159; Sullivan, 1977a: pp. 216-218) was a powerful pro-
Roman king using the title "philocaesar" even before Vespasian's arrival in the east. An early supporter of the
Flavians (*Hist.* 2.81), he was rewarded with *ornamenta consularia* (*RE* 3A.796.4, and, in particular, Bosworth, 1980: p.
269). As a group, these kings were consistently pro-Roman,
using their Roman names on official documents and coins (see,
for example, A.H.M. Jones, 1938: p. 219) and regularly displaying the title "philocaesar". One of their major contri-
butions to the Flavian cause was money: note Tacitus'
introduction of Antiochus - *uetustis opibus ingens et
inseruientium regnum ditissimus*: *Hist.* 2.81.1.

    18. An assault was made on Gabara (*BJ* 3.132), a minor
stronghold without defences.

    19. The problem of which calendar (or calendars)
Josephus uses has been discussed by many scholars. The
standard view is that of Niese, 1893: pp. 193 ff., who argues
for the Tyrian system: Niese's solution has been accepted by
Weber, 1921 and by Michel and Bauernfeind, 1962. Nicols,
however, convincingly argues that Josephus' dates should be
regarded as transliterations of Julian dates (1978: pp. 40-46)
and his argument has been accepted in the text.

    20. Josephus (*BJ* 3.397) referring to himself in the
third person, states that "Titus' pleading with his father was
the main influence in saving the prisoner's life".

    21. He foretold the elevation of both Vespasian and
Titus to the principate, so he claims: "You will be Caesar,
Vespasian, you will be emperor, you and your son here" (*BJ*
3.401). His prophecy was noted by other writers - Suetonius

(*Vesp*. 5.6) and Dio (66.1.4).

22. This is the earliest evidence of Mucianus' arrival in the east. McGuire, 1980: p. 56, mistakenly assumes that Titus was sent to effect a reconciliation between Vespasian and Mucianus.

23. Gischala did not rate very highly with Vespasian, it would seem: "To meet these rebels (at Gischala), Vespasian sent Titus with 1,000 cavalrymen, and dismissed *legio X* to Scythopolis; with the two remaining legions he returned to Caesarea to rest" (*BJ* 4.87-88).

24. *BJ* 4.121 ff.; Schürer, 1973: pp. 496 ff.

25. Nicols, 1978: pp. 52-54.

26. For the date of Nero's death, see Bradley, 1978: p. 292, and, for the length of time for word to reach Caesarea, Weber, 1921: p. 141; Homo, 1949: p. 51.

27. Homo, 1949: p. 41; Fortina, 1955a: p. 42 n. 16: cf. Durry, 1964.

28. Mattingly, 1930: p. 215, Nos. 870-872. These coins, issued in 77-78, have Titus on the obverse, with the legend *T. Caes. imp. Aug. f. tr. p. cos. VI censor*; on the reverse, Victory is represented standing on a prow, and the legend *uictoria naualis* is visible. For similar coins, see Madden, 1881: p. 223; Mattingly and Sydneham, 1926: p. 108, Nos. 789-790; McCrum and Woodhead, 1966: No. 47.

29. See note 25. Vespasian was therefore informed about Vindex and his plans before the proclamation of the revolt.

30. Plutarch, *Galba* 4.2.

31. He was able to put into practice the lessons learned from Sosibius and Narcissus.

32. See note 10.

33. *ceterum hic Syria, ille Iudaeae praepositus, uicinis prouinciarum administrationibus inuidia discordes, exitu demum Neronis positis odiis in medium consuluere, primum per amicos, dein praecipua concordiae fides Titus praua certamina communi utilitate aboleuerat, natura atque arte compositus adliciendis etiam Muciani moribus*: *Hist*. 2.5.

34. Josephus assigns the resumption of action in Judaea to June 69 (*BJ* 4.502), but it may well have started somewhat earlier; see note 38.

35. According to Plutarch (*Galba* 11.1), a number of senators came to Narbo to meet Galba and told him to hurry on to Rome; he had not left Spain before the middle of August and it was October before he reached the capital (Syme, 1980: p. 9). The senators, who were notoriously slow travellers, had themselves covered over 750 miles in the time it took Galba to travel 180, an action typical of his excessive caution. This was the problem Vespasian faced: Galba's hesitation to confirm his appointment resulted in the postponement to 69 of the campaign planned for 68 (*BJ* 4.497).

36. There is no reason to believe that Galba wanted to

adopt Titus; see Büchner, 1964: pp. 12 ff.; Urban, 1971: p. 96.

37. Sherwin-White, 1966: pp. 26-27.

38. If Josephus' chronology is correct (*BJ* 4.502), and the campaign of 69 did not begin until June of that year, then presumably Galba still had not confirmed Vespasian's command by the end of 68; but if hostilities recommenced in March, it is just possible that notice of confirmation reached Palestine before Titus' departure.

39. This is clearly Tacitus' opinion. The entire passage is crucial:- *ubi Corinthi, Achaiae urbe, certos nuntios accepit de interitu Galbae et aderant qui arma Vitellii bellumque adfirmarent, anxius animo paucis amicorum adhibitis cuncta utrimque perlustrabat: si pergeret in urbem, nullam officii gratiam in alterius honorem suscepti, ac se Vitellio siue Othoni obsidem fore: sin rediret, offensam haud dubiam uictoris, set incerta adhuc uictoria et concedente in partis patre filium excusatum. sin Vespasianus rem publicam susciperet, obliuiscendum offensarum de bello agitantibus* (*Hist.* 2.1); i.e. "At the city of Corinth in Achaea, he was reliably informed of Galba's death, and met those who assured him that Vitellius was arming for war. In his anxiety, he summoned a few of his friends and carefully examined the position from both points of view. He felt that if he went on to Rome, he could expect no thanks for a gesture intended to honour another and would be a hostage in the hands of either Vitellius or Otho. If, on the other hand, he returned to Judaea, the conqueror would certainly be offended, though so long as the issue of the struggle was still in doubt and provided his father joined the winner, then he, the son, would be forgiven. But if Vespasian claimed the principate, men who had to think of war would inevitably forget such slights".

40. Despite Chilver, 1979: p. 164, it is hard to believe that Titus did not, at the very least, pay his respects to Mucianus on his way through Syria: see *Hist.* 2.74.

41. Suetonius is quite definite:- *post Neronem Galbamque Othone ac Vitellio de principatu certantibus in spem imperii uenit*: *Vesp.* 5.1. According to Dio, Vespasian reached his decision whilst Otho and Vitellius were engaged in civil war (Xiphilinus, 196.1-3; Zonaras, 11.16 n. 49).

42. For the various calendars, see Nicols, 1978: pp. 42 ff.

43. Niese, 1895, in the critical apparatus to *BJ* 4.550.

44. Weber, 1921: pp. 156 ff.

45. For these possibilities, see Nicols, 1978: p. 63.

46. Some of the implications of the famous *cunctatio* are discussed by Béranger, 1953: pp. 137 ff.

47. The date of Paetus' arrival can be determined from *BJ* 7.39 ff. Titus celebrated his father's birthday (Nov. 17) at Berytus in 70 and then proceeded to Syria; by that time Paetus was already on his way to Syria (*BJ* 7.59). See J. and

J. Balty, 1977: pp. 122-123.
  48. Collega (*RE* 21.2269.74) was legate of the *IV Scythica* in 70 (*BJ* 7.58) and possibly in the preceding year. He was rewarded for his support of the Flavians with an early consulship before 75: Gallivan, 1981: p. 220. For his status in Syria following Mucianus' departure in 69, see Eck, 1982: p. 289 with n. 25 (cf. p. 285 n. 11) and, for his appointment as consular governor of the Cappadocia-Galatia complex in 73/74, *ibid.*, pp. 293 ff.
  49. Titus' enduring fame has been guaranteed by the significance of Jerusalem in religious tradition: see Brandon, 1957.
  50. *BJ passim*; *Hist.* 5.1; Dio, 66.7; Aurelius Victor, *De Caes.* 11.11; Orosius, 7.9; Eutropius, 7.21; Sulpicius Severus, *Chron.* 2.30; Silius Italicus, *Punica* 3.605-606; Valerius Flaccus, *Arg.* 1.13-14. Note especially *ILS* 264 (=McCrum and Woodhead, 1966: No. 53):- *senatus populusque Romanus imp. Tito Caesari diui Vespasiani f. Vespasian[o] Augusto pontif. max. trib. pot. X imp. XVII [c]os. VIII p. p. principi suo quod praeceptis patr[is] consiliisque et auspiciis gentem Iudaeorum domuit et urbem Hierusolymam omnibus ante se ducibus regibus gentibus aut frustra petitam aut omnino intemptatam deleuit.*
  51. Schürer, 1973: pp. 501 ff.; Smallwood, 1976: pp. 316 ff.
  52. For the personal enmity between Josephus and John of Gischala, see *BJ* 2.585 ff. Gry, 1948: pp. 215-226, has discussed passages from Jewish literature referring to the fall of Jerusalem; a similar study on Christian writers was conducted by Giet, 1952: pp. 325-362. These investigations have produced little information on the siege itself and so Josephus' account remains pre-eminent. The older view of the political sympathies of the Zealots (as found, for example, in Cust, 1924: p. 130) has now been largely rejected, mainly because of the discovery of the Judaean scrolls (see Yadin, 1962) and the excavation of Masada (1955/1956, 1964/1965). Literature on both is extensive. A comprehensive account of the discovery of the scrolls and their significance may be found in Wilson, 1969, which also has a useful section on the excavations at Masada (pp. 195-211). These two events have resulted in a resurgence of interest in Jewish political factions, particularly in the Zealot movement. Though the earlier view has not been rejected by all scholars (see Richmond, 1962: pp. 142-155), a more sympathetic appreciation of the Zealot ideology is generally accepted (Appelbaum, 1971: pp. 155-170). The earlier work of Roth, 1959b: pp. 33-40 and 1959c: pp. 332-355, follows along similar lines, regarding the Zealots as a political and ideological movement.
  53. The topography and fortifications are discussed in some detail by Josephus, *BJ* 5.136-247, and also by Abel, 1949: pp. 238-258; Hubbard, 1966: pp. 130-154; Avi-Yonah, 1968:

pp. 98-105 and 1975: pp. 211-219 (general), 220-228 (walls), 228-237 (Antonia), 236-238 (Upper City), 238-240 (Lower City), 241-242 (Bezetha).
    54. Tacitus (*Hist*. 2.82.3) implies that Titus did not accompany Vespasian to Egypt. However, it is quite clear that he did in view of Josephus' detailed account of Titus' march back from Alexandria (*BJ* 4.659-663).
    55. On the size of the army, see *BJ* 5.39 ff.; Schürer, 1973: pp. 501-502. For A. Larcius Lepidus Sulpicianus, see *PIR*² L 94; *RE* 12.800.11; Syme, 1936: pp. 238-245; Houston, 1971: pp. 140-142. His career is known from a fragmentary inscription from Antium, *ILS* 987. He seems to have come to this command straight from a quaestorship in Crete-Cyrene (he and his son Priscus are the last attested quaestorian legionary legates) and so was one of the group of officers who obtained quick promotion from Vespasian. Subsequently, he became proconsular legate of Pontus-Bithynia and apparently died there, or not long after his return to Rome. For M. Tittius Frugi, see *PIR*¹ T 208 (Dessau); *RE* 6A.1567.29. He received a suffect consulship in Dec. 80, but no other post is attested. According to Dessau, he might be the subject of the acephalous *ILS* 988 who was apparently awarded double military *dona* by Titus, but this is by no means certain, and the inscription could well refer to Sex. Vettulenus Cerialis (see note 15). Aspects of his career have been discussed by Houston, 1971: p. 254; B.W. Jones, 1975a: p. 460; Devreker, 1977: p. 237. For C. Aeternius Fronto, see *PIR*² L 287; Houston, 1971: pp. 297-298 (but note that Houston preserves the incorrect form of his name, C. Liternius Fronto); Brunt, 1975a: p. 143; Bastianini, 1975: p. 276. Amongst the junior officers attached to the army of Titus was Ti. Julius Celsus Polemaeanus (*PIR*² J 260), a Romanised Greek from Ephesus, afterwards suffect consul (92); he served as tribune of the *III Cyrenaica*
    56. On him, see *PIR*² A 846; *RE* 1.2632.68.
    57. The career of Ti. Julius Alexander has been the subject of many studies. See, in particular, *PIR*² J 139; Turner, 1954: pp. 54-64; Houston, 1971: pp. 292-294 and especially p. 292 n. 16 for some earlier studies; Schürer, 1973: pp. 456-458 and 501-502; Brunt, 1975a: p. 143; Bastianini, 1975: p. 274 and 1980: p. 77; Sullivan, 1977d: pp. 932-934. Nothing is known of him after his two early posts (*epistrategus* of the Thebaid, ca. 42 and procurator of Judaea, 46-48) until 63 when he appears as military adviser to Corbulo (*inlustris eques Romanus minister bello datus*: *Ann*. 15.28). Presumably, he had acquired considerable military experience during the interval, since he held the same sort of post under Titus (after an appointment to the prefecture of Egypt and the control of the two legions there), and, subsequently, also commanded the praetorians in Rome.
    58. According to Perowne, 1958: p. 173, the Antonia had

at its base a great artificial ditch which had to be filled in to allow the engines to come to close quarters with the fortress. This involved the construction of causeways, inclined ramps made of stone, wood and earth.

59. On the council meeting, see Pflaum, 1950: pp. 144-145.

60. The precise date is discussed by Schürer, 1973: p. 506 n. 115.

61. *Titus* 5.2; *BJ* 6.316; Orosius, 7.9; some of the implications of the salutation are discussed in notes 80 and 81.

62. See Marsden, 1969: pp. 99 ff., 174 ff., for the traditional Roman tactics, and pp. 90, 175, 185, for particular reference to Titus in the siege of Jerusalem.

63. Two instances of unwarranted personal intervention (*BJ* 5.81-97 and 281) occurred before Agrippa's wall was taken (May 5), two more (5.287-288 and 310-311) before the second wall fell (May 14), another two (5.339-341 and 486-488) occurred before the construction of the wall around the city (ca. early June) and two more subsequently (6.70 and 132-135). In the last instance, he was persuaded by the entreaties of his staff (cf. 5.88 for similar blunt speaking) to remain at the Antonia: he would, they said, "achieve more by sitting still [there] as director of the contest of his troops than by going down and exposing himself in the forefront" (6.133).

64. Note the comments of Abrahams, 1927: p. 34: "... it is Titus' tactics that seem to lack genius. He was prompt enough in countering the Judaean devices after they had done their damage; he showed less foresight in anticipating them. The attack was made by rule; the defence broke through all rules".

65. *fertur Titus adhibito consilio prius deliberasse an templum tanti operis euerteret. etenim nonnullis uidebatur aedem sacratum ultra omnia mortalia inlustrem non oportere deleri, quae seruata modestiae Romanae testimonium, diruta perennem crudelitatis notam praeberet. at contra alii et Titus ipse euertendum in primis templum censebant quo plenius Iudaeorum et Christianorum religio tolleretur: quippe has religiones, licet contrarias sibi, isdem tamen ab auctoribus profectas; Christianos ex Iudaeis extitisse: radice sublata stirpem facile perituram*: *Chron.* 2.30.6-7. Note that the Flavian poet Valerius Flaccus had no hesitation in praising Titus for his active role in the deliberate destruction of the Temple. According to him, Domitian described in his poetry *Solymo nigrantem puluere fratrem,/spargentemque faces et in omni turre furentem*: *Arg.* 1.13-14. The later writer Orosius (5th century A.D.) was equally direct, though, like Sulpicius Severus, he also imported Christianity into the deliberations: *quod tamen postquam in potestatem redactum opere atque antiquitate suspexit, diu deliberauit utrum tamquam incitamentum hostium incenderet an in testimonium uictoriae reseruaret.*

sed Ecclesia Dei iam per totum orbem uberrime germinante, hoc
tamquam effetum ac uacuum nullique usui bono commodum
arbitrio Dei auferendum fuit. itaque Titus, imperator ab
exercitu pronuntiatus, templum in Hierosolymis incendit ac
diruit: 7.9.5-6.

66. That his source was Tacitus has been argued by
Bernays, 1885: pp. 159 ff.; Wolff-Beck, 1903: pp. 469-470;
Barnes, 1977: pp. 224-231. Objections have been raised by
Weynand, *RE* 6.2703; Fortina, 1955a: pp. 66-69 n. 46;
Montefiore, 1962: pp. 158 ff., though largely countered by
Barnes. Sometimes, however, the passage is printed as a
Tacitean fragment, e.g. in the *OCT* and the Teubner editions of
1912 (Halm) and 1969 (Koestermann); as Barnes points out (p.
231), "a firm distinction must always be drawn between fragments which preserve the actual words of a lost work, reports
of its contents, and traces of it surviving in later writers".
The passage from Sulpicius, he argues, should be allocated to
the final category. Earlier scholars, e.g. Valeton, 1899: p.
106, argue that the source was either Pliny the Elder or M.
Antonius Julianus. They note that Minucius Felix, a Christian
writer who lived in the first half of the third century,
suggested a comparison between the Roman accounts of Jewish
affairs given by Josephus and Antonius Julianus, the latter's
work being entitled *De Iudaeis* (*Octauius* 33.4); so an account
of the war, supplied by an important contemporary Roman
official present at Titus' deliberations, could have provided
a version independent of, but equally authoritative to, that of
Josephus. But there are problems. Not all scholars accept
that the writer of the *De Iudaeis* was the procurator of 70
(Syme, 1958a: p. 178, identifies them, but in *PIR*² A 843 and
A 846 they are accorded separate entries). Montefiore, 1962:
pp. 156-170, argues that they are identical and that Julianus
was the source used by Sulpicius Severus, a view that Barnes,
1977: p. 228 n. 15, dismisses as "totally implausible".
Whilst certainty is impossible, the evidence does suggest that
Sulpicius had access to Tacitus and made use of him (note *at*
contra alii in note 65: compare *at contra reus*, *Ann.* 4.28)
and it has yet to be shown that the procurator of 70 wrote the
De Iudaeis.

67. Barnes, 1977: p. 228.
68. Smallwood, 1976: pp. 325-326.
69. This is argued convincingly by Montefiore, 1962: pp.
156-170, Weiler, 1968: pp. 139-158 and Lifshitz, 1977b: pp.
466-468. Montefiore, p. 162, comments "it is known that Titus
later wished to be thought clement, and Josephus would have
furthered his wishes as much as he could". Fortina, 1955a: p.
69 n. 46, however, argues against this on the grounds that
Josephus did not fail to mention other actions of Titus that
illustrate his cruelty (on which, see Schürer, 1973: pp. 506-
507) and he cites those scholars who agree with his proposal
that Josephus' version of the Temple's destruction is to be

preferred (p. 67). His argument does not convince.

70. For Sex. Lucilius Bassus, see Houston, 1971: pp. 149-150; *PIR*² L 379; Devreker, 1980: p. 81; and, for Flavius Silva, see Eck, 1970: pp. 93-111; *PIR*² F 368; McDermott, 1973b: pp. 335-351; Schürer, 1973: p. 515; Devreker, 1980: p. 85. The literature on Masada is enormous; for a convenient list, see Schürer, 1973: pp. 484-485.

71. This is the reason given by Josephus (*BJ* 7.20). It is not particularly convincing, since in the winter of 66/67 he had crossed from Achaea to Alexandria (*BJ* 3.8). Casson, 1959: pp. 39, 220, points out that the lack of navigational reference points because of extensive cloud cover represented a greater danger than winter storms: for a list of comments from ancient writers on the risks of winter voyages, see Rougé, 1952: pp. 316-325, but this does not disprove the argument of Saint-Denis, 1947: pp. 196-214, that the sea lanes remained open, particularly to commercial traffic. If Josephus' reason is to be rejected, it may have been that, for Vespasian and his advisors, the eastern origins of their movement were still too fresh in men's minds and therefore Titus' arrival at such a time would have been premature.

72. *quin etiam Vologaesus Parthorum rex missis ad senatum legatis de instauranda societate hoc etiam magno opere orauit, ut Neronis memoria coleretur*: Suet., *Nero* 57.2. On Zeugma in general, see Frézouls, 1977: pp. 184-185.

73. For Izates, see *PIR*² J 891, and, for Monobazus, *PIR*¹ M 491.

74. See note 47.

75. For the date of these changes, see Bosworth, 1976: pp. 63-78 and Mitford, 1980: pp. 1180-1182.

76. He entered "the city" on April 25, 71 at about 7 a.m., according to a recently published papyrus - *P. Oxy.*2725. Most scholars suppose that Alexandria is meant, although, as Bowman, 1976: p. 157, points out, it could well be Memphis. McGuire, 1980: pp. 70-71, discusses Suetonius' implication (*Titus* 5.2) that the Apis incident caused hostility to Titus, thus prompting his hasty return to Rome. According to her, this is chronologically impossible: there was no time for what was supposed to have happened in the second half of June 71 - the rumours concerning his involvement to reach Rome, the report of Vespasian's negative reaction to reach Alexandria, Titus' hurried departure and also his arrival in Rome.

77. *quare festinans in Italiam, cum Regium, dein Puteolos oneraria naue appulisset, Romam inde contendit expeditissimus inopinantique patri, uelut arguens rumorum de se temeritatem: ueni, inquit, pater, ueni*: *Titus* 5.3.

78. Mattingly, 1930: pp. xlv, 113 (A.D. 71) and 150 (A.D. 73).

79. Tacitus describes the custom as follows:- *sed Tiberius pro confecto interpretatus id quoque Blaeso tribuit ut imperator a legionibus salutaretur, prisco erga duces*

honore qui bene gesta re publica gaudio et impetu uictoris
exercitus conclamabantur; erantque plures simul imperatores
nec super ceterorum aequalitatem. concessit quibusdam et
Augustus id uocabulum ac tunc Tiberius Blaeso postremum: *Ann.*
3.74.

80. Philostratus may be referring to this when he comments:- "When Titus had been declared emperor in Rome and had been judged to deserve this reward, he left to share his father's power" (*Vit. Apoll.* 6.30). Similarly, Dio notes "Thus was Jerusalem destroyed... In consequence of this success, both generals received the title of *imperator*, but neither got that of *Iudaicus*, although all the other honours... were voted to them" (66.7.2). Titus used the title only as a *cognomen* during his father's lifetime but it does appear, erroneously, as a *praenomen* on inscriptions from outside Rome. Compare... *T. Caesar Vespasianus imp.* (*ILS* 8903) with... *imp. Tito Caesare Aug. f...* (*ILS* 8904, from Melik Scherif in Armenia Minor). For a discussion of the need for the senate's confirmation, see Kornemann, 1930: p. 61.

81. This is argued by Hoffmann, 1883: pp. 1-13, discussing *BJ* 6.316 ff., 341 ff.; 7.6-15, 17-19, 23-24, 37-40, 118. Henderson, 1927: p. 11, suggests that Vespasian may have associated his son with him as a partner because of his apprehension at Titus' proposed revolt in the east, a theory completely unsupported by the ancient evidence.

82. Their identity has never been established. Even Crook, 1951: p. 165, "hesitates to say ... whether it was they (i.e. Mucianus and his group) who spread the rumours".

83. He is not recorded as having made this claim explicitly, but his later "concatenation of powers without precedent or subsequent parallel" (Crook, 1951: p. 164) suggests that he may have.

84. *ILS* 264 = McCrum and Woodhead, 1966: No. 53. See note 50.

85. In 44 Agrippa was seventeen, and his sisters Berenice, Mariamme and Drusilla sixteen, ten and six respectively (*AJ* 19.304).

86. On his education, see Schürer, 1973: p. 471 with n. 1 for some examples of his preference for his Roman name on his coins. All members of the family had been entitled to call themselves Julius since Antipater received the citizenship from Caesar, but Agrippa was the first to do so in official documents. Note also Sullivan, 1977d: pp. 329-345.

87. Augustus was well aware of Herod's defects: he is supposed to have said that he would rather be Herod's pig than one of his sons (Macrobius, *Sat.* 2.4.11).

88. For Berenice and Antonia, see *PIR*[2] B 108 and A 885.

89. He even managed to dissuade Gaius from persisting in his project of having his statue set up in the temple at Jerusalem (*AJ* 18.289 ff.).

90. Josephus has two versions of his role in the

accession. In the *BJ* (2.206 ff.), Agrippa has a passive function whilst Claudius takes the initiative; but, in *AJ* 19.236 ff., Agrippa is virtually in charge, and Claudius' role is that of an imbecile, so frightened as to be on the point of giving up the favour conferred on him by fortune; on these discrepancies, see Scramuzza, 1940: pp. 58-59. In either case, Claudius showed his appreciation, confirmed Agrippa in his possessions and supplemented them with Judaea, Samaria and the tetrarchy of Abilene; he was also granted *ornamenta consularia*, whilst his brother Herod, married to his niece Berenice, received the small kingdom of Chalcis and *ornamenta praetoria*.

91. For the extent of Agrippa's kingdom at various periods, see Frankfort, 1962: pp. 659-672; Schürer, 1973: pp. 472-473 with notes 7-8.

92. *IGRR* 3.1244: see Schürer, 1973: p. 475 n. 15; Sullivan, 1977b: pp. 329-351.

93. For his activities in the war and subsequently, see Schürer, 1973: pp. 474-483; Sullivan, 1977d: pp. 329-345.

94. The career of this remarkable woman has been the subject of many studies. See *PIR*[2] J 651; *RE* 3.287.15; Macurdy, 1935: pp. 246-253 and 1937; Mireaux, 1950; Crook, 1951: pp. 162-175; Jordan, 1974; Sullivan, 1977d: pp. 310-313; McDermott and Orentzel, 1979: pp. 32-38; Rogers, 1980: pp. 89-85; McGuire, 1980: pp. 97-99, 107-108; Martinet, 1981: pp. 68-70, 73-74. Macurdy, 1935: p. 252, describes her as follows: "Like Cleopatra, she is always vital and in action, subduing the hearts of men by her charm and cherishing the ambition to be the greatest in the world". Wilcken (*RE*) also points out that it was her misfortune that Titus was no Antony. It was this parallel that most concerned Vespasian.

95. Sabinus II was probably dismissed by Galba ca. Nov. 68 and reappointed by Otho in March of the following year: Nicols, 1978: pp. 61-67.

96. Price, 1919: pp. 39-40; Mooney, 1930: p. 484, notes 107 and 108 below.

97. *nec minore animo regina Berenice partis iuuabat, florens aetate formaque et seni quoque Vespasiano magnificentia munerum grata*: *Hist.* 2.81.

98. Her descent from the Hasmoneans may be traced through Mariamme, her great-great-grandmother who married Herod the Great (*BJ* 1.241, 262, 344, 432-436).

99. For Marcus, see *PIR*[2] J 138, and, for his father, note 6 above. Evidence for their wealth is discussed by Fuks, 1957-1964: pp. 197-200 (Marcus) and pp. 201-203 (Gaius - the Alabarch's correct *praenomen*, according to Fuks, p. 200); see also Turner, 1954: pp. 54 ff. The marriage between Marcus and Berenice was one of the many instances of close association between the two families: *ibid.*, p. 58; Sullivan, 1953: pp. 67-70. Fuks, 1948/1949: pp. 15-17, suggests that the marriage took place in 43 or 44; Mireaux, 1950: pp. 59-60,

prefers an earlier date, whilst Schürer, 1973: p. 572 n. 59, argues that Berenice was probably only promised in marriage to Marcus and that she was aged thirteen when she married Herod of Chalcis.

100. For him, see Schürer, 1973: pp. 571-573; A.H.M. Jones, 1938: pp. 139, 206-207, 209, 216-218.

101. One of the best-known accounts of her and her brother is to be found in the twenty-fifth chapter of the Acts of the Apostles, where Luke describes the meeting between the two Hellenised Jewish royalties and the Hellenised Jew, Paul.

102. She is regularly referred to as "queen": see Macurdy, 1935: pp. 246-249, for a survey of the epigraphic evidence, and, in particular, *AE* 1928, 82 (=Macurdy, 1935: pp. 247-248), where she is assigned the title *regina* and, if the reconstruction is correct, where her name appears before that of Agrippa.

103. The evidence for an incestual relationship is not very convincing. Josephus was prejudiced against Agrippa because of his patronage of Justus of Tiberias, and, in the *AJ*, published certainly after Titus' death and probably after those of Berenice and Agrippa, he attacked their reputations, even though he had written sympathetically of them in his earlier works (see note 90 for similar inconsistency). Hence *AJ* 20.145 should be read with considerable scepticism. Juvenal's reference has similar validity: *deinde adamans notissimus et Berenices/in digito factus pretiosior: hunc dedit olim/barbarus incestae, dedit hunc Agrippa sorori...* (6.156-158). Even if Agrippa and Berenice had married, they would have incurred no stigma in Roman law (though they would certainly have in Jewish law); philadephic marriages *sociatis externo more in matrimonium regnumque*, as Tacitus says of Tigranes III and Erato of Armenia (*Ann.* 2.3), were recognized. C. Julius Antiochus IV, the Flavian supporter, was married to his sister Iotape (see *PIR²* J 47 and J 149) and Gaius had considered introducing the custom to Rome by marrying his sister Drusilla (after whom Berenice's youngest sister was named).

104. Agrippa attempted at times to advance the tenets of Judaism. The marriage which he had arranged for his sister Drusilla with Epiphanes, son of Antiochus IV of Commagene, had to be broken off when he refused to be circumcised, but Azizus, king of Emesa, accepted Agrippa's terms and married her: see Sullivan, 1977a: pp. 215-216. Agrippa's other efforts to promote Judaism are discussed by Schürer, 1973: pp. 475-476, as are those of Berenice who, according to Schürer, p. 475, "was as bigoted as she was dissolute".

105. *BJ* 2.426 (her palaces); *Vita* 119 (her massive corn granaries); Juvenal, 6.151 ff. (her jewelry); *Hist.* 2.81 (her wealth).

106. Mireaux, 1950: pp. 145-146, comments that "dans la

Guerre juive, Bérénice disparaît du récit à partir du moment
où Titus entre en scène".

    107.   She had left Polemo in 66 (Schürer, 1973: p. 474;
Sullivan, 1977d: pp. 919-927), and, by the end of 68, her
affair with Titus was common knowledge (*Hist.* 2.1.1-2). They
may have met at Ptolemais early in 67 - this is the view of
Mireaux, 1950: p. 147: "la première entrevue de Titus et de
la reine eut lieu sans doute à Ptolemais dans l'hiver de 67".

    108.   There can be no doubt that Berenice was living with
Agrippa in 67/68; after leaving Polemo, she returned to him
and appears with him in Josephus. It would seem more likely
that the affair with Titus had its origins in the summer of
67, at the palace in Caesarea Philippi, rather than at the
base camp in Ptolemais during the winter.

    109.   Note Pliny's comment on Asinius Rufus:- *nam in
hoc quoque functus est optimi ciuis officio, quod fecunditate
uxoris large frui uoluit, eo saeculo quo plerisque etiam
singulos filios orbitatis praemia graues faciunt*: *Ep.* 4.15.3.

    110.   See Charlesworth, 1926: pp. 1-16.

    111.   Mommsen, 1895: p. 540.

    112.   Tacitus (*Hist.* 2.79) states that "Alexander made
his legions swear allegiance to the new emperor on July 1"
and that "on July 3 the army of Judaea had taken the oath
before Vespasian in person"; by the middle of July, all the
Syrian legions had also taken the oath (2.81). On the other
hand, Josephus, *BJ* 4.585 ff., 601, claims that the legions of
Judaea first proclaimed Vespasian and that they did so after
Vitellius' arrival in Rome in the middle of July.

    113.   Syme, 1939: p. 497, refers to him as "that
irreproachable and academic Piso whom Galba unwisely adopted
to a four days' partnership of the purple".

    114.   Mattingly and Sydenham, 1926: p. 8.

    115.   Josephus presents the authorized version: the
acclamation was the spontaneous movement of patriotic
soldiers angry at hearing of Vitellius' attacks on Italy and
Rome; the reluctant Vespasian had to be forced into accepting
the purple (*BJ* 1.24; 4.585 ff., 601). This is the impression
that the Flavians wanted to convey. On this in general, see
Briessmann, 1955: pp. 2 ff.

Chapter Three

ROLE UNDER VESPASIAN

INTRODUCTION

The disasters of the years 68-69 had had a profound effect on
the empire, leaving it financially impoverished and beset with
wars in Batavia and Judaea as well as with civil strife. The
principate had come close to disintegration at its very core.
The Julio-Claudian dynasty had enjoyed the prestige accruing
from divine ancestry through Julius Caesar, and from the
almost legendary idealization of Augustus; with the death of
Nero, however, the army's role in the imperial selection
process was only too clear. As Tacitus saw, the well-hidden
secret of the principate had been revealed: it seemed
possible for an emperor to be chosen outside Rome (*Hist*. 1.4).
The task of rehabilitation fell to Vespasian who insisted on a
standard of firmness and sobriety considered characteristic of
the revered past. Suetonius' anecdotes at least confirm and
illustrate the official line. When a young officer reeking
with perfume came to thank Vespasian for his commission, the
emperor promptly withdrew it and informed him that it would
have been better had he smelt of garlic (*Vesp*. 8.3); when the
marines asked for a special shoe allowance on the grounds that
they were constantly marching from Ostia and Puteoli to Rome,
he curtly dismissed them and made them do the journey barefoot
- and Suetonius adds that "they have done so ever since"
(*Vesp*. 8.3).
     The financial stringencies advocated by the new regime
were intended to enable the empire to recover from the
impoverishment caused by the constant warfare, but reforms
based solely on these policies would have been inadequate to
restore the security of the principate itself[1]. Legal
validity for all the usual powers (*Hist*. 4.3.3) of an emperor
was of primary significance, and was obtained before Jan. 9,
70 by the *Lex de imperio Vespasiani* together with the *senatus
consultum* contained therein[2]. Yet the problem that beset
Galba, advancing age, also faced Vespasian, and it was
fortunate for the new regime, as Mucianus had pointed out

(*Hist.* 2.77), that the emperor had a son who was *capax imperii* and who had served with distinction in the Judaean campaign. As far as Vespasian was concerned, highlighting the military achievements of his heir and giving constitutional solidity to his position were as essential for Titus' position as for his own. So the precariousness of the principate in 70 produced conditions suited to the enhancement of Titus' status and reputation.

Military and political influence had, from the earliest days, gone hand in hand, and the benefits of military renown had always been appreciated by Roman emperors and others. To gain the rewards deemed appropriate, such achievements had to be suitably advertised and presented, but it was hardly necessary to go so far as to emulate Cornificius who "so prided himself upon having saved his soldiers that, even when he was back in Rome, he always had himself conveyed on the back of an elephant whenever he dined out" (Dio, 49.7.6): his persistence paid off and within a year of his return he was awarded the consulship (35 B.C.). Vespasian's methods were more subtle[3]. The captive Josephus was commissioned to extol the achievements of father and son in Judaea; *Iudaea capta* appeared on numerous coins throughout the empire[4]. A major beneficiary of all this was Titus who had completed the campaign with his siege of Jerusalem. His role in the subjugation of the province prior to that had been commensurate with what was to be expected of a quaestorian legionary legate who was the son of the supreme commander. In the dynastic interests of the new regime, however, he had to be represented as playing a significant part in the whole campaign and therefore was beside his father in the triumph celebrating the Jewish victory, an honour permitted to no one apart from the emperor since 22 when Blaesus shared in the triumph with Tiberius (*Ann.* 3.74.4).

The elaborate "double" triumph was celebrated only a few days (*BJ* 7.120) after Titus' arrival in Rome in June[5]. Josephus found it "impossible to describe adequately the magnitude of the spectacle" (*BJ* 7.132), but did his best (*BJ* 7.123-157), noting that "the city of Rome kept festival that day for her victory in the campaign against her enemies, for the termination of her civil dissensions, and for her dawning hopes of felicity" (*BJ* 7.157). This was a significant comment, since it indicated clearly the aims of the dynasty's propaganda: peace, security, and hopes for the future in which Titus was to have a prominent role. The joint triumph also emphasized Titus' position in the new regime - it is of some significance that the senate had originally recommended separate triumphs (*BJ* 7.121). In the procession, the dress and posture of Vespasian and his son were identical, as were their prayers and sacrifices (*BJ* 7.124 ff.); from this time on, all imperial acclamations were jointly credited to them, and from July they shared tribunician power. Josephus' account

strongly suggests that the triumph was intended to indicate
Titus' role precisely.

TITUS: PARTICEPS IMPERII

So, in the interests of establishing the dynastic nature of
the new regime, Titus received precise honours. In fact, he
assumed an unprecedented position of power which clearly
marked him out as heir-apparent. He was awarded, in conjunc-
tion with his father, almost every imperial office. Within
three years of his return to Rome, he held proconsular
imperium and *tribunicia potestas*, wielded the powers of the
censorship and was granted a number of imperial salutations;
he also became praetorian prefect. To maintain the distinction between the respective positions of father and son, some
of the titles held by Vespasian were omitted in Titus'
formula: *Augustus, pater patriae* and *pontifex maximus* appear
for Vespasian alone. Again, the titles which were held
concurrently by Vespasian and Titus reflected the preeminence of Vespasian, for the numerical value of Titus'
tribunician power, imperial salutations and consulships was
consistently kept below that of Vespasian. Of the titles
that Titus did not receive, however, *pater patriae* and
pontifex maximus could not, by their very nature, be held by
two people, and, even with the latter, an effort was made to
parallel Vespasian's usage, for Titus appears as *pontifex*.
Thus, on an inscription of 79 Vespasian is described as
... *Augustus pontifex maximus trib. pot. X imp. XX cos. IX
pater patriae*, whilst Titus' titles are given as ... *Augusti
filius pontifex trib. pot. VIII imp. XIIII cos. VII*[6]. He was
always *Augusti filius* during his father's reign. He may well
have regarded himself as co-ruler and he was indeed extremely
powerful; but that was far from being co-ruler. There is no
hint in the titulature of equality: Titus' position is always
indicated quite precisely - he was the second most powerful
man in the empire and the heir-apparent, but nothing else.
  Titus' position during Vespasian's reign is described by
Suetonius as follows:-
  From that time (his return to Rome in 71) he never ceased
  to act as the emperor's partner and even as his protect-
  or. He took part in his father's triumph and was censor
  with him. He was also his colleague in the tribunician
  power and in seven consulships...He also assumed the
  command of the praetorian guard, which before that time
  had never been held except by a Roman knight[7].
The significance of each of these offices merits considera-
tion.

TRIBUNICIA POTESTAS

Despite the controversy over the relative significance of
imperium and *tribunicia potestas*, it seems clear that the
latter was one of the most important titles held by the early
emperors[8], and it always retained a certain significance, for
the bearer was recognized by the senate as an emperor or heir.
Claimants to the throne who failed to gain senatorial
recognition (e.g. Pescennius Niger and Clodius Albinus) also
failed to assume *trib. pot.*[9] As well as this, the annual
increase of its number was used to indicate the years of the
holder's reign; and for this purpose it had disadvantages,
especially when conferred on heirs long before their accession,
for their tribunician number did not correspond with the years
of their rule. Titus' assumption of *trib. pot.* prior to his
reign was not without precedent; both Tiberius and Agrippa
held it for limited periods under Augustus. But his policy
was not followed consistently by later emperors, perhaps as
they felt that there was little or no opposition to the
principle of hereditary succession. Vespasian, however, meant
to establish a dynasty, despite hostility to the principle[10].
He wanted to mark Titus out as his destined successor, but
because of his age and the conditions, including civil war,
under which he had seized power, Vespasian found himself in
precisely the same position as had Augustus: he feared the
possibility that the empire would disintegrate on his death.
Hence he used the same solution as Augustus.
      Titus assumed the title in 71; probably it was conferred
on July 1, for his tribunician numbers on coins and inscriptions run consistently with Vespasian's but always two fewer[11].
He does not seem to have altered the date after Vespasian's
death on June 24, 79. In brief, the purpose of the title for
Titus was to ensure his smooth accession to the principate -
it indicated senatorial approval.

IMPERIAL SALUTATIONS

The significance of imperial salutations within the official
titulature is not without interest[12]. From the time of
Claudius, emperors seem to have indicated by the *praenomen* of
imperator the salutation they received on their accession,
and, starting with *imp. II*, to have included in the "Republican" part of their formula any salutations granted for victories subsequently won under their auspices. Normally,
salutations were the prerogative of the emperor only, and not
awarded to subordinate heirs[13]; here, as elsewhere, Titus'
position was anomalous. He received fourteen salutations
during his father's reign, though he did not share in the
first six awarded to Vespasian. The precise occasions giving
rise to Titus' salutations are far from certain, apart from
his first - he was acclaimed by his troops on the day of the

capture of Jerusalem and the burning of the Temple (*BJ* 6.316; *Titus* 5.2) and was described as *imperator* on an inscription from the first months (before April) of 71. The remaining thirteen were awarded as follows: *Imp. II* in 71, *III* and *IV* in 72, *V* in 73, *VI-VIII* in 74, *IX-XII* in 76, and *XIII-XIV* in 78[14]. Of major importance, apart from his unprecedented number of salutations as heir-apparent, was his policy on his accession. Unlike his predecessors, he did not regard his acclamation on June 24, 79 as meriting a salutation, presumably preferring to see his initial award in 71 as indicating that he was co-ruler with Vespasian.

IMPERIUM

The nature of Titus' *imperium* has frequently been discussed[15]. The ancient literary evidence is inadequate, the numismatic and epigraphic inconsistent. Suetonius' comment on Titus' journey to the oracle of Venus on Paphos has often been cited but to little real effect[16]. It is not clear whether Titus was encouraged to hope for imperial power or for command in Judaea[17]. Again, Josephus' version of a speech Titus delivered on the fall of Jerusalem has been pressed into service[18]. The problems involved have been considered already, but essentially Titus' alleged description of Vespasian and himself as "autokratores" is not a definite indication that *imperium* had been conferred on Titus[19]. The epigraphic and numismatic evidence records his titles with varying degrees of accuracy and consistency:- *imp.* occurs in four different positions, viz. (*imp.*) *Titus* (*imp.*) *Caesar* (*imp.*) *Vespasianus* (*imp.*), but it is never found as a *praenomen* in documents from Rome[20]. The presence of *imperator* in any of these positions presumably implies some sort of *imperium* for Titus, but its inconsistent location, together with the absence of *Augustus*, leaves no doubt that it was secondary to Vespasian's. Probably, it was conferred towards the end of 70 or else in the first months of 71 before the celebration of the triumph[21].

Now, the bronze coins of 71 that refer to Titus as *imperator designatus* should not be regarded as accurate[22]. It used to be thought that the term indicated an early attempt to define Titus' precise constitutional position. But he had already been acclaimed *imperator* by his troops on the fall of Jerusalem and the title was already in use before April 71[23].

CONSULSHIP

Before he left Alexandria for the siege of Jerusalem in 70, Titus' position in the new regime was precisely indicated: two days after his thirty-first birthday he was declared consul with his father, both *in absentia*[24]. His appointment as ordinary consul, colleague of his father, was a prelude to the status he was to acquire as *particeps imperii*.

During the next nine years, Titus held six consulships, always as *ordinarius* with Vespasian as colleague[25]. Only in the years 71 (when the Jewish triumph was celebrated), 73 (the year of his censorship) and 78 (the year when no member of the family held a consulship), did Titus omit the office. It was an unprecedented monopoly intended in the first instance to enhance the family's status as well as Titus'. If Vespasian's senators shared Pliny's feelings on their consular policy[26], then it may well have been counterproductive, for, although the real power of the consulship had virtually disappeared with the advent of the principate, the emotional attitude to the old Republican offices was very much alive, and the autocracy of Nero's reign had led to a revival of such sentiments. So whilst Vespasian's and Titus' consistent tenure of the consulship was intended to provide an aura of legality as well as enhancing the dynasty's status, it could well be that, for once, Vespasian miscalculated, and succeeded only in underlining the undisguisedly autocratic nature of the new regime. Titus' unprecedented number of consulships, far surpassing those held by imperial heirs in previous reigns[27], was yet another indication of his prominence during the reign of his father. From the very beginning, Vespasian's dynastic policy was blatantly obvious and centred on Titus.

CENSORSHIP

His *censoria potestas* is frequently attested in literature, on coins and on inscriptions[28]. It has sometimes been assumed that he was designated to the office as early as the period July-Dec. 71[29], but, if that were so, then a formal election must have been held by the senate and a decision announced, presumably at the time of the Judaean triumph. But no record of any such election survives, and, far more importantly, the Flavians did not consider it necessary to enter upon the actual duties of the office until nearly two years later. Designations extending over a considerable period of time were not regular, and the one inscription on which it occurs is probably to be assigned to late 72 or early 73[30].

The office was rarely assumed during the empire. In 22 B.C., the last non-imperial censors, Munatius Plancus and Paullus Aemilius Lepidus, were appointed; when they failed to complete their *lustrum*, Augustus himself took over but never again resorted to the office[31]. Seventy years later, in the seventh year of his reign, Claudius assumed it with L. Vitellius as his colleague[32]. It was not until a quarter of a century later that it was again revived, probably in April 73. The earliest known inscriptions recording it are from this period and the comments of Censorinus and Pliny the Elder seem consistent with such a date. According to Censorinus, the *lustrum* was completed in 74[33]. Other scholars argue that therefore the censorship lasted from 71 until 74: they regard Pliny's testimony[34] that the duties of the office had been undertaken *intra quadriennium* as meaning "during four years" and so assign Vespasian's and Titus' assumption of it to 71. Mommsen, however, shows that their interpretation was almost certainly incorrect and offers the alternative "four years ago" - four years before the date when Pliny was writing[35]. So all depended on the epigraphic and numismatic evidence: scholars have generally accepted that they assumed the office early in 73[36] and probably in April, the Republican date.

As colleague with his father, Titus naturally collaborated with him in performing the duties associated with the office, and presumably supervised the census of citizens, the revision and reorganization of the senatorial and equestrian orders, together with the adlections *inter tribunicios*, *inter praetorios* and *inter patricios*. He also shared in the grant of *ius Latii* to all the *ciuitates* of Spain, perhaps yet another belated tribute to Galba's memory and intended to add weight to the officially inspired rumour that that *nobilis* had planned to adopt Titus. His name appeared with Vespasian's on inscriptions commemmorating this grant and probably he shared with him the responsibility for the *cura morum*[37].

The array of powers seemingly involved in the office is paralleled by the varied suggestions made by modern scholars to establish the reasons for assuming it. One function of the censor was to replenish the senate. It had been depleted through civil war, capable men were needed, and those who assisted in the usurpation had to be rewarded and their future loyalty guaranteed. The censorship could be seen as providing a cloak of legality to this necessary if at times somewhat sordid operation. It has also been argued that it provided a balance to the Flavians' humble background, that it justified their broadening of the empire's social and political structure[38] and that its revival was consistent with Vespasian's "Augustanism"[39], his deliberate intention to evoke memories of a revered past age. Evidence can be elicited to support each of these contentions. Numerous adlections were made[40]; the expansion of the empire's social and political structure is shown, in the west, by the numerous grants of *ius Latii*, and, in the east, by the growing proportion of "eastern" senators in highly significant consular posts in the reigns of Domitian and Trajan[41]. So, whilst certainty is impossible, it could well be that the essential reason for assuming the office was the large number of adlections *in senatum* and, more importantly, *inter patricios* that were regarded as vital. It is not unlikely that some 150 such awards were made[42], an operation of the magnitude to require a suitable legal disguise.

PRAEFECTUS PRAETORII

In addition to the powers inherent in his various offices, Titus was also made praetorian prefect: traditionally, it has been assumed that he received the appointment in 71 and that no colleague was assigned to him[43]. Neither assumption has ancient authority.

The post was traditionally reserved for men of equestrian rank, and so this was one of the rare occasions when Vespasian dispensed with traditional practice. But he had substantial reasons for his action. It was essential to detect and prevent any discontent among the praetorian cohorts whose numbers and loyalty could have represented a perennial source of worry to the new regime, for their power was immense, and their location at the very centre of the empire gave them an importance out of all proportion to their numbers. This had been demonstrated in the fall of Nero and of Galba[44]. Nero's position became impossible with the desertion of the guard at the instigation of its prefect Nymphidius Sabibus, and, by transferring allegiance from Galba to Otho seven months later, the praetorians were even more directly responsible for Galba's collapse. Hence the Flavians paid particular attention to this position.

Suetonius' statement (*Titus* 6.1) that only Roman knights had previously held the praetorian prefecture is completely incorrect. Early in 70 or late in 69, Marcus Arrecinus Clemens, brother of Titus' first wife Arrecina Tertulla[45], was appointed (*Hist.* 4.68) to the post by Mucianus, possibly on the advice or instructions of Vespasian. The circumstances were as follows: the loyalty of Arrius Varus was suspect (*Hist.* 4.68); Mucianus and the ambitious Domitian had to leave soon for Gaul and wanted to leave Rome in safe hands; Varus was therefore moved to the control of the grain supply and replaced by Clemens[46]. This rearrangement has provoked much comment: it has even been suggested that Clemens was Mucianus' supporter and, by implication, an enemy of Titus[47]. Yet Vespasian was emperor, even if still in Egypt, and it is hard to believe that at Berytus (July 69) the question of a suitable prefect had not been near the top of the agenda[48]. Vespasian was too careful to leave such a vital appointment to someone else. As happened with other posts, he turned to his relatives: L. Caesennius Paetus (Syria), Q. Petillius Cerialis Caelius Rufus (Britain) and, possibly, T. Flavius Sabinus III (Pannonia)[49] were all early postings. Whilst there is no evidence that the recommendation came from Vespasian and was made originally at Berytus, the significance of the post was such that normal prudence, a quality he possessed in abundance, demanded that the emperor alone should nominate the "guardian of his sacred side"[50].

It has also been suggested that Titus "wrested"[51] the post from Clemens on his return in 71 so as to counter the growing influence of Mucianus. Apart from the alleged motive, which will be discussed later, the question of timing is important. It is indeed possible that Titus became prefect at around the time of his triumph; but no ancient authority asserts it[52]. Clemens received a suffect consulship in 73, and, when he was designated to it early in the previous year, that might mark his retirement from the prefecture. Vespasian had no reason to be displeased with his performance, as far as can be ascertained, and hence would probably have eased him out at the earliest opportunity rather than bluntly dismiss him. His future career (governor of Spain, consul for the second time and probably city prefect during Domitian's absence at the Dacian wars) strongly suggests that his service as prefect during the regime's early days was adequate. Perhaps he was moved gently aside in much the same way as Domitian was to "transfer into the most noble order" his praetorian prefect, L. Julius Ursus[53].

Titus may well have had a colleague in this post. It is very likely that Ti. Julius Alexander held the praetorian prefecture. Last attested in the literary sources at Titus' council of war (*BJ* 6.242) that was discussing the fate of the Temple, he could well have accompanied Titus to Rome. His declaration for Vespasian on July 1 deserved its reward. A papyrus names him as prefect of the praet(orians)[54], a post for which he was admirably qualified. As an administrator and chief of staff to Corbulo and Titus, he had distinguished himself, displaying in addition a remarkable dexterity in deserting a sinking ship at precisely the right time. His reputation as prefect might have been as bad as Titus', if, as has been suggested, Juvenal's famous comment is to be applied to him[55].

Titus' activities as prefect seem to have gone beyond the regular and accepted processes of Roman law: in fact, he was "somewhat arrogant and tyrannical" (*Titus* 6.1). Recently, it has been conjectured that, though Titus and Vespasian refused to accept charges of *maiestas* (Dio, 66.9.1, 19.1), Titus found an effective substitute in the doctrine of the *manifestus*[56]. Usually, this is explained as extrajudicial punishment of a manifest criminal: the punishment of such a person required no charge (and therefore no trial) but rather was the result of popular pressure. Titus seems to have gone so far as to encourage the latter (*Titus* 6.2) in the theatre and camp, but definite victims of the "technique" are unattested, apart from A. Caecina Alienus.

TITUS CO-RULER?

The unprecedented honours accorded Titus in the early part of the reign clearly indicate his father's desire that he should participate very actively in the administration of the empire. His anomalous position was, to some extent, the result of

efforts to legitimize their usurpation of power and to perpet-
uate the dynasty. On the other hand, Titus himself may well
have had some influence on his father's decision. Some have
argued that he insisted on various honours as his due for his
part in the events of 69, and also so as to counter Mucianus'
growing power[57]. It must be admitted that his role in organizing support for Vespasian was vital - his tactful handling
of Mucianus, his influence on Agrippa II and Berenice, his
negotiations with Ti. Julius Alexander. Inevitably, he would
be rewarded. Again, his father was sixty, and four emperors
had died in the previous twenty months: it was essential that
he assign as much responsibility as he reasonably could to his
thirty-year-old son. Yet, Vespasian was always emperor and
Titus the heir: *Augustus* and *Augusti filius*, these titles
accurately indicate the place of each. Nor is there even a
rumour or hint in the literary sources that Titus, on his
return from Judaea in 71, was in a threatening mood, demanding
offices and honours. He had no need to act in that way, for
Vespasian had obviously explained carefully what he had in
mind for him, perhaps in the winter of 70/71 that they had
spent together in Alexandria.

Of some relevance is the work-load undertaken by diligent
emperors[58]. Vespasian had been in a position to witness the
debacle resulting from indolent and incompetent leadership:
he did not spend all his time in Greece sleeping. Undoubtedly,
he was well aware of the magnitude of the task he had vigor-
ously fought for and willingly assumed. He meant to found a
dynasty, as he made clear at every opportunity, and equally he
wished to ensure that his son who was to succeed him was
properly prepared and supervised. In Judaea, Ti. Julius
Alexander's role was to check Titus' recklessness as well as
guide him in military matters. Now, in the administrative
field, the task was Vespasian's. Thus, as Suetonius points
out, Titus bore most of the routine burdens of administration,
performed the functions of imperial secretary, conducted
official correspondence, drafted edicts and even took over the
task normally assigned to a quaestor of reading imperial
speeches to the senate (*Titus* 6.1).

On the other hand, Vespasian was not idle (*Vesp.* 21).
There can be no doubt that the new administration was efficient, for both father and son worked hard at their tasks, with
Vespasian always the director. Frequently, the phrase "co-
rule" has been applied to this period[59], yet that is not the
impression conveyed by the accounts of Vespasian's reign left
by Suetonius and Dio. In the former, it is Vespasian who
created new provinces (revoking the freedom granted by Nero:
Vesp. 8.4), who sent new legions to Cappadocia after
appointing a consular governor instead of an equestrian as
formerly (8.4), who had new buildings built (8.5) and
instigated legal (10), cultural (17) and other (9) reforms.
There is no hint whatsoever of Titus' participation: he had

other tasks to perform (*Titus* 6.1). Again, Suetonius' anecdotes about Vespasian are most instructive. It was he who poked fun at Demetrius and at Mucianus' lack of masculinity (*Vesp.* 13), who promoted Mettius Pompusianus to consul after being warned of him (14) and who would reject a funeral worth ten million sesterces, offering instead to accept 100,000 at once with permission to toss him into the Tiber when he was dead (19). Anecdotes on *auaritia* (16) were directed at the person who formulated the financial policy. He laughed at efforts to trace the Flavii back to the founders of Reate and to a companion of Hercules (12): Titus' reactions were not recorded. Most significant, though, was the famous urinal anecdote, where Vespasian, with the image of the blunt, slightly coarse countryman, instructed (23.3) his son on the finer points of efficient financial management. For Suetonius, this was not a discussion between two partners (despite *Titus* 6.1); rather it was the master and his apprentice. Dio's briefer account conveys a similar impression. What was significant was Vespasian's relationship with Phoebus (65.11. 2), Mucianus (13.1-2), Helvidius Priscus (13.3) and Caenis (14), whilst the comparative status of father and son was once again indicated by the urinal anecdote (14.5).

TITUS AND MUCIANUS

Titus' alleged rivalry with Mucianus has been the subject of some dispute. The question is essential for an assessment of Titus and demands re-examination. On the one hand, it has been argued that Mucianus and a group of supporters opposed Titus, that the alliance maintained some coherence even after Mucianus' death and was dissolved only with the execution by Titus of Eprius Marcellus and Caecina Alienus in 79[60]. Recently, this reconstruction has been dismissed as fanciful[61]. Both arguments require careful assessment. For the sake of convenience, Vespasian's reign will be considered in two separate sections, the first ending in 75 with the arrival of Berenice in Rome, and the second with the executions of 79.

The argument that Titus and Mucianus were bitter rivals in the early seventies may be outlined as follows: Mucianus, as *de facto* head of state in 70, eliminated pretenders to the throne, ordered other executions, appointed generals and, at the same time, secured the escape from prosecution of Eprius Marcellus and Vibius Crispus, both *amici* of Nero and known delators who had been facing attack from Helvidius Priscus and his supporters for their past activities. Despite a rebellious senate, posts of some significance were provided for them by Mucianus, a three-year appointment as proconsul of Asia for Marcellus and a similar term in Africa for Crispus. Thereby, he gained their constant support, they became members of his group. An indication of his power and influence was Tacitus' comment in the *Dialogus* (the dramatic date of which is 74) that Marcellus and Crispus were "leading men in the emperor's friendship and carried all before them"[62]. Then, when Titus and Vespasian were in Alexandria in 70, Titus (according to Tacitus) urged his father to be lenient with Domitian, despite the rumours of his behaviour in Rome: "As for friends, time, altered circumstances, fortunes, perhaps their passions or their errors, may weaken, may change, may even destroy their affection"[63]. But what was really worrying Titus was not Domitian's activities in Rome, but rather those of the great *amicus*, Mucianus, who may even have spread rumours about Titus' disloyalty in the east. Indeed, Titus' hurried return in 71 was prompted by the possible effect of these rumours on his father. He then insisted on being granted extraordinary powers, in particular that of praetorian prefect, as a *quid pro quo*, to counter Mucianus' influence, and this involved the dismissal of Arrecinus Clemens, one of Mucianus' group. The final piece of evidence is the continued absence of Berenice, whose arrival in Rome can be explained only by the death of Mucianus; it was he who blocked her return[64].

Objections have been raised to this reasoning, basically on the grounds that Mucianus' individual assertion of power must have ended with the return of Vespasian. According to Tacitus, this was understood before the attempt was made to challenge Vitellius: "I shall place myself before Vitellius, and you before me... We shall not hold the same position in success as in failure, for, if we win, I shall have the position you choose to give"[65]. He could expect to retain considerable influence, primarily in an advisory capacity, but this does not imply that he was allowed to exercise authority independent of the emperor. Similarly, Eprius Marcellus and Vibius Crispus may well have been supported by Mucianus, but they did not owe their place to him. They were the type of competent and proven administrators that Vespasian needed to organize the provinces and deliver the much-needed revenues. Nor was Arrecinus Clemens an adherent of Mucianus, for his loyalty belonged to his Flavian relatives and especially Vespasian[66].

Whilst these objections are generally valid, they seem to miss the central issue, the character of Vespasian. There is no hint in the ancient sources that anyone other than he was in charge. Titus obviously had far more power than Tiberius did under Augustus, but he was still *Augusti filius* and not *Augustus*.

The hostility between Titus and Mucianus is supposed to have been obvious as early as 70; reports of Titus' disloyalty were rife, so it is argued, and therefore he countered with allegations against his father's prominent *amicus*, Mucianus. Now, in 70, both Vespasian and Titus were in Alexandria but there is no indication that rumours of Titus' disloyalty were circulating at that time. On the contrary, it was his behaviour immediately before and during his leisurely tour of the east at the end of 70 that gave rise to them. Earlier in the year, he had not even had the chance to be disloyal. As for the behaviour of the *amici*, it is clear that what was worrying Titus was Flavian solidarity. The context makes this obvious:-

> It was said that Titus before his departure had a long interview with his father, in which he implored him not to let himself be easily excited by the reports of slanderers, but to show an impartial and forgiving temper towards his son. 'Legions and fleets,' he reminded him, 'are not such sure bulwarks of imperial power as a numerous family. As for friends time, altered circumstances, fortunes, perhaps their passions or their errors, may weaken, may change, may even destroy their affection. A man's own race can never be dissociated from him, least of all with princes, whose prosperity is shared by others, while their reverses touch only their nearest kin. Even between brothers there can be no lasting affection, unless the father sets the example'. Not so much reconciled towards Domitian as delighted with Titus' show of brotherly love, Vespasian...[67]

Titus' point was that, whilst the affection bestowed by one's friends could well be transitory, that which existed between members of a family, especially one that meant to be established as a dynasty, had to resist "time, altered circumstances, fortunes, passions and even errors". Vespasian was not the only one with dynastic ambitions. Again, Tacitus' report of Vespasian's reaction to the speech contains no hint whatsoever that either of them were thinking of Mucianus: Domitian was causing all the bother.

Again, Titus' supposed insistence[68] on being appointed praetorian prefect has no ancient authority whatsoever, nor indeed has the assumption that the post was conferred on him in 71 at the same time as his other powers. It could well be that in 72, around the time of Arrecinus Clemens' designation to the consulship, Titus (and possibly Ti. Julius Alexander) replaced him as prefect. Either interpretation is possible on the evidence we have, and, in fact, it is not even certain that Titus was the direct successor of Clemens.

Of critical importance is the role assigned to Eprius Marcellus and Vibius Crispus. Tacitus' comment (*Dial.* 8) on their power and influence is quite significant - *principes in Caesaris amicitia*: they were *amici Caesaris* and very powerful ones at that[69]. Any connection that may have existed between them and Mucianus was substantially less significant. An examination of the consular *fasti* for 74 is illuminating. Vespasian (*cos. V ord.*) and Titus (*cos. III ord.*) opened the year and were followed by Ti. Plautius Silvanus Aelianus, L. Junius Q. Vibius Crispus, Q. Petillius Cerialis Caesius Rufus and T. Clodius Eprius Marcellus, all suffect consuls for the second time[70]. Senior administrators of varying talent, they were rewarded for their loyalty to the dynasty. Mucianus, as was only proper, had received greater and somewhat earlier honours - a second consulship in 70 and a third in 72[71], both suffect. The four consulars, on the other hand, had to wait until the expiry of their appointments, some overseas, and then were promoted *en masse*. It was probably in 76 that L. Tampius Flavianus and M. Pompeius Silvanus Staberius Flavinus also received their iterated consulships[72]. These six senior consuls were Vespasian's elder statesmen, honoured in some cases for loyalty to the Flavians, or at least timely acceptance of them, and in others for efficiency as well. In a sense, the unusual series of consulships revealed and was intended to reveal the stability of the new regime. Immediately following the usurpation of power in 69, there had been the inevitable period of confusion, marked most obviously by the problems Mucianus faced with a rebellious and fractious senate[73]. Its conclusion was indicated by Vespasian's return to Rome by the autumn of 70 and by the consulships awarded to the loyal legionary legates of 69/70[74]. Next came the turn of his more elderly supporters. Stability could be openly advertised. Loyalty had been at a premium and was duly rewarded, with almost mathematical precision - a series of ordinary consulships for Titus (*cos. IV ord.* in 75), two further suffect consulships to Mucianus, an additional one for the senior administrators and promotion to the *fasces* (sometimes prematurely) for the legionary commanders. In all this, there was not the slightest hint of factions or of disloyalty: if they existed, neither Vespasian nor the literary sources were aware of them.

Amongst the supposed supporters of Mucianus, Vibius Crispus merits attention. Noted as he was for his ability to swim with the stream[75], he was well aware of the direction of the current in the first years of Vespasian's reign. Helvidius Priscus learned this lesson to his cost. Vespasian may have been reluctant to kill him, but kill him he did[76]. Vibius would not have been so foolish, and in any case was not endowed with sufficient courage, to side with Mucianus against Vespasian's son and heir-apparent. Had Mucianus in fact been attempting to organize a faction against Titus, he too, almost certainly, would have shared Helvidius Priscus' fate, for Vespasian was genuinely quite upset at any suggestion that Titus should not succeed him[77]. Finally, Vibius Crispus' full name is not without significance. The "L. Junius" recalls Vespasian's brother-in-law, L.(Junius)Caesennius Paetus: the origin of the common item could be the result of an adoption and may hint at some connection between Vibius and the imperial family[78].

TITUS, BERENICE AND THE CONSPIRACY OF 79

The supposed rivalry between Titus and Mucianus has also been connected with two incidents from the second part of Vespasian's reign, the arrival of Berenice in Rome in 75 and the execution of Eprius Marcellus and Caecina Alienus in 79[79].
The literary evidence concerning Berenice is somewhat inconsistent. Suetonius describes Titus' passion for her, his resultant unpopularity and eventual dismissal of her *inuitus inuitam*, but gives no hint of two separate returns (*Titus* 7). Dio (65.15.3), on the other hand, assigns her arrival in Rome to 75. According to his account, she went to live with Titus in the palace and her brother received *praetoria ornamenta*. Popular disapproval, however, led to her dismissal at around the time that the Celtic chieftain Julius Sabinus and his wife were put to death (79). The opposition to her presence included the attacks of two Cynic philosophers, Diogenes and Heras, who had managed to slip back into the city despite their earlier expulsion; for their impudence, the former was flogged and the latter beheaded. Dio's account of Vespasian's reign then ends with the affair of Marcellus and Caecina (66. 15.3-4). In the section dealing with Titus' own reign, Berenice is recorded as having returned "again"[80]: the context is highly laudatory and the implication is that her return was very brief (66.18.1). Of the other ancient authorities, Aurelius Victor repeats the version of Suetonius with the implication that Berenice came back to Rome on one occasion only (*De Caes.* 10.7). His epitomator, however, provides a more extensive account, still following Suetonius, but adding the extraordinary comment that "Caecina, the ex-consul was invited to a meal, and hardly had he left the room when Titus ordered him to be slain on suspicion of having raped his wife Berenice"[81].
From this, it emerges that Berenice must have returned in 75 and remained in Rome, not for a year as is sometimes claimed[82], but until the conspiracy of Eprius Marcellus and Caecina. Her second return in Titus' reign was far briefer. The recent argument that she must have received an immediate summons to the capital in 71[83] has the same strength and weakness as the alleged hostility between Titus and Mucianus - a certain attractiveness and even logic, but no ancient evidence. Her absence until 75 has been ascribed to the influence of Mucianus who is alleged to have insisted on it as a *quid pro quo* for the honours awarded to Titus; and the opposition to her was removed only by his death, which must therefore have occurred in 75[84]. But there is no precise indication in our sources of when Mucianus died: all that can securely be established is that it was before 77[85]. Her absence can more reasonably be ascribed to Vespasian, who had no intention of appearing to reverse the victory at Actium and welcome a second Cleopatra to Rome. Once again, Titus' role

in the regime was revealed. All vital decisions were made by the emperor, albeit after consultation with Titus and others - but by him nonetheless.

Much more controversial is the conspiracy of Eprius Marcellus and Caecina Alienus[86]. On the one hand, it is seen as an extension of the rivalry between Titus and Mucianus, with Eprius assuming the latter's mantle on his death and re-establishing his "group". Diogenes' and Heras' return was secured by them so as to arouse hostility to Titus and weaken his position. He certainly responded promptly to their presence. Then, it is argued, the feud centred on the succession problem. By 79, Vespasian was probably showing signs of ill-health; Titus feared that his opponents, senior Vespasianic *amici*, might be powerful enough to prevent his accession and so he struck first[87]. This reconstruction is admittedly attractive. On the other hand, the problem is to determine whether the opposition that certainly existed after 75 was directed at Titus personally or at the regime in general. Titus was a very convenient focal point as heir-apparent openly living with Berenice, but what was at stake was the existence and continuity of the dynasty. Vespasian, well aware of this, surely instructed his praetorian prefect to take appropriate action. Helvidius Priscus had previously suffered for his temerity in attacking the emperor's dynastic plans; following the next attack, Diogenes was flogged and Heras beheaded; then, in 79, Marcellus and Caecina were put to death. Again, the evidence pointing to a reformed anti-Titus coalition is particularly fragile: it is limited to the supposed arrangement of the return of Diogenes and Heras, which could surely have been accomplished without such eminent support.

The essence of the problem is the nature of the conspiracy of 79, for that is surely what it was. The literary sources provide abundant evidence. According to Suetonius and Dio, Caecina was invited to dine with Titus, and was cut down by the guard before he could leave the room at the end of the meal. Both suggest that the action was justified: Suetonius reports that Titus had an autographed copy of a speech that Caecina was preparing to deliver to the troops (*Titus* 6.2), whilst Dio comments on the fact that Caecina already had armed support (65.16.3-4). No doubt it was not forgotten that, ten years previously, he had been instrumental in eliciting support for Vitellius[88]. Less clear is the precise role of Eprius Marcellus whose participation in the conspiracy is attested by Dio alone; more obscure still are the motives that prompted their action. All that can be said with certainty is that a conspiracy had been formed and armed support for it secured. As ever, Vespasian's reaction to threats aimed at the dynasty was prompt.

Berenice's presence during the last years of his reign merits attention. There is no reason to doubt the consistent

tradition that Titus' accession was greeted with hostility.
According to Suetonius, it was feared that he would be a
second Nero (*Titus* 7.1), and amongst the reasons adduced for
such an attitude was Titus' notorious passion (*insignem
amorem*) for Berenice. She was indeed far from unobtrusive.
Quintilian's statement on her is interesting:

> Again, some have been judges in cases where their own
> interests were involved. I note, for instance, in the
> book of observations published by Septimius that Cicero
> appeared in such a case, while I myself, when I appeared
> on behalf of Queen Berenice, actually pleaded before
> her[89].

The context deals with civil proceedings before a *iudex*,
hardly a post to be occupied by a foreign princess, and it is
even less likely that she presided over any sort of Roman
court. Possibly, as has been suggested, she was present on
some occasion when the imperial *consilium* was dealing with a
matter that concerned her or in which she was thought to have
expertise[90]. At all events, it must have exacerbated the
situation and aroused opposition to her on political grounds
as well. Small wonder, then, if she was widely regarded,
especially by senators, as an ambitious eastern queen unable
to disguise her intention of becoming empress of Rome. Her
position in the city became untenable during the last year of
Vespasian's reign. The epitomator's remark that Caecina was
killed *ob suspicionem stupratae Berenicis* (*Epit. de Caes.*
10.4), though not supported by any other ancient authority,
may reflect, not only the extent and persistence in tradition
of the hostility with which she was regarded, but also the
fact that she left Rome soon after the suppression of the
conspiracy hatched by Eprius Marcellus and Caecina Alienus -
hence, for the epitomator, *post hoc, ergo propter hoc*.
Unfortunately for her, the removal of these two senior
senators must have aroused such ill-feeling that some gesture
of appeasement was essential, and her reputation made her the
ideal choice, despite Titus' attitude (*inuitus inuitam*: *Titus*
7.2). She was always unpopular in Rome and was only admitted
in 75 because, presumably, Vespasian felt that the regime was
stable enough (witness the four iterated consulships of the
previous year) to withstand the increased hostility. But the
conspiracy of 79 and its suppression necessitated a concession
to senatorial opinion and she was sent away. Her second
return in Titus' reign was almost certainly not at his instigation, and its brevity demonstrates that he made his choice
and would not impair his *auctoritas* by allowing her to remain
in his capital.

THE ROLE OF MUCIANUS

If the supposed rivalry between Titus and Mucianus is to be
rejected, a re-examination of their relationship and roles

during the seventies is desirable. Let it be noted that in outlook and behaviour they were not dissimilar. In a comparison of Titus' reputation before and after his accession, one scholar has suggested that perhaps "he laid aside one mask to assume another, a move that could well be attributed to the cynical refinement and poetic versatility of a graduate of Nero's court"[91]: these characteristics were not lacking in Mucianus. Both of them were cultivated diplomats with loose morals. Such similarity might well appear disadvantageous to the development of a satisfactory relationship between them, but there is no evidence that it was in fact so. Mucianus' activities during the early years of Vespasian's reign until his death were tangential to those of Titus and do not in any way suggest that he was trying to create an anti-Titus coalition; rather he was persevering in the role that he had assumed in the last years of the previous decade. He still preferred to wield influence behind the scenes[92] and avoid the dangers of supreme power. His talent was for organization and his contacts had served Vespasian well.

Now his role in the Corbulonian circle must be stressed. The influence and indeed the existence of such a group, though often debated[93], must still be regarded with not a little scepticism, for Corbulo's insistence on harsh discipline and his tendency to avoid set battles in favour of strategic manoeuvring[94] were characteristics not appreciated by every soldier and officer. On the other hand, his protracted command, from 55 to 66, must have led them to expect substantial rewards and promotion: "twelve years with the eastern armies offered an unrivalled opportunity for extending a general's *clientela* among troops and officers"[95]. But just as his patronage had been cultivated assiduously, so too his demise in 66 would have been greeted with extreme chagrin. Vespasian's appointment later in that same year was not welcomed, for lacking consular parentage as did Corbulo's own legates[96], he hardly seemed to be an adequate replacement. He could not be expected to assume his predecessor's patronage responsibilities. It is noteworthy that, according to Suetonius (*Vesp.* 4.6), he had to restore discipline on his arrival in the east, a puzzling statement in view of the standards demanded by Corbulo over a considerable period of time. Perhaps he was greeted by his troops' ill-concealed annoyance at the loss of their prospects, exacerbated by the fact that their new commander had just severed his own friendship and his son's marital connection with the group to which Corbulo had himself been allied[97]. In these circumstances, the unanimous support accorded him by all seven eastern legions three years later requires explanation.

Of these seven, three (*V Macedonica, X Fretensis* and *XV Apollinaris*) served in Judaea in 67 and the following years under the aegis of Vespasian: no doubt he and his legates (Sex. Vettulenus Cerialis, M. Ulpius Traianus and Titus) secured their loyalty and, later, appropriate rewards were distributed. But the four that remained in Syria (*III Gallica, IV Scythica, VI Ferrata* and *XII Fulminata*) had had little or no direct contact with Vespasian, and the credit for their prompt adherence to the Flavian cause belongs surely to Mucianus: a term as governor of Lycia during and presumably under Corbulo's command must have brought him into close contact with the legates of these legions and with others as well, and he exploited the acquaintance[98].

The *III Gallica* had been part of Corbulo's army for many years. Its legate around 64 had been T. Aurelius Fulvus who later received an early consulship and probably patrician status; after governing Spain, he received the *fasces* for the second time (85, *cos. ord.*) and held the city prefecture. He was consistently loyal to all the Flavians and his descendants included the future emperor Antoninus Pius[99]. The *IV Scythica* had been in Syria since 56: after being involved in Caesennius Paetus' disgrace at Rhandeia, it seems to have played a minor role for the rest of the sixties. Its legate in 70, and probably before that time, was Cn. Pompeius Collega, who also obtained a suffect consulship, possibly patrician status and a consular command, the new Cappadocian-Galatian complex[100]. The *VI Ferrata* had been in Syria from the time of Augustus and had formed part of Corbulo's army since 55/56: its legate in the late sixties was almost certainly M. Hirrius Fronto Neratius Pansa who later achieved rewards similar to those of the other Syrian legates - a consulship, patrician status and a consular command (also Cappadocia-Galatia, succeeding Pompeius Collega)[101]. The *XII Fulminata* had long served in Syria and was defeated on two separate occasions, by the Parthians at Rhandeia, and, with A. Caesennius Gallus as legate, by the Jews in 66. He later received the *fasces* and followed Neratius Pansa in Cappadocia-Galatia: whilst his probable relationship to L. Caesennius Paetus suggests close but unattested imperial connections, it does not seem to have accelerated his career. Perhaps his legateship was quaestorian, like that of Titus[102].

These four legions had served many years in the province, and, since 67, under the command of Mucianus himself[103]. He had had ample opportunity to forge contacts with the senior officers in the last years of Corbulo's command and could now take advantage of his earlier work. All his diplomatic skills were clearly necessary, when the time came, to convince them that Vespasian's patronage was worth securing[104]. There is, of course, no direct evidence that this was in fact the order of events, but it does seem very likely in view of the unanimous support Vespasian received from legates who knew of him but had perhaps never even seen him. Mucianus' influence can be discerned in their subsequent rewards. It is almost as if he saw to it that they received a certain minimum level - a consulship, patrician status and a consular command. But, as must be stressed, we have no direct evidence whatsoever (and can expect none) of the motives behind these appointments made in the seventies, yet it is not unreasonable to suggest that they came at the instigation of Mucianus.

Other former associates of Corbulo may have been approached by him. Rutilius Gallicus, probably governor of Galatia in the sixties, may well have come into contact with his counterpart in Lycia, and both would presumably have been under Corbulo's authority. From Galatia, he seems to have gone to Asia as *legatus pro praetore*. His rewards for supporting the Flavians in 69/70 were substantial - an early consulship, consular appointments in Africa and Germany and further honours under Domitian. Whilst certainty is impossible, it could be that Mucianus' knowledge of the man enabled him to use the arguments most appropriate to secure his allegiance[105]. A. Marius Celsus[106] joined Corbulo in 63 together with the legion *XV Apollinaris* which he brought from Carnuntum (*Ann.* 15.25.3). The support he provided for the Flavians in the civil war is not recorded. Indeed, he consistently appeared on the losing side, but the fact that he was appointed to Lower Germany and then Syria early in the reign suggests, though does not prove, that he had more than ability to recommend him[107]. Again, Mucianus would have been able to speak with authority on Celsus and would also have known how to convince him of the advantages of supporting the Flavians.

By their very nature, political manoeuvres such as the above are not recorded and can never be retrieved with any degree of certainty. All that can be securely established is that, in each instance, the common factor was an association with Corbulo and, in view of Mucianus' character and past service under that general, he emerges as the likeliest candidate to have convinced them that Vespasian would provide all that they could have expected from Corbulo; indeed, only he seems to have been in a position to persuade them. In the seventies, he continued for a time as a figure of power and influence behind the scenes, ensuring that the appropriate patronage was distributed to the deserving. There was, of course, the distinct possibility of conflict with Titus; but there is no evidence that it occurred, and in view of Vespasian's undoubted if unobtrusive control of affairs, it is highly unlikely that any such division would have been permitted to endure.

Mucianus had been a successful organizer and diplomat, and was destined for a similar role in the new regime, as can be seen from his control of the senate during the early part of 70. His difficulties were many - the confusion prevalent in the *curia*, Domitian's attitude and behaviour, and the moves against alleged delators, starting with P. Egnatius Celer[108]. All were dealt with competently and smoothly. Again, this was the role expected of him in subsequent years. With the advantage of his experience, and the *dignitas* conferred by

iterated consulships, he was the ideal intermediary between
emperor and senate.

Particularly revealing is the incident that occurred
early in January 70, the demotion and quick reinstallation of
Tettius Julianus[109]. He first appears in Tacitus (*Hist.* 1.79)
as quaestorian legionary legate of the (Moesian) legion *VII
Claudia*, awarded *ornamenta consularia* by Otho in 69: later in
the same year Aponius Saturninus attempted to murder Julianus
(now apparently designated to the praetorship for 70), compelling him to abandon his command and flee to save himself:-

> Aponius Saturninus, the governor of Moesia, ventured to
> commit an appalling act (*pessimum facinus*). He sent a
> centurion to assassinate the commander of the seventh
> legion, Tettius Julianus. The motive was a private
> dispute, camouflaged as a bid to help the Flavian cause.
> Julianus discovered that he was in danger, and seeking
> the help of natives who knew the geography of the area
> intimately, made his escape through the trackless wilds
> of Moesia to the region south of the Balkan range.
> Thereafter, he took no part in the civil war, finding a
> number of excuses for spinning out his journey to
> Vespasian and in response to the latest news alternately
> loitering or hurrying forward[110].

He delayed joining the Flavians and soon paid the price, being
stripped of the praetorship "ostensibly for abandoning his
legion when it rallied to Vespasian, but in reality so that
the vacant post could be transferred to Plotius Grypus"[111].
Soon after, however, probably at the second meeting of the
senate for 70 (January 3[112]), "he had his praetorship restored
to him when it was discovered that he had taken refuge with
Vespasian, while Grypus retained his office"[113]. So Mucianus
received two versions of Julianus' behaviour, the second of
which forced him to reverse his original decision. The first
account, hostile to Julianus, probably emanated from Aponius
Saturninus who had already tried assassination and so would
hardly feel any qualms at charging Julianus with desertion.
Subsequently, it was discovered (*cognitus est*) that Aponius'
version had been fabricated. It is highly likely that this
information was provided by Vipstanus Messalla, who had been
tribune *laticlavius* of the legion *VII Claudia* at the time of
the attempted assassination[114] and would therefore have been
one of the very few to know precisely what had happened and to
be in a position to convey the information to Mucianus: he
was certainly in Rome in January 70, since he is attested as
speaking in the senate on behalf of his half-brother Regulus
(*Hist.* 4.42). Again, Vipstanus was clearly upset at Aponius'
action; he wrote an account of the civil war which Tacitus
used[115] and it was probably from this work that Tacitus
obtained the phrase *pessimum facinus* to describe the attempt
on Julianus' life[116].

If this speculative restoration is correct, then Mucianus

was faced with a delicate problem, for Julianus' brother-in-law had been one of the "principal accountants and paymasters of the Flavian party"[117]. He was the powerful freedman Tiberius Julius Aug. lib., soon to become the new regime's finance minister[118], as Mucianus knew full well. On the other hand, Mucianus needed the support of Aponius in his struggle with Antonius Primus (*Hist.* 4.39 ff.)[119], and Julianus himself was at least guilty of "extended procrastination"[120] in joining the Flavians, though was hardly alone in this. Yet, Mucianus could not afford to alienate the eminent finance minister, and hence the praetorship was restored. Problems of this nature could safely be left to him. No doubt there were other occasions in the early seventies when political debts had to be paid and difficult choices made, when decisions had to be taken promptly whilst causing minimum offence. Julianus' reinstatement could be regarded as illustrative of the role that Vespasian envisaged for Mucianus, the highly placed administrator with diplomatic skill and the requisite *auctoritas* to ensure compliance by all parties. He was not to be the regime's enforcer.

On the other hand, there are hints in the sources that Mucianus' influence was less obvious as the reign progressed and that he withdrew from the centre of affairs to concentrate on literature. His literary output was certainly substantial during this period. He collated and edited versions of ancient speeches and documents, including those of Pompey, Crassus and other prominent Republican politicans: his *libri actorum* were composed in eleven books and his *epistulae* in three (*Dial.* 37). No doubt the task was necessary in view of the damage to the official records that had occurred when Vitellius' legions stormed the Capitol in December 69, but his reported boast that he had made an emperor (*Hist.* 4.4.1) may reflect the bitterness and frustration that he felt in later years and that virtually forced him to turn to other activities: according to Suetonius (*Vesp.* 13), he also treated Vespasian with scant respect at this time. The elder Pliny cited him by name on thirty-two occasions, using him for information about Asia, Syria, the Greek islands and as an eyewitness for a number of exotic animals; in the *Naturalis Historia*, he was listed among the authorities for eighteen of the thirty-seven books[121]. The precise extent of Mucianus' output cannot be determined, but he was clearly a prolific writer, and much of his work could well be assigned to a period of virtual retirement - he was already dead when Pliny was writing (*NH* 32.62). The decline in his political influence could perhaps be assigned to the period after 72, when he attained the rare distinction of a third consulship; that award may well have represented both the culmination and the conclusion of his effective participation in the new regime. None of this, though, can be interpreted as evidence for a plot against Titus; indeed, any association he may have had with Vibius Crispus and Eprius Marcellus would have been severed as they saw his influence waning[122]. He was disrespectful towards Vespasian and no doubt quite bitter, but was criticized mildly and in private - witness Vespasian's comment to a friend that he at least was a man (*Vesp.* 13). But, whilst insults were tolerated (*Vesp.* 14), an attack on imperial dynastic policy would not have been accepted. Mucianus' survival is definite evidence that, in Vespasian's eyes, bitterness and disrespect did not constitute treason.

SUMMARY OF TITUS' ROLE

Titus' precise role in the seventies should be seen in the light of Vespasian's dynastic plans and judged in accordance with the existing procedure for establishing the succession. Previous emperors had considered the problem and produced various solutions: some hedged their bets by suggesting more than one candidate, some left the decision as late as possible, and no one established a standard formula or precise definition of the heir's status and powers. Vespasian, an excellent judge of tactics with a well-attested capacity for *cunctatio*[123], solved the problem with what appears to be uncharacteristic rapidity. He immediately and publicly declared his intention of establishing a dynasty; there was no subterfuge. As soon as Titus returned from Judaea, Vespasian used every means at his disposal to delineate the status and powers of his heir. At the age of sixty, with the deaths of four emperors in the past two years still fresh in everyone's mind, he had neither time nor use for *cunctatio*. Stability was vital, and in his considered judgement, a new dynasty was the only way to maintain it. His son's position had to be clearly established and be seen to be established.

Titus was heir-apparent and had been granted unprecedented powers: his long-held *tribunicia potestas*, intended to show that his role as heir had senatorial recognition, almost guaranteed a smooth transition to his father's throne, whilst his salutations, *imperium*, consulships, censorship, and praetorian prefecture increased both his power and his status. It was almost inevtiable that his responsibilities as praetorian prefect would result in a loss of popularity (*Titus* 6.2), but this was a risk that his father was prepared to take, and one that probably did not concern him overmuch, since he himself could not afford to incur the odium inevitably attached to the regime's enforcer. He deliberately fostered a quite different image: he assiduously attended the sessions of the senate, requested advice, was affable, easily accessible, forgetful of insults, tolerant of jokes and gibes, and even fond of occasional obscenity to be expected in a general known to have been able to mix with his men. Executions were to be regarded as an unfortunate necessity that caused him much distress: Suetonius accurately reflects

the official version in his comment that Vespasian "certainly
never took pleasure in the death of anyone, but even wept and
sighed over those who suffered the punishment they deserved"124. But, behind this carefully constructed facade, it was
clear that he was *Augustus*, and Titus *Augusti filius*. The
persistence of the urinal anecdote in the literary tradition
(*Vesp.* 23.3; Dio, 65.14.5) reflects the contemporary or near
contemporary view that their respective roles were those of
master and apprentice.

The theory that Titus and Mucianus were rivals is
untenable. Mucianus' role in the early seventies was
consistent with his activities in the previous decade, and
his awards were appropriate to the part he had played in
securing Vespasian's accession and superior to those of everyone else, apart from Titus and Vespasian himself. His
subsequent loss of influence may well have resulted in resent-
ment and bitterness, but not in action against Titus. Had
Mucianus intrigued against him as he had against Antonius
Primus, he would have shared Helvidius Priscus' fate, for
Vespasian was, undoubtedly, always in command. On the other
hand, Titus was his heir-apparent, very powerful indeed, but
never co-ruler.

NOTES

1. For the problems facing Vespasian and the solutions
he proposed, see *inter alia*, *CAH* 11, pp. 1-19; Homo, 1949:
p. 137; Waters, 1963: pp. 198-218.
2. For the text of the *Lex de imperio Vespasiani*, see
McCrum and Woodhead, 1966: No. 1. Numerous discussions on
its significance are available, the most recent and authoritative being that of Brunt, 1977a: pp. 95-116; his note 1 on
p. 95 lists other studies on the topic. He argues convincingly that the *senatus consultum* almost certainly antedates Jan.
9 - see, in particular, pp. 102-105.
3. For Cornificius, see *PIR*² C 1503; Syme, 1939: pp.
238-239. There were few who failed to realize the political
advantages to be gained from military glory. The deliberate
policy of Augustus to promote his image as a successful
commander was followed by his successors, even (and perhaps
particularly) if they had not distinguished themselves in
war: note Suet., *Gaius* 43 ff. (and especially 47), and also
Claud. 17.3. Tiberius also made political capital out of his
northern campaigns (*Tib.* 9.2).
4. For a list of these, see Mattingly, 1930: pp. 44-46;
Blamberg, 1976: pp. 44-45, 92-93. There is also a useful
discussion by Kneissl, 1969: pp. 42-43.
5. For the month, see Chambalu, 1885: pp. 502-517.
According to Josephus (*BJ* 7.121), "they decided to celebrate
their achievements by one triumph in common, though the senate
had decreed a separate triumph to each". The triumph is also

mentioned by Suetonius, *Titus* 6.1 and *Vesp.* 8.1, and by
Orosius, 7.9. See also *CIL* 6.945 (from the arch of Titus);
Kleiner, 1962: pp. 42-43; Instinsky, 1948: pp. 370-371,
where the author stresses Vespasian's role in his son's
military reputation; Barini, 1952: pp. 96-100; McGuire,
1980: pp. 77-79.

    6. *ILS* 254 - McCrum and Woodhead, 1966: No. 87.

    7. *neque ex eo destitit participem atque etiam tutorem*
imperii agere. triumphauit cum patre censuramque gessit una,
eidem collega et in tribunicia potestate et in septem consul-
atibus fuit ... praefecturam quoque praetori suscepit numquam
ad id tempus nisi ab eq. R. administratam: *Titus* 6.1.

    8. Hammond, 1959: p. 72, discusses this point.

    9. For discussions on its significance in the days of
Augustus, see Grant, 1946: pp. 444-454; Chilver, 1950: pp.
408 ff.; Béranger, 1953: pp. 96-105; Lacey, 1979: pp. 28-38.

    10. Vespasian's determination is well attested: *Vesp.*
25; Dio, 66.12.1. See also Mattingly, 1930: p. xliii;
Carcopino, 1949: pp. 265-267; Homo, 1949: pp. 289-295. The
growing disillusionment with the principle of hereditary
succession is discussed by Béranger, 1939: pp. 171-187; for
the hostility aroused by the position of Titus, see below.

    11. e.g. *ILS* 246 (of A.D. 72) with Vespasian as *trib.*
pot. IV and Titus *II*; compare *ILS* 254 (of 79) where the
numbers are *X* and *VIII* respectively. There is no precise
evidence to indicate the day it was conferred, but it must
have been in the period June 14 - Sept. 7: *CIL* 16.24, from
Sept. 8, 79 and *ILS* 16.26, from June 13, 80, both show *trib.*
pot. IX for Titus. The likeliest date is July 1, the
anniversary of Vespasian's *dies imperii*. See Chambalu, 1882:
pp. 7-10; Hammond, 1938: p. 36; Fortina, 1955a: pp. 90-91
n. 12; Buttrey, 1980: p. 25.

    12. See Hammond, 1959: pp. 76-79.

    13. *ibid.*, pp. 77, 109 n. 115.

    14. In *CIL* 6.1984 (= McCrum and Woodhead, 1966: No. 152:
from Rome, on which see note 20) Titus is named *imperator:-*
... adlectus ad numerum ex s. c. T. Caesar Aug. f. imperator
imp. Caesare Vespasiano Aug. III M. Cocceio Nerua cos...; it
must be earlier than April, when the suffect consuls are
attested (see Gallivan, 1981: p. 187). A correlation of
Vespasian's and Titus' salutations was established by Chambalu
1882: pp. 28-31; Pick, 1885a: pp. 237-238; Mattingly, 1930:
pp. xxiv-xxv. Their work has been revised and substantially
corrected by Buttrey, 1980: pp. 18-27, who conveniently lists
the evidence for each salutation on pp. 18-19: his conclusions have been accepted in the text.

    15. Mommsen, 1887-1888: II^2 1164 n. 1; Meyer, 1900: p.
24; McFayden, 1920: p. 65; Kornemann, 1930: p. 60; Fortina,
1955a: pp. 64 ff. They argue that he held a secondary proconsular *imperium*, similar to that bestowed by Augustus. The
award is held to have been made either in 71 or else in 70,

after he was saluted as *imperator* by the Judaean army; for
the latter date, see the argument advanced by A.R. Birley,
1975: p. 152, who comments that "it is not unreasonable to
suppose that the senate met to confer *imperium* on Titus before
the end of the year 70". Few scholars would go as far as
Hammond, 1956: p. 81, who suggests that "possibly the precise
nature of his *imperium* was never actually determined and it
was simply assumed by himself and Vespasian that as heir he
had a power and titles second only to those of his father":
when the senate conferred it, they surely distinguished
between the *imperium* of father and son.

16. The only passage that may suggest a special *imperium*
for Titus in 69 is the following:- *dum de nauigatione
consulit* (sic.*Paphiae Veneris oraculo*), *etiam de imperii spe
confirmatus est. cuius breui compos et ad perdomandam Iudaeam
relictus...*: *Titus* 5.1-2. J.C. Rolfe, in the Loeb edition,
translates the passage as follows:- "Visiting the oracle of
the Paphian Venus, to consult it about his voyage, he was
also encouraged to hope for imperial power. Soon realising
his hope (Rolfe adds in a footnote 'By the accession of his
father Vespasian'), and left behind to complete the conquest
of Judaea..." Commentators have differed on its interpretation. According to Price, 1919: p. 27 n. 5, *imperii* has a
general reference to empire, whereas for Mooney, 1930: p. 478,
it refers either to Titus' own rule or to his position in
Vespasian's reign. Hübner, however, 1963: pp. 13-14, inter-
prets it as indicating Titus' period of co-rule, as does
Martinet, 1981: p. 42, who regards Titus as the "Mitregent
seines Vaters".

17. It could be argued that Titus was hoping for control
of the Judaean campaign, which he was indeed given some months
later (Nicols, 1978: p. 73).

18. *BJ* 6.341: Hoffman, 1883: pp. 1-13, argues this at
some length, discussing also *BJ* 6.316 ff.; 7.6-16, 17-19,
23-24, 37-40, 118.

19. See the discussion of Hammond, 1956: p. 79. Note
also *ILS* 264, indicating that Titus fought in Judaea *praeceptis patris consiliisque et auspiciis*: but as Hammond (p. 79)
points out, it does not definitely "disprove a secondary
imperium".

20. On the coins from Asia,*imp*(*erator*) as a *praenomen* is
found for Titus: see Mattingly, 1930: p. lxix, Nos. 477-479
(Asia Minor, uncertain mint, 73), 496 (Antioch, 69-70), 522
and 524 (?Tyre, ?69). But the coins ascribed by Mattingly to
"60-70" or "?69" were almost certainly minted later: see the
comments of Buttrey, 1980: p. 21. The title also appears on
inscriptions from many areas outside of Rome, e.g. from Spain
(*CIL* 2.2477: Jan.-June 79), Gallia Belgica (Newton, 1901: No.
203: 72-73), Africa proconsularis (*CIL* 8.875: Jan.-June 72),
Numidia (*CIL* 8.10116: Jan.-June 76), Bithynia (*CIL* 3.6993:
Jan.-June 78), Pisidia (Newton, 1901: No. 196: 73-79), Armenia

Minor (*CIL* 3.306: Jan.-June 75), Umbria (*ILS* 260: Jan.-June 73) and Herculaneum (*CIL* 10.1420: Jan.-June 72). It is generally agreed that Titus' use of *imperator* as a *praenomen* was restricted to areas outside of Rome and did not conform with official usage; see Kornemann, 1930: p. 62 with n. 6; *RE* 6.2712; Hammond, 1959: p. 77. Sometimes, it is found immediately after the *praenomen* i.e. *Titus imp*....: e.g. *CIL* 2.4251, 3.2917, 3.11194-11196, 7.1204-1205. For examples of *Titus Caesar imp*. or *Caesar Titus imp*., see *CIL* 6.235, 2053-2054, 2.3732, and, for the fourth position, McCrum and Woodhead, 1966: Nos. 93, 102 and 478. The position of the title within his imperial formula is discussed by Newton, 1901: p. 11 n. 6; Price, 1919: p. 29; Hammond, 1957b: p. 27. Note, however, Buttrey, 1980: p. 4, who comments that such "variations and inconsistencies ... are notorious and have, not infrequently, been explored in the hope of wringing some constitutional significance from them".

21. See A.R. Birley, 1975: p. 152 (cited note 15 above).
22. For these coins, see Mattingly, 1930: p. xxx, and Nos. 528, 752 and 798. The legend was read as *imperator designatus* by Mommsen, 1871: pp. 459-461 and 1887: pp. 31-35; Mattingly, 1930: p. xxx; Fortina, 1955a: pp. 88-90. Pick, 1885a: pp. 192-197, argues that *designatus* can not refer to *imperator*, whilst Hammond, 1956: p. 80, dismisses the controversy on the grounds that the legend was an error originating in the mint itself. For a more detailed discussion, see Buttrey, 1980: pp. 40-44, who forcibly argues that the title *imperator designatus* "can now be·retired as an illusion".
23. See note 14.
24. *consulatum absentes inierunt*: *Hist.* 4.38; similarly *Hist.* 4.3. According to Dio, the consular office was assumed by Vespasian and Titus whilst the former was in Egypt and the latter in Palestine (66.1.1). But, in Jan. 70, both were in Alexandria, as Tacitus indicates (*Hist.* 4.51, 52). They still held it on May 24, despite the comments of Degrassi, 1952: p. 20, who cites March 7 as the last attested date. The inscription referring to their tenure on May 24 (McCrum and Woodhead, 1966: No. 191) is noted by Gordon, 1955: pp. 194-195.
25. For his first consulship, see note 24. The others were held in 72 (*cos. II*: *ILS* 246), 74 (*cos. III*: *CIL* 7.1204), 75 (*cos. IV*: *CIL* 6.32361), 76 (*cos. V*: *ILS* 8904), 77 (*cos. VI*: McCrum and Woodhead, 1966: No. 7), and in 79 (*cos. VII*: *ILS* 254). They are discussed by Chambalu, 1882: pp. 10-16; Weynand, *RE* 6.2713-2715; Fortina, 1955a: p. 79; McGuire, 1980: pp. 83-84.
26. Pliny refers to the Flavians as *miseros ambitionis qui ita consules ut semper principes erant*: *Pan.* 58.
27. Prior to his accession, Tiberius held two consulships, in 13 B.C. (Suet., *Tib.* 9; Dio, 54.25.1) and in 7 B.C. (Dio, 55.8.1). Drusus the elder and Gaius Caesar each held

one, in 9 B.C. (Dio, 55.1.1) and A.D. 1 (Dio, 55.10.6),
respectively; whilst Germanicus and the younger Drusus had
two each, Germanicus in A.D. 12 and 18 (Suet., *Gaius* 1; *Ann.*
2.53), Drusus in 15 and 21 (Dio, 57.14.1; *Ann.* 1.55).
Claudius was *cos. suff.* in 37 (Dio, 59.6.6). Apart from
Gaius, who held the *fasces* in four of the five years of his
reign, the Julio-Claudian emperors themselves tended to avoid
the office, quite unlike the first two Flavians: Augustus
had four consulships between 23 B.C. and A.D. 14 (and another
nine before that time), Tiberius held three consulships during
his reign, with four each by Claudius and Nero. For the
details, see Hammond, 1933: pp. 85-87, 249-250.
    28. *Titus* 6.1; *Vesp.* 8.1; Pliny, *NH Praef.* 3, 3.66,
7.162; H.A. *Marc. Anton.* 1; Aurelius Victor, *De Caes.* 9.9;
Censorinus, *De Die Natali* 18.14. For the numismatic evidence,
see Mattingly, 1930: Nos. 86 ff., 667 ff. and index, and, for
the epigraphic, *DE* 2, p. 173 (Kalopothakes).
    29. *T. Caesari Au*(g. f.) *Vespasiano im*(p.) *trib. potest.*
co(s.) *censori desi*(g.) *collegioru*(m) *omnium sacerd*(oti): *ILS*
258.
    30. See Buttrey, 1980: pp. 3, 22. He points out that,
whilst "the unnumbered title *COS* or *TRP* or *IMP* is normal for
the first occasion on which the title is taken, ... the
reverse is not necessarily true; numeration may be omitted,
so that simple *COS* does not surely mean *COS PRIMO*, rather than
COS ITERUM, COS TERTIO or the like" (p. 3) - thus, for
instance, *CIL* 11.3605 with *cos. IV tr. p. imp. X.* Therefore,
ILS 258 (note 29) should not automatically be assigned to 71,
as, for instance occurs in McCrum and Woodhead, 1966: p. 48;
it could just as well be dated to the latter half of 72, when
Titus was *cos. II tr. p. II.* In addition, the designate
censorship is not mentioned on the other inscriptions of 71
or on most of those of 72 (see Buttrey, 1980: p. 22). In
these circumstances, there is no reason whatsoever to assume
that Vespasian and Titus were designated censors before 72.
Presumably, it occurred towards the end of that year or else
early in 73. Indeed, "no monument certainly datable to 72
gives Titus as *censor designatus* or *censor*" (*ibid.*, p. 23).
    31. For the evidence, see Hammond, 1959: p. 120.
    32. *ibid.*, p. 124 n. 188.
    33. *lustrum ab imperatore Vespasiano V et (T.) Caesare*
III cos. factum est: Censorinus, *De Die Natali* 18.14. On his
reliability, see Kubitschek, *RE* 3.1918.
    34. *accedunt experimenta recentissimi census quem intra*
quadriennium imperatores Vespasiani pater filiusque censores
egerunt: Pliny, *NH* 7.162.
    35. Mommsen, 1887-1888: II^2 352 n. 3.
    36. One inscription (*CIL* 8.875) which seems to date
from the period between January and June 72 (*trib. pot. cos.*
II for Titus) also shows *(c)ensori.* It is very fragmentary
(what survives is divided, with *trib. pot. cos. II* on the

front of the tablet and *(c)ensori* on the back) and therefore
may be rejected as evidence for dating the assumption of the
censorship. Another problem is *CIL* 5.4312: (*imp. Caesar
Ves)pasianus A(u)gust(us pont. max. trib. po)t. IIII imp X p.
p. cos. I(II)I censor...* Since it does not show Vespasian's
fifth consular designation, it probably dates to the period
Jan.-March 73; however, it is very fragmentary and may well
have originally read *censor designatus*. The earliest reliable
epigraphic records date to 73, e.g. *ILS* 260, which lists Titus
as *censor cos. II des. III* (after March 73), *trib. pot. II*
(before July 73). Similarly, *CIL* 2.5217, with Vespasian as
censor cos. IIII des. V trib. pot. IIII, must be assigned to
the period between March and July 1, 73. As Newton, 1901:
p. 30, points out, "it seems best to accept the month of
April, a very natural time, in the year 73, as the date at
which Vespasian and Titus entered upon the censorship". The
title is common enough on inscriptions and still appears after
74, e.g. Titus is *censor* in *CIL* 2.3250 of 76. For the appearance of the title even after the office had lapsed, see
Buttrey, 1980: p. 4.

   37. For the powers, privileges and duties of the censor,
see Hammond, 1959: pp. 128-166; Suolahti, 1963: pp. 25-73.

   38. Such is the view of Weynand, *RE* 6.2655; Homo, 1949:
p. 285. Henderson, 1927: pp. 33-34, argues that the censorship was an overt move towards absolutism, since the senate,
the only remaining institution with any power to oppose the
emperor, was now legally and practically dependent on the two
Flavian censors for their positions. Charlesworth (*CAH* 11,
pp. 417-418) also discusses the enervating effect it had on
the senate. However, many of the *adlecti* did not receive
accelerated promotion subsequently - quite the contrary: see
note 40 below.

   39. See Hammond, 1959: p. 86; Isager, 1976: pp. 64-71.

   40. The adlections of 73/74 have been the subject of a
number of recent studies. Of particular importance are those
of Eck, 1970: pp. 103-105; Houston, 1977: pp. 35-63;
Devreker, 1980: pp. 70-87. Of course, adlection to the
senate could and did occur at times other than during an
imperial censorship. A number of Vespasian's supporters were
so honoured in the period 69-72: see Devreker, pp. 80-81.
However, adlection in 73/74 or in the preceding years did not
automatically mean that subsequent favours could be expected,
as the belated consulships of Ti. Julius Celsus Polemaeanus
(92), A. Julius Quadratus (94), C. Caristanius Fronto (90),
Raecius Gallus (?84) and even M. Cornelius Nigrinus Curiatius
Maternus (83) indicate: for the evidence, see *ibid.*, p. 82.
For the adlections to the patriciate, see Eck, 1970: pp. 108-
109. It must be stressed that the names of only a few of the
adlecti in senatum or *inter patricios* have survived: see
Houston, 1977: p. 37.

   41. Newton, 1901: pp. 31-34 (*ius Latii*); Devreker, 1980:

p. 87 and 1982: pp. 492-516 (eastern senators).

    42. For the basic calculation, see Houston, 1977: p. 37.

    43. Passerini, 1939: p. 288:- "(Tito) rivesti la pre-fettura dopo il trionfo celebrato nel 71, e la tenne fino alla morte del padre"; many assume that he had no colleague, e.g. Durry, 1968: p. 377:- "(Vespasien) donnait une marque d'honn-eur et de méfiance (aux cohortes) unique dans l'histoire de la garde: la nomination comme seul préfet du prétoire de son fils et co-régent". For a discussion of the role and duties of the praetorian prefect, see Durry, pp. 168-169.

    44. Suet., *Nero* 47-48 (praetorians abandon Nero), *Hist.* 1.5, 14, 18: Dio, 64.3 (strained relations between Galba and the praetorians), Suet., *Galba* 19-20 and *Otho* 5-6: *Hist.* 1.37-41: Dio, 64.5-6: Plutarch *Galba* 24-27 (Galba assassin-ated). For a discussion of these events, see Wellesley, 1975: pp. 20 ff., 71-73.

    45. For his career, see B.W. Jones and R. Develin, 1976: pp. 79-83.

    46. See Wellesley, 1975: pp. 212-213.

    47. Crook, 1951: p. 166 n. 23:- "Arrecinus Clemens (was) another of Mucianus' men".

    48. At the conference (*Hist.* 2.81 ff.), *multos praefect-uris et procurationibus, plerosque senatorii ordinis honore percoluit, egregios uiros et mox summa adeptos* (82). Arrecin-us Clemens had gained senatorial rank by the end of 69 (*Hist.* 4.68) and it is possible that the award was made at Berytus: he was certainly *egregrius* and was later *cos. II* (A.D. 85) and possibly *praefectus urbi* (B.W. Jones and R. Develin, 1976: p. 82).

    49. For Caesennius Paetus and Petillius Cerialis, see Eck, 1982: p. 287. Townend, 1961: pp. 60 ff., suggests that T. Flavius Sabinus (= Sabinus III), son of Vespasian's brother, might have been sent to Pannonia.

    50. Martial, 6.76.1 on Domitian's praetorian prefect, Cornelius Fuscus.

    51. Crook, 1951: p. 166 n. 23.

    52. The prefecture of Titus is referred to by Suetonius, *Titus* 6.1; Pliny, *NH Praef.* 3; Aurelius Victor, *De Caes.* 9.11, *Epit. de Caes.* 10.4.

    53. There is a useful discussion of Domitian's transfer (*cum ... Iulium Ursum... in amplissimum ordinem transtulissem*) of Ursus by Syme, 1958a: pp. 635-636; Ursus eventually received a third consulship, in 100 - Zevi, 1972: p. 438.

    54. That he held this post as Titus' colleague has been argued by Turner, 1954: pp. 54 ff.:- "It is an attractive speculation that Alexander was his colleague, and that ... the two continued in Rome a partnership which had succeeded brilliantly in Palestine" (p. 64); for the papyrus referring to him as prefect, see McCrum and Woodhead, 1966: No. 329.

    55. Juvenal's advice on how to spend the day included:- *sportula, deinde forum iurisque peritus Apollo/atque*

triumphales, inter quas ausus habere/nescio quis titulos Aegyptius atque arabarches/ciuus ad effigiem non tantum meiere fas est (1.131-134). Turner's comment (1954: p. 63) is worth citing:- "For the unnamed 'Egyptian and arabarch', towards whose statue Juvenal recommends the action of dogs against lamp-posts, no candidate except Alexander has been put forward by commentators".

56. Baumann, 1974: pp. 182-188; for instances of the *manifestus* doctrine during the empire, see McGuire, 1980: p. 90.

57. e.g. Crook, 1951: pp. 162-175.

58. For a discussion of this, see Millar, 1977: pp. 203-272 and especially p. 209.

59. "He was in practice, if not in theory, co-emperor and more" (Crook, 1951: p. 164); "... quasi-equal colleague" (Hammond, 1956: p. 82); "Titus and Vespasian were associated in an unofficial Doppelprinzipat" (McGuire, 1980: p. 76); "... genuine co-ruler" (Rogers, 1980: p. 90). See also note 16 above.

60. Crook, 1951: pp. 162-175.

61. Rogers, 1980: pp. 86-95.

62. *nunc principes in Caesaris amicitia agunt feruntque cuncta*: Dial. 8.3.

63. *nam amicos tempore, fortuna, cupidinibus aliquando aut erroribus imminui, transferri, desinere*: Hist. 4.52.

64. Crook, 1951: pp. 162-166.

65. *me Vitellio antepono, ti mihi...inter nos non idem prosperarum aduersarumque rerum ordo erit: nam si uincimus, honorem quem dederis habebo*: Hist. 2.77.

66. Rogers, 1980: p. 90.

67. *Titum, antequam digrederetur, multo apud patrem sermone orasse ferunt ne criminantium nuntiis temere accenderetur integrumque se ac placabilem filio praestaret. non legiones, non classis proinde firma imperii munimenta quam numerum liberorum; nam amicos tempore, fortuna, cupidinibus aliquando aut erroribus imminui, transferri, desinere: suum cuique sanguinem indiscretum, sed maxime principibus, quorum prosperis et alii fruantur, aduersa ad iunctissimos pertineant. ne fratribus quidem mansuram concordiam, ni parens exemplum praebuisset. Vespasianus haud aeque Domitiano mitigatus quam Titi pietate gaudens...*: Hist. 4.52.

68. Crook, 1951: p. 165.

69. Crook, 1955: pp. 155, No. 66 and 163, No. 139.

70. Equini, 1967: pp. 11-17; Dusanic, 1968: pp. 59-74; Gallivan, 1981: p. 214.

71. Gallivan, 1981: p. 213. On both occasions, Mucianus' colleague was one of Vespasian's relatives - in 70, Q. Petillius Cerialis Caesius Rufus, his son-in-law, and in 72, T. Flavius Sabinus (= Sabinus III), his nephew.

72. Gallivan, 1981. p. 201.

73. Evans, 1979: pp. 198-202.

74. e.g., in 70, M. Ulpius Traianus of the *X Fretensis* and L. Annius Bassus of the *XI Claudia*: see Gallivan, 1981: p. 187, for the date. As Syme, 1958a: p. 593 n. 2, notes in reference to Traianus, Bassus and others, "speedy consulates now come to sound men among the legionary legates of the Dalmatian and eastern armies".

75. *ille...numquam derexit bracchia contra/torrentem*: Juvenal, 4.89-90. Syme, 1958a: p. 100, describes him as "skilfully navigating the surges of civil war".

76. Dio, 65.13.3.

77. A.R. Birley, 1975: p. 143.

78. Syme, 1977: p. 47.

79. Crook, 1951: pp. 167-175.

80. In both sections (66.15 and 18), the account of Xiphilinus survives and clearly indicates two separate returns. Her arrival in 75 can be deduced from 66.15.1, where Dio mentions Vespasian's temple of Peace in the year of his sixth consulship (75), whilst her first dismissal occurred around the time that Julius Sabinus and his wife were executed. She arrived "again" in Titus' own reign (66.18.1).

81. *Caecinam consularem adhibitum cenae, uixdum triclinio egressum, ob suspicionem stupratae Berenicis uxoris suae iugulari iussit*: *Epit. de Caes.* 10.4.

82. e.g. by A.H.M. Jones, 1938: p. 258.

83. Jordan, 1974: pp. 209 ff., argues that her arrival should be placed in 71 because she was then "at the height of her power". She may well, as Crook, 1951: p. 166 points out, "have expected an immediate summons to the capital", but Dio's evidence is clear: she arrived after the dedication of the temple of Peace in 75.

84. Crook, 1951: p. 166.

85. That Mucianus was alive in 74 is shown by *Dial.* 37. 2; he was dead when Pliny's *NH* was published in 77 (*NH* 32. 62).

86. Marcellus and Caecina were unlikely associates in a conspiracy, in view of their past careers and attitudes to the imperial government, though that, of course, hardly disproves the existence of an alliance. T. Clodius Eprius Marcellus (*PIR*² E 84; *RE* 6.261) was some twenty years older than Caecina, born ca. 18 (praetor in 48: *Ann.* 12.4; *ILS* 992) probably in Capua (*Dial.* 8). He commanded *legio XIV* under Claudius (*SEG* 18 (1962) 196, No. 587) and governed Lycia-Pamphylia ca. 53-55 (*ibid.*; *Ann.* 13.33). Accused of *repetundae*, he was acquitted (*Ann.* 13.33) and became proconsul of Cyprus between 57 and 62 (*SEG, loc. cit.*) and consul in Dec. 62 (Gallivan, 1974: p. 310). He acquired great wealth, especially from his activities as a delator under Nero: joining with Cossutianus Capito in 66, he secured the condemnation of Thrasea Paetus, for which he received five million sesterces (*Ann.* 16.22 ff.). He remained in Rome during Galba's reign, throughout 69 and in the first months of 70,

when he was active in senatorial debates, coming into conflict
with Thrasea's son-in-law Helvidius Priscus (*Hist.* 2.53, 95;
4.6-8, 10, 43; *Dial.* 5). Proconsul of Asia for the unusually
long term of three years (70/71 - 72/73: Eck, 1982: pp. 287-
291), he could well have been involved in Vespasian's reorganisation of the east; it may be conjectured that the chief
motive behind the appointment was the need for an efficient
agent to ensure completeness and uniformity in the task: see
McElderry, 1913: pp. 117-118; Syme, 1956: p. 268; Crook,
1955: p. 163; Kreiler, 1975: p. 22. His second consulship
was awarded in 74 (with Q. Petillius Cerialis Caesius Rufus:
Gallivan, 1981: p. 214), and during his lifetime he held three
priesthoods (*augur*, *curio maximus* and *sodalis Augustalis*: *ILS*
992). He was an *amicus* of both Nero and Vespasian (Crook,
1955: p. 163, No. 139). Despite his reputation (*inuisum*:
Hist. 2.53), he must have been an administrator of considerable competence in view of his appointment to Asia at such a
time and for so unusually long a term. His careful manoeuvring had enabled him to survive and thrive under various
emperors, and at the age of sixty he was a highly unlikely
associate of A. Caecina Alienus (*PIR*² C 99; *RE* 3.1238.10).
Quaestor of Baetica in 68 (and so aged about thirty-six at
the time of the conspiracy), he was appointed to the command
of a legion in Upper Germany (the *IV Macedonica*, according to
Alföldy, 1967: p. 8) in return for his prompt support of
Galba's rebellion, but, punished for embezzlement, he deserted
to Vitellius and was one of his earliest supporters (*Hist.*
1.53). He invaded Italy with thirty thousand men, fought
Otho's forces and accompanied Vitellius to Rome (*Hist.* 1.61
ff., 2.17-56; Plutarch, *Otho* 5.18; *BJ* 4.547) where he was
made consul with Valens (Townend, 1962: pp. 113 ff.). Again
he defected, this time to the Flavians (*Hist.* 2.99, 3.13). No
posts or honours are recorded for him under Vespasian, though
he is attested as one of his *amici* (Crook, 1955: p. 155, No.
66). Houston, 1971: p. 357, comments on him as follows:- "It
seems at least probable that Caecina, who had deserted Nero
for Galba, Galba for Vitellius, and Vitellius for Vespasian,
and who was ambitious, envious (cf. *Hist.* 2.99-101) and still
young, might have looked forward to the reign of Titus with
some misgivings, and therefore have hoped to gain favour by
supporting another candidate, if he himself could not claim
the throne". See also Briesmann, 1955: pp. 28-45: Chilver,
1956: pp. 203-205; McGuire, 1980: pp. 92-94.

    87. Crook, 1951: pp. 170-171; Crook implies that there
was no conspiracy, but the comments of Suetonius (*Titus* 6.2)
and Dio (65.16.3-4) suggest the contrary.

    88. *studia militum inlexerat*: *Hist.* 1.53. Rogers, 1980:
pp. 93-94, argues cogently that Caecina "had the oratorical
ability with which to harangue and influence troops as well as
the ambition to risk the punishment resulting from failure...
(Therefore) the threat to the stability of the Flavian dynasty

was not imagined or contrived - it was real. Titus acted, not to eliminate those who were trying to force the dismissal of Berenice, but to preserve the continued role of his father and himself".

89. *fuerunt etiam quidam suarum rerum iudices. nam et in libris obseruationum a Septimio editis adfuisse Ciceronem tali causae inuenio, et ego pro regina Berenice apud ipsam eam dixi*: Inst. 4.1.19.

90. Crook, 1951: p. 170, who suggests that the *consilium* may have been discussing her dismissal or retention.

91. Garzetti, 1974: p. 259.

92. As Tacitus notes, Mucianus was *dispositu prouisuque ciuilium rerum peritus*: Hist. 2.5. See also Waters, 1963: p. 212.

93. e.g. by Syme, 1958a: pp. 789-790 and 1970: p. 27; Nicols, 1978: pp. 118-119.

94. For his reputation as a strict disciplinarian, see *Ann.* 13.36, and Frontinus, *Strat.* 4.1.21, 4.2.3 - *disciplina correcta*. His approach to warfare was criticized by Caesennius Paetus who *despiciebat gesta (Corbulonis), nihil caedis aut praedae, usurpatas nomine tenus urbium expugnationes dictitans*: *Ann.* 15.6. Note also Corbulo's comment that *bellum habere quam gerere malebat*: *Ann.* 15.3.

95. Syme, 1958a: p. 789. For a discussion of Corbulo's command, see Magie, 1950: pp. 554 ff., 1411-1412; Schieber, 1976: pp. 42-51; Chaumont, 1976: p. 115.

96. The attested legates of the seven eastern legions in the late sixties were T. Aurelius Fulvus (*III Gallica*) replaced by C. Dillius Aponianus, Cn. Pompeius College (*IV Scythica*), Sex. Vettulenus Cerialis (*V Macedonica*), M. Hirrius Fronto Neratius Pansa (*VI Ferrata*: almost certainly), M. Ulpius Traianus (*X Fretensis*) replaced by A. Larcius Lepidus Sulpicianus, A. Caesennius Gallus (*XII Fulminata*) and Titus (*XV Apollinaris*) replaced by M. Tittius Frugi. Only Titus seems to have had a father of consular status.

97. Vespasian's friendship with Thrasea Paetus and Barea Soranus is noted by Tacitus, *Hist.* 4.7. For Titus' and Corbulo's connections with the group, see B.W. Jones, 1973a: p. 87.

98. For the nature of Mucianus' command under Corbulo, see Sherk, 1951: p. 32; Syme, 1958a: p. 790.

99. For the *III Gallica*, see *RE* 12.1519 ff., and, for Aurelius Fulvus, *PIR²* A 1510; Alföldy, 1969: pp. 19-21; Houston, 1971: pp. 28-30; B.W. Jones and R. Develin, 1976: p. 82; Nicols, 1978: p. 100.

100. For the *IV Scythica*, see *RE* 12.1556, and, for Pompeius Collega, *PIR¹* P 458; Houston, 1971: pp. 205-207; Nicols, 1978: pp. 106-107 (where the possibility of his adlection *inter patricios* is discussed); Gallivan, 1981: p. 202.

101. For the *VI Ferrata*, see *RE* 12.1587 ff., and, for

Neratius Pansa, *PIR*[1] H 129 (there is no entry for him yet in *PIR*[2]); Torelli, 1968: pp. 170-175; Houston, 1971: pp. 111-117; Camodeca, 1976: pp. 19-38; Vidman, 1981: pp. 377-384; Gallivan, 1981: pp. 204-205.

102. For the *XII Ferrata*, see *RE* 12.1705, and, for Caesennius Gallus, *PIR*[2] C 170; Houston, 1971: pp. 37-38; Syme, 1977: pp. 45-46 and 1980: p. 73; Nicols, 1978: pp. 107-108; Gallivan, 1981, p. 210.

103. Titus was sent from the siege of Gamala to Syria in Sept./Oct. 67 (*BJ* 4.32) to visit and, presumably, welcome him.

104. There is, inevitably, no direct evidence of these activities; for the suggestion that he wrote to Vettius Bolanus, who had been a senior praetorian legate in Armenia in 62 (*Ann*. 15.3) and therefore another possible member of Corbulo's "group", see Nicols, 1978: p. 120. Mucianus was adept at working behind the scenes, e.g. he urged Plotius Grypus to forward hostile accounts of Antonius Primus' activities to Vespasian (*Hist*. 3.52).

105. For Q. Julius Cordinus C. Rutilius Gallicus, see Sherk, 1951: p. 26; Houston, 1971: pp. 219-230; Bosworth, 1973: pp. 62-70; B.W. Jones and R. Develine, 1976: pp. 81-82 (his career under Domitian); Nicols, 1978: pp. 121-122; Gallivan, 1981: p. 200; Eck, 1982: pp. 293-294 (his post in Africa).

106. For his *praenomen*, see Syme, 1981: p. 134. His career is discussed in *PIR*[1] M 233 (but he is not to be identified with the *cos. ord.* of 62·, P. Marius, who is now known to lack a *cognomen*: *RE* Suppl. 14.276) and by Syme, 1958a: p. 682. Nicols' suggestion (1978: p. 121) that he turned to writing history after being disillusioned by the events of 69/70 must be rejected, since he is now known to have been appointed by Vespasian to two consular provinces, Lower Germany and Syria, in the first years of the reign (Rüger, 1979: pp. 187-200; Syme, 1981: pp. 133-134).

107. For the evidence, see Syme, 1981: pp. 133-134.

108. For the details, see *Hist*. 4.39 ff.; Evans, 1979: pp. 198-202.

109. For a detailed discussion of this incident, see Evans, 1978: pp. 102-128.

110. *Aponius Saturninus Moesiae rector pessimum facinus audet, misso centurione ad interficiendum Tettium Iulianum septimae legionis legatum ob simultates, quibus causam partiam praetendebat. Iulianus comperto discrimine et gnaris locorum adscitis per auia Moesiae ultra montem Haemum profugit; nec deinde ciuili bello interfuit, per uarias moras susceptum ad Vespasianum iter trahens et ex nuntiis cunctabundus aut properans: Hist. 2.85.*

111. *(Tettio Iuliano praetura,) tamquam transgredientem in partis Vespasiani legionem deseruisset, (ablata) ut in Plotium Grypum transferretur: Hist. 4.39.*

112. For the date, see Evans, 1978: p. 115 n. 53.

113.   *redditur Tettio Iuliano praetura, postquam cognitus est ad Vespasianum confugisse : Grypo honor mansit*:   *Hist.* 4.40.

114.   The second version could hardly have come from Alexandria: see Evans, 1978: p. 116.   Vipstanus, on the other hand, was given temporary control of the *VII Claudia* (*Hist.* 3.9).

115.   Tacitus cited him on two occasions, *Hist.* 3.25 and 28.   He described the role of the Danubian army in the war with Vitellius, but the extent to which Tacitus relied on him is in dispute: see *RE* 9A.171.

116.   Milns, 1973: p. 294.

117.   Evans, 1978: p. 112.

118.   Experienced financial administrators were essential in time of civil war, as Mucianus stressed:- *sed nihil aeque fatigabat quam pecuniarum conquisitio: eos esse belli ciuilis neruos dictitans Mucianus*...:   *Hist.* 2.84.   Such was Tiberius' role in 69/70 and he was appropriately rewarded: between 69 and 71 his two sons were adlected into the equestrian order, he himself appeared in the Jewish triumph (Statius, *Siluae* 3.3.140), was appointed *praepositus a rationibus* (*ibid.* 86-88) and, in 73, was also adlected *inter equestres* (*ibid.* 143).   Whilst his precise position in the late sixties is uncertain (see the discussions of Weaver, 1972: pp. 286-288;   Evans, 1978: pp. 111-112:   in general, they argue for a financial procuratorship in the eastern provinces), Mucianus would have been only too well aware of his standing in Vespasian's eyes.

119.   Mucianus was particularly thorough in arousing opposition to Primus.   Plotius Grypus, for instance, who almost certainly replaced Tettius Julianus as legate of the *VII Claudia* under Aponius Saturninus, had received hints from Mucianus to report unfavourably on Primus;   these accounts were then forwarded to Vespasian (*Hist.* 3.52).   It would be reasonable to suggest that he intended to enlist the support of Aponius Saturninus, Grypus' superior.

120.   Evans, 1978: p. 123.

121.   He is used for Book 2.13, 16, 19, 31, 33, 35-36. His writings on geography are mentioned in 3.59;   4.66 ff., 77;   5.50, 83, 132:   on Asia in 7.36, 159;   16.213;   31.19; 36.131:   on Lycia in 12.9;   13.88;   31.33:   on Syria in 5.128:   on the Greek islands in 2.231;   11.167;   19.12; 31.16;   34.36:   and on animals in 7.36;   8.6, 201, 215;   9.33, 80, 94, 182;   32.62.

122.   Vespasian had acted in this way when his friendship with Thrasea and Soranus (*Hist.* 4.7) was likely to prove dangerous, and Vibius Crispus was noted for his ability to "swim with the stream" (Juvenal 4.89-90).

123.   e.g. Vespasian's advice to his troops during the siege of Gamala (whilst Titus was visiting Mucianus in Syria: see note 103):-"incautiousness in war and mad impetuosity are

alien to us Romans" (*BJ* 4.35); and again, not long afterwards,
when his generals urged him to take advantage of the dissension within the Jewish ranks and attack Jerusalem at once, he
told them that they "were gravely mistaken as to the right
policy, and were anxious to make a theatrical, though
hazardous, display of their gallantry and arms without regard
to expediency and safety ... for success obtained by sitting
still is more fruitful than when won by the uncertainty of
arms"(*BJ* 4.368, 372).

    124. ... *neque caede cuiusquam umquam laetatus iustis
suppliciis inlacrimauit etiam et ingemuit*: *Vesp.* 15.

Chapter Four

REIGN OF TITUS

ACCESSION

Vespasian died suddenly on June 24, 79[1]. Although suffering
from gout (Dio, 66.17.1), he was apparently still in good
general health and the sources suggest that his final illness
was of short duration. Towards the summer of 79, however, he
contracted a slight fever in Campania, forcing him to return
to Rome at once; but, as was his custom, he spent the summer
at Aquae Cutiliae in his native Sabine country to take
advantage of its medicinal baths[2]. There his fever worsened
and his "excessive use of the cold waters" (*Vesp.* 24) led to
further complications, which, however, were not serious enough
to prevent him from transacting his *munera imperatoria*: he
even received an embassy in bed. Following a sudden attack of
diarrhoea, however, he unexpectedly died in the arms of his
attendants, as he struggled to his feet (*Vesp.* 24). In
Suetonius' detailed account, there is no hint whatsoever of
foul play, and the subsequent rumour, believed by the emperor
Hadrian (Dio, 66.17.1), that he had been poisoned by Titus,
would appear to be without foundation[3]. On the other hand, it
did reflect the consistent tradition of the new emperor's evil
reputation and the fear that he would be a second Nero (*Titus*
7.1; *Epit. de Caes.* 10.5)[4].
    Reports of his ruthlessness, extravagance and licentious-
ness were no doubt rife[5], though possibly exaggerated in the
sources so as to highlight his supposed sudden change of
character[6], whilst his affair with Berenice was still as fresh
in men's minds[7] as were the executions that had occurred only
a short time before. Almost overnight, however, he changed
for the better: "no fault could be found in him, but, on the
contrary, the highest virtues" (*Titus* 7.1); he dismissed his
favourite boys and Berenice as well, on her second return to
Rome (*Titus* 7.2; Dio, 66.18.1); he assumed the office of
pontifex maximus "to keep his hands unsullied and was true to
his word" (*Titus* 9.1); he executed no senators or anyone else
(Dio, 66.19.1); no petitioner was sent away without at least

some encouragement (*Titus* 8); a day when he had conferred no favour was a day wasted (*ibid.*). As he himself put it, "it is impossible for me to be insulted or abused in any way, for I do nothing that deserves censure and I care nothing for what is reported falsely" (Dio, 66.19.1-2). In all this, one can discern his father's touch. He had learned one lesson well at least. It was important to create an image of moderation, co-operation and affability. The truth is far harder to disentangle. As has been pointed out[8], he was in many ways a typical product of the Neronian age; he had the versatility and cynical refinement to be expected of a graduate of that court. He could well have laid aside one mask to assume another.

Categorizing of individuals as "bad" or "good" is one of the most persistent traits of human thought in all ages[9]. As early as the second century, all deceased emperors were classified as either *diuus* or *hostis*[10], and the tendency is obvious in the ancient writers on the Flavian era. Domitian was a bad man and, by implication, a bad ruler; but, since Titus was regarded as a good ruler, he must therefore have been of good character as well. The contrast with his brother was too obvious to be missed. For Suetonius, Domitian's deterioration in character from *clemens* to *saeuus* (*Dom.* 10.1) marked the beginning of the decline in his reign[11]. Hence the stress on Titus' personal excellence. He was almost as insistent on being regarded as *clemens* as his father was on establishing a dynasty[12]. Reported public declarations of his own excellent character by any emperor should in any case always be regarded with extreme scepticism, a principle to be applied all the more rigorously when two other factors intrude - a reign of extreme brevity and the ancient fondness for contrast that could be given full play when the rollowing ruler was a younger brother (the inevitable *odium fraternum*), last member of a dynasty, and, supposedly, of evil character.

The transfer of power from father to son was achieved without any serious difficulty. The various powers already held by Titus were no doubt immediately confirmed by the senate, whilst his assumption of the titles *Augustus, pontifex maximus* and *pater patriae* together with the use of *imperator* as a *praenomen* suggest the passing of senatorial decrees that authorized these changes. No direct evidence of such senatorial activity, however, has survived[13]. An interesting feature is the absence of a fresh salutation at the time of his accession. Normally, *imp. I* was used to mark that particular event, but, from Titus' point of view, an increase in numeration would have been inconsistent, since he was not, as were most incumbents, lacking previous salutations. In fact, he was *imp. XIV* on Vespasian's death[14], and more importantly, he obviously preferred to think of himself as co-emperor under Vespasian, a claim that would be negated, or at least seriously weakened, by an additional salutation to mark what he had virtually regarded as his role since 71. It was not an unintelligent posture to adopt if there was any hostility or unease at the prospect of his period of rule. Transition from father to son could be made to seem less harsh and abrupt, and give far less scope for claims that the best man should rule, if it were simply a question of a co-ruler assuming slightly more power. Essentially, though, the credit for the transfer of power, apparently managed with remarkable ease, within a decade of a disastrous civil war and the disappearance of the century-old Julio-Claudian dynasty, must be ascribed to Vespasian.

On the other hand, Titus was faced with problems on the dynastic level, firstly from disillusion with the hereditary principle on the part of at least some senators together with the concomitant belief that the "best man" should rule, and secondly from the attitude and actions of Domitian. As was to be expected, Titus' accession evoked, if not direct opposition, at least apprehension from various quarters (*Titus* 6.2), for this was the first occasion on which a non-member of the Julio-Claudian family had come to power by virtue of the hereditary principle. Augustus, though presenting himself as *princeps* or "first citizen", knew full well that his authority was enhanced by the descent of the Julian *gens* from Venus and, more particularly, by the state's recognition of his adoptive father Julius as *diuus*. The Flavians had less impressive antecedents. Since the reign of Nero in particular the concept of the emperor as the *uir optimus* had gained some currency, and Titus had aroused some hostility on this score, mainly from Helvidius Priscus whose attitude has been summarized as follows:-

> Constitutionally, the choice of a *princeps* lay with the senate, and a man was to be chosen in the public interest as the person best fitted for the task. There was no reason to think that Titus or Domitian fulfilled this criterion. In practice the succession had been dynastic from the first, and it had given Rome a series of rulers, every one of whom in senatorial opinion had proved a tyrant. The crimes and follies of Nero had resulted in civil war that imperilled the very fabric of the empire. Galba (having no heir in his family) had allegedly proclaimed a very different principle: the adoption of the best man to be marked out by consent[15].

Yet this had not occurred in practice: Piso was chosen by a coterie. Again, in his *Panegyricus*, Pliny comments that "if a man is destined to rule the people, one and all, he must be chosen from among them all"[16]. So he must be chosen "from among" (*ex*) and not "by" (*ab*) all; in fact it was to be Trajan himself who should select his successor[17], the approval of the senate and people would come later[18]. This was hardly the position of Helvidius Priscus, and although it would be wrong to regard the *Panegyricus* as a philosophical treatise providing a considered contemporary view of the succession problem, it does represent one of the very few statements on the topic that can be assigned to the period in question. This divergency between Pliny and the Stoics renders difficult any attempt to assess the practical effect of these under-currents in the early eighties, and, indeed, the extent to which such views were held by members of the upper classes.

Only one attempt on Titus' life is attested, and there is no prima facie evidence to suggest that the inspiration came from Helvidius' principles: he himself had served under various emperors and did not advocate attacks on the establish-ed order[19]. All that is known is that two patricians were found guilty of aspiring to the throne: Titus warned them "to abandon their attempt, pointing out that the imperial power was the gift of fate" (*Titus* 9.1). Typically, Suetonius provides a more detailed account of the aftermath, intended to reinforce the image of Titus' *clementia*: he reassured the mother of one of the conspirators, invited them both to dinner[20], and, the following day, deliberately placed them next to him at a gladiatorial show and allowed them to inspect the contestants' weapons when they were offered for his inspection. The mask may have slipped slightly, though, when he added that "danger threatened them both, but at a future time and from another" (*Titus* 9.2)[21].

DOMITIAN

However, if rumour is to be believed, the most serious threat to Titus came from his brother. Suetonius' allegations are quite specific: Domitian consistently plotted against his brother openly and in secret (*Titus* 9.3; *Dom*. 2.3); for some time he considered offering the troops a double donative (*Dom*. 2.3); he spread rumours that Titus had interfered with Vespasian's will and so deprived him of his rightful inherit-ance, since his father had left them as joint rulers (*Dom*. 2.3); and he almost openly stirred up disaffection in the armed forces (*Titus* 9.3). It was also alleged that even prior to Titus' accession it had been found necessary to curb Domitian's rising ambition (*Hist*. 4.51; *Dom*. 1.3). In particular, he had attempted to suborn Petillius Cerialis (*Hist*. 4.86); he wanted to be given command of the proposed campaign against the Alani (*Dom*. 2.2), and even tried to bribe oriental kings to request his leadership in similar circum-stances (*Dom*. 2.2)[22].

Other incidents have been adduced as evidence of personal enmity between the brothers: it was alleged that Titus had been intimate with Domitia Longina (*Titus* 9.2; Dio, 66.26.4); although declared *consors successorque* (*Titus* 9.3), Domitian was given none of the other powers held by Titus for most of Vespasian's reign, despite his wish to be his brother's equal in power and rank (*Dom*. 2.1); Pliny claims that Julius Bassus' friendship with Domitian caused Bassus to fear Titus (*Ep*.

4.9.2); Titus awarded a consulship to Aelius Lamia, the first
husband of Domitia Longina (*Dom*. 1.3), as an insult to his
brother; Domitian prohibited the castration of young males
(*Dom*. 7.1) because of Titus' fondness for eunuchs (*Titus* 7.1);
and after his brother's death, Domitian bestowed no honour on
him except deification (*Dom*. 2.3)[23].

In all, there seems to have been two distinct, though
closely related,allegations. Domitian saw himself as his
brother's equal in rank and status both in 69 and in 79: the
circumstances were different, but on each occasion he acted
illegally; secondly, in their personal relationship, mutual
antipathy was often evident. Now Tacitus' account of Domitian's behaviour in 69 is very obviously slanted in favour of
Titus, particularly with the strongly drawn parallel between
the former's supposedly treasonable activities in the closing
chapter of Book *IV* and Titus' achievements in Judaea with
which the following one opens[24]: Domitian ceased to perform
even his trifling official duties, assuming a mask of simplic-
ity and moderation in an effort to conceal his real character,
whereas Titus was portrayed as dignified, energetic, affable
and as able to mix with the ordinary soldiers without impair-
ing his *auctoritas*. This would represent an interesting
reversal of roles, for Domitian's alleged attempt to conceal
his real nature accords ill with his well-attested readiness
to blush[25]; it was Titus who was far more experienced in the
skills of diplomacy. The accuracy of the charges against
Domitian has been impugned on a number of occasions, in
particular with the recent progress towards rehabilitating his
much maligned character, and, to some extent, the traditional
interpretation has been modified[26]. But whilst charges of
suborning Cerialis and encouraging mutiny in the army would
appear to lack substance, Suetonius' claim that he wished to
be equal to his brother in power and rank (*Dom*. 2.1) should
surely be accepted: less certain are the precise steps, if
any, that he took to achieve this.

With regard to their personal relationship, the evidence
for Titus' supposed dislike of Domitian is not at all convincing. The award of a suffect consulship to Aelius Lamia was
remarkable, not so much because he was Domitia Longina's
first husband (*Dom*. 1.3: cf. 10.2), but rather from the fact
that he held it for five and a half months, a term of
unparalleled length in the Flavian era[27]. He was very much
Titus' appointee, but hardly promoted in this way merely to
spite Domitian. Again, Titus' failure to grant his brother
the unusual powers he himself had held must be put into
perspective. He was aged forty and his accession occurred
after ten years of peace. Vespasian, at the age of sixty,
came to the throne after a disastrous civil war and the deaths
of four emperors in little more than eighteen months. The
principate itself had come close to disintegration. He had to
establish a new dynasty, a task rendered all the more difficult

by the fact that it lacked the prestige of its Julio-Claudian
predecessors. The pressure on Titus was incomparably less
severe. He perhaps felt that he could wait until later in his
reign before assigning the appropriate powers to Domitian[28].
Mutual hostility is neither the likeliest nor the most obvious
explanation. As for Domitian's dislike of Titus, the evidence
is not entirely persuasive. Even Suetonius is suspicious of
the alleged affair with Domitia - she would have boasted of it
if it were true (*Titus* 9.2); his *consecratio* of his brother
is not an indication of antipathy towards him and it is
difficult to believe that this was the motivation for prohib-
iting the castration of young males. The reported complaint
of Julius Bassus could best be described as second-hand
(Pliny's version of Bassus' explanation for his fear of Titus),
difficult to assess precisely, and not a little unconvincing.
Much more significant is the difference in age and upbringing
between the brothers. Whilst Titus' early years in the
forties coincided with one of the "peaks" in the family's
fortunes (and hence he secured a court education), his
brother's were spent in the decline of the fifties: socially
and politically, his education was incomparably inferior[29].
Again, as Titus was absent on military service in Germany,
Britain and Judaea during Domitian's early teens, he would
have had little opportunity to get to know his young brother.
These factors would have accentuated their natural differences: the self-assured, gregarious and successful Titus
must have had little in common with his retiring, uncertain
and suspicious younger brother. Mutual ignorance and incom-
patibility rather than antipathy may have characterized their
relationship.

Nor was there any pressing need to strengthen the dynasty
itself. The extraordinary powers accorded to Titus in 71 were
appropriate to those troubled times when the empire was under
the control of the sixty-year-old Vespasian who lacked imperial antecedents. But now the dynasty appeared more solidly
established, having survived with ease the crucial test of
its founder's death. In such conditions, Titus' approach to
the question of his own successor was perfectly proper. In a
sense, his choice had already been made by fate, for, with no
sons of his own, his brother Domitian was the inevitable
choice. Furthermore, during Vespasian's reign, Domitian had
been granted singular honours, but his status had been kept
distinctly inferior to Titus'[30]. He had held six consulships,
one ordinary and five suffect[31], but was assigned no share in
supreme power - the title *imperator* did not occur in any form
in reference to him prior to his own accession. Like Titus,
he had been given the name *Caesar*, which he used as a *praenomen*, and had received the title *princeps iuuentutis*,
appropriate to a junior heir[32]. From the first day of his
brother's reign, however, he was nominated "partner and
successor" (*Titus* 9.3); he remained *Caesar* and *princeps*

iuuentutis[33], and the suffect consulship of 80 to which he had been designated two months before Vespasian's death was now converted into an ordinary consulship[34]. But he did not receive *tribunicia potestas*[35] or any form of *imperium*. In short, he received no real promotion beyond the consulship of 80 and that of 82 to which he was designated by Titus before his death[36].

This was eminently fair and consistent. Domitian was young and inexperienced, whilst his brother was just over forty and could reasonably expect to rule for another twenty years or so, in view of the age at death of his predecessors who had not died violently[37]. None of them, apart from Vespasian, had assigned substantial powers to an heir-apparent in the first years of their reign. Domitian may well have been dissatisfied with the arrangement: he probably expected much more[38]. Again, Titus perhaps meant to keep his options open, with his brother's position vague enough to allow for future changes in the dynastic arrangements. His second wife had been divorced fifteen years previously and remarriage was a definite possibility. Berenice was now obviously an unacceptable candidate, but there were others of suitable pedigree: no doubt he recalled that the father of his childhood friend Britannicus had married for the third time at the age of about forty-eight and was over fifty when his son was born[39]. Alternatively, Julia's marriage to Vespasian's grand-nephew, T. Flavius Sabinus (= Sabinus IV), could well produce children[40].

His accession was appropriately commemorated on the coinage. No attempt was made to hide his military prowess; after all, his achievements in war provided the basis of his reputation (*Hist.* 5.1). Stress, however, was laid on the peaceful and constitutional nature of the transfer of power. On one coin, he was depicted as receiving the *palladium*, symbol of Rome's eternity, from a helmeted Roma[41]; here, the reference was to the military exploits by which Vespasian and Titus "raised up" Roma, an event commemorated on the coinage[42] as early as A.D. 71. On the other hand, a number of sestertii issued by Titus depicted his father, now a god, handing over to Titus the *regimen orbis*, symbolized by a globe over a rudder[43]. Both father and son appeared togate on these coins. So the actual transfer of power from father to son was depicted in strictly constitutional and civilian terms. No longer was Titus shown spearing an enemy or standing victorious amongst captive Jews; instead, a togate emperor presided over a *congiarium* or clasped hands with his brother Domitian[44].

So the accession was smoothly accomplished. Vespasian had prepared Titus carefully. His early training had been conducted in the imperial court itself by the best available instructors; he had seen active military service in a responsible position and acquired diplomatic experience under the aegis of his father, and had been supervised by the able

Ti. Julius Alexander in Jerusalem and by Vespasian himself in
the seventies when he was assigned a substantial proportion of
an emperor's routine work. He had certainly acquired a reputation for brutality and immorality, but its significance
should not be exaggerated. The regime needed an enforcer, one
that Vespasian could trust absolutely, and since the latter
was eminently shrewd and his judgement of the dynastic
situation close to faultless, it is clear that, in his eyes,
assigning such a role to Titus posed no real threat to the
dynasty's continuity. In this connection, his reaction to
Berenice's activities is particularly relevant: so long as
she represented no danger to the dynasty, he was apparently
unconcerned, but, once she did, she was immediately dismissed.
He had a fine sense of judgement. Titus' accession, then, had
shown the success of Vespasian's efforts to establish the
legitimacy of the Flavian regime and to entrench his elder
son as unassailable heir to the throne.

CHARACTER OF REIGN

From the outset, Titus asserted the Augustan qualities of his
regime. Tiberius and his successors had emphasized connections with Augustus and insisted on their descent from the
deified founder of the line as the basis for their own rule[45].
Vespasian's accession in 69 had, even more urgently, required
a similar stabilizing element: accordingly, he sought to
recall the aura of the Augustan age by, *inter alia*, erecting a
temple of Peace in 71, minting coins bearing legends reminis-
cent of Augustus[46] and even modelling his own official title
exactly on that of Augustus. Titus undertook measures based
on those implemented in the previous reign but adapted to suit
the altered circumstances. His policy was sound. He had to
establish a basis for the legitimacy of his own rule.
    His intentions were revealed and advertised on his coins,
most clearly on those which were essentially his, the unique
Restoration issues. In general, they reproduced types of
previous emperors and members of their families, but only of
those who, in his view, deserved to be remembered - Augustus,
Agrippa, Tiberius, Drusus (son of Tiberius), Livia, Germanicus,
Agrippina the elder, Claudius and Galba, with Augustus,
Claudius and Galba being by far the most popular[47]. The
restored type appeared on the obverse, whilst the reverse
contained Titus' own titles, e.g. *Diuus Augustus Pater* (obv.);
*imp. T. Caes. diui Vesp. f. Aug. p. m. tr. p. p. p. cos. VIII
s. c. Rest.* (rev.)[48]. The concept was unique. These coins
differed significantly even from previous issues of Vespasian
which had drawn heavily on Augustan types, in that they
reproduced precisely the earlier coins and contained the
specific statement that Titus was restoring them. To ensure
their wider circulation, they were issued only in aes. His
aim was not to preserve the memory of famous coins of the

early empire;   rather, they provided a link with respectable
predecessors, made clear by the portrait on the reverse and at
times by a reverse type remarkably similar to those of both
Augustus and Vespasian, e.g. one of the Galba Restoration
coins shows, as well as *imp. T. Vesp. Aug. Rest. s. c., Pax*
with a torch in the right hand firing a heap of arms, and
holding cornucopiae in the left hand[49]:   she is identically
portrayed on a Vespasianic and an Augustan coin[50].   He under-
lined his intentions by the simultaneous issue of *Diuus
Augustus Vespasianus* sestertii, where his father, now deified,
was portrayed with precisely the same attributes as the
deified Augustus on the Restoration coins, i.e. togate,
radiate, seated left and holding a long vertical sceptre[51].
In this way, he emphasized his relationship with the two *diui*
who had established dynasties.

A similar purpose can be discerned in the publicity given
to his childhood friendship with Claudius' son, Britannicus;
he meant to establish his personal connections with the more
respectable members of the Julio-Claudian family.   Thus he had
two statues made of his friend, one of gold which was set up
in the palace, and another of ivory which was carried in the
Circus and which Titus publicly honoured by personally parti-
cipating in the dedicatory procession (*Titus* 2).   Presumably,
his intention was to distance himself publicly from any
Neronian overtones of the past decades in much the same way as
his father had in his somewhat unusual addendum to Plautius
Silvanus' honorific inscription: "He governed Moesia in such
a way that the honour of his triumphal decoration should not
have been delayed to my time"[52].   In general, the members of
the new dynasty presented themselves as the legitimate
successors of the Julio-Claudians, obscuring, as far as
possible, the essentially military origins of their usurpation
of power.   Consequently, any connection with Claudius had
obvious value as propaganda - Claudius, but not Nero, appears
in the *Lex de Imperio Vespasiani*.   On the other hand, the
Flavians dissociated themselves from Nero by honouring
Britannicus and stressing Nero's involvement in his murder.

TITUS' OFFICIALS

But, apart from these public declarations of imperial policy,
there is some evidence to suggest that Titus was very much his
own man and that, unlike his brother, he had no intention of
merely following the guidelines of Vespasianic policy.   An
indication of this emerges from his senior senatorial and
equestrian appointments, and whilst the brevity of his reign
renders extremely difficult and hazardous any examination of
his attitude in this regard, some general observations can,
nonetheless, be tentatively offered.

For Titus' consuls, see Tables 9 and 10.   Vespasian had
regarded the ordinary consulship as the virtual preserve of

TABLE 9:   THE CONSULS OF TITUS' REIGN

79	March/June	L. Junius Caesennius Paetus
		P. Calvisius Ruso Julius Frontinus
	Sept./?Oct.	T. Rubrius Aelius Nepos
		M. Arrius Flaccus
80	To 13 Jan.	Imp. Titus Caes. Vespasianus Augustus VIII
		Caes. Domitianus VII
	13 Jan./Feb.	A. Didius Gallus Fabricius Veiento II
	13 Jan./June	L. Aelius Plautius Lamia Aelianus
	March/April	Q. Aurelius Pactumeius Fronto
	May/June	C. Marius Marcellus Octavius P. Cluvius
		Rufus
	Nov./Dec.	M. Tittius Frugi
		T. Vinicius Julianus
81	Jan./Feb.	L. Flavius Silva Nonius Bassus
		L. ?Asinius Pollio Verrucosus
	March/April	M. Roscius Coelius
		C. Julius Juvenalis
	May/June	L. Vettius Paullus
		T. Junius Montanus
	July/Aug.	C. Scoedius Natta Pinarius
		T. Tettienus Serenus
	Sept./Oct.	M. Petronius Umbrinus
		L. Carminius Lusitanicus

For the evidence, see Gallivan, 1981: p. 215

TABLE 10:   POSSIBLE CONSULS OF TITUS' REIGN

79 or 80	M. Atilius Postumus Bradua
ca. 80	...Asprenas
ca. 80	P. Nonius Asprenas Caesius Cassianus
ca. 80	L. Salvius Otho Cocceianus

For the evidence, see Gallivan, 1981: pp. 202-212

the Flavian family: hence he held the post in 70, 71, 72, 74, 75, 76, 77 and 79, and, in the same period, only four of the *consules ordinarii* were non-Flavians, viz. M. Cocceius Nerva (71), L. Valerius Catullus Messallinus (73), D. Junius Novius Priscus (?Rufus) and L. Ceionius Commodus (78). In 80, the first year of his reign, Titus held this post with Domitian[53], but the consuls of that year had been designated by Vespasian before his death in June 79, Titus' only change - as far as is known - being the substitution of Domitian for his father[54]. Thus only the consuls of 81 and 82 can fairly be regarded as Titus' own appointees: in 81, Titus withdrew from the ordinary consulship, nominating L. ?Asinius Pollio Verrucosus and L. Flavius Silva Nonius Bassus, whilst he was designated for the following year (with Domitian) but died before he could assume the post[55]. This could well be interpreted as a deliberate departure from Vespasian's policy, and if so, it was understandable, in so far as Titus probably felt that the family's *dignitas* was firmly established, and hence was prepared to admit non-Flavians to a prestigious post. Certainly he was more adventurous than his younger brother who held the ordinary consulship consistently from 82 to 89[56] Again, whilst four appointments in a brief reign can hardly be regarded as certain evidence of a definite policy, the fact that the pattern is so different (Vespasian was in power for eight years and Domitian for seven before two non-Flavians were admitted to the ordinary consulship) suggests that Titus was not prepared to follow slavishly the policy directions laid down by his father.

Nothing is known of L. Asinius Pollio Verrucosus[57] beyond his ordinary consulship of 81, but presumably he was a descendant of the patrician Asinii, one of the great houses of the empire. A collateral branch of the family, the Asinii Marcelli, were prominent from ca. A.D. 50 to 150, and earlier Asinii had had close connections with Germanicus[58], as had some of the Flavians' early patrons, the Vitelli and the Pomponii[59]. It was an unexceptionable appointment. The fact that nothing further is known of him is not particularly significant and certainly does not indicate that he lost favour under Domitian. Whilst the Flavians were generally reluctant to employ patricians (other than the *adlecti* of 73/74) in military provinces, there were other positions available. Apart from the urban posts open to ex-consuls, patricians were appointed to the senatorial provinces of Africa and Asia[60], and the fasti of proconsular Africa are incomplete for the early nineties when Pollio would have been eligible for such a post[61]. L. Flavius Silva Nonius Bassus was also a patrician, but of more recent standing, having been adlected to that rank in 73/74[62]. Indeed, it is possible that Silva was related to the imperial family[63]. As military tribune in the *IV Scythica*, he could well have served under Corbulo, many of whose former senior officers found high

favour with Vespasian. Certainly such a connection would not
have been a disadvantage. After his tribunate of the people,
presumably held late in Nero's reign, he emerged as legate of
the *XXI Rapax* in Germany: he may well have replaced the
unnamed legate of that legion during the civil war[64], serving
under Titus' brother-in-law, Q. Petillius Cerialis Caesius
Rufus. His subsequent double adlection *inter praetorios* and
inter patricios and service as a legate of the newly established province of Judaea, when he brought the Jewish war to
its conclusion with the capture of Masada[65], marked him out
for the future preferment which he achieved in 81. After
Titus' death, all that is known of Silva is his lavish gift of
an amphitheatre to his home town of Urbs Salvia[66]. He could
well have held a senior post under Domitian, but, unfortunately, relatively few of the consular legates from his early
years are known. It should not, however, be assumed that his
service to Titus disqualified him in Domitian's eyes. A
newly found inscription can easily fill in a lacuna in our
knowledge. Julius Frontinus, it used to be assumed, must have
fallen foul of Domitian because no post was attested for him
between 81 and 96[67]; it is now known that he served in
Domitian's war against the Chatti and was proconsul of Asia
ca. 85[68]. M. Cornelius Nigrinus Curiatius Maternus' career
has recently been revealed[69]; from comparative obscurity, he
has emerged as one of Domitian's most eminent senators,
holding a suffect consulship and governing three imperial
consular provinces between 81 and 96. Another factor not to
be ignored is premature death[70]. Under these circumstances,
it would be most unwise to assume that our ignorance of
Asinius Pollio's and Flavius Silva's careers after 81 must be
explained by Domitian's hostility to his brother's appointees.
        Whilst no substantial conclusions can be drawn about
Titus' attitude to these senior appointments, it could be
tentatively suggested that, unlike Vespasian and Domitian, he
favoured the approach of many earlier emperors, leaving the
ordinary consulship to eminent senators whose support was
vital for the preservation of the regime. In this sense, he
would have been closer to Trajan and Hadrian rather than to
his father and brother.
        The prolongation of L. Aelius Lamia Plautius Aelianus'
term as suffect consul in 80 is of some interest, even though
the consuls for that year were designated by Vespasian. As
has been shown recently, the normal duration of suffect
consulships under the Flavians was two months[71], though there
are possible exceptions - Domitian and L. Pasidienus Firmus in
75, and Domitian in 77[72]. Lamia, on the other hand, is
attested as suffect on January 14, 80 and was still in office
on June 13[73]. Vespasian's death in June 79 forced Titus to
revise the designations for 80 and therefore Domitian was
elevated to the vacant ordinary consulship, leaving Lamia as
the colleague of Fabricius Veiento, *cos. II suff.* In March

and April, he remained in office with a new colleague, Q. Aurelius Pactumeius Fronto, and retained the post for the following term (May/June), with C. Marius Marcellus Octavius P. Cluvius Rufus, an unusually long tenure[74]. It is possible that another of the designated consuls had died before assuming office, but, in any case, Titus must have decided that there was no need to add other consuls to his father's list. If Lamia was the son of Plautius Silvanus[75], then the favour shown him by Titus is understandable. Vespasian had honoured his father and other senior Neronian consulars, some of whom had less obvious claims to Flavian patronage than had the Plautii. It would be perverse to resort to *odium fratern-um* as an explanation for the honour; the award of two additional terms as suffect consul to a senator of his lineage was hardly intended as an insult to Domitian. The latter may well have interpreted it as such, but on very insubstantial grounds: Lamia had been the first husband of Domitian's wife, Domitia Longina. However, neither his illustrious ancestors and descendants[76], nor his rather wry sense of humour (*Dom.* 10.2),could preserve him from execution during Domitian's reign.

Amongst the most significant of an emperor's officials were the governors of his consular provinces. Of those then attested (Tables 11, 12 and 13), five were almost certainly first appointed to their provinces by Vespasian and some of these had already served in another imperial consular province during that reign, i.e. Cn. Julius Agricola (Britain since 77/78), D. Junius Novius Priscus (Lower Germany since 78/79), C. Calpetanus Rantius Quirinalis Valerius Festus (Spain since 78/79 and Pannonia earlier in the reign), L. Ceionius Commodus (Syria since 78/79) and T. Atilius Rufus (Pannonia in 79/80 - and subsequently, in 83, Syria)[77]. Three others were possibly appointed by Titus, i.e. Q. Corellius Rufus and L. Funisulanus Vettonianus, both consuls in Sept./Oct. 78, and subsequently governors of Upper Germany (Sept. 82) and Dalmatia (before 84) respectively[78]; C. Vettulenus Civica Cerialis, brother of Sex. Vettulenus Cerialis (Titus' fellow legate during the Judaean war), is attested in 82 as governor of Moesia, a province previously governed by his brother[79]. Finally, the legate of Cappadocia-Galatia in 80/81, A. Caesennius Gallus, almost certainly came to the province in that year[80]. He was related to the Flavians and, like his two immediate predecessors in that province (M. Hirrius Fronto Neratius Pansa and Cn. Pompeius Collega), had formerly served as one of Corbulo's legates. It is also possible that he succeeded Atilius Rufus in Syria[81]. The most remarkable feature is the obvious continuity of administration from reign to reign. The high standard of Flavian provincial governors has long been recognized: efficient governors were appointed and retained in office, though not usually for more than three years in one province. Service in more than one area at this level was not

TABLE 11:   SENATORIAL ADMINISTRATORS OF A.D. 79/80

GOVERNORS OF IMPERIAL CONSULAR PROVINCES[a]

SENATOR	PROVINCE
Cn. Julius Agricola	Britain
M. Hirrius Fronto Neratius Pansa	Cappadocia-Galatia
?L. Funisulanus Vettonianus	Dalmatia
D. Junius Novius Priscus	Lower Germany
?Q. Corellius Rufus	Upper Germany
T. Atilius Rufus	Pannonia
C. Calpetanus Rantius Quirinalis Valerius Festus	Spain
L. Ceionius Commodus	Syria

PROCONSULS OF SENATORIAL CONSULAR PROVINCES[a]

M. Ulpius Traianus	Asia

GOVERNORS OF IMPERIAL PRAETORIAN PROVINCES[a]

L. [?Antonius Saturninus]	Judaea
T. Tettienus Serenus	Lugdunensis
T. Aurelius Quietus	Lycia-Pamphylia

IURIDICI OF IMPERIAL PRAETORIAN PROVINCES

?? C. Salvius Liberalis Nonius Bassus	Britain[b]
Ti. Julius Celsus Polemaeanus	Cappadocia-Galatia[c]

PROCONSULS OF SENATORIAL PRAETORIAN PROVINCES[a]

C. Cornelius Gallicanus	Baetica
[--Ma]rcius [---]tesinus	Cyprus
Velius Paullus	Pontus-Bithynia

NOTES TO TABLE 11

a	Eck, 1982: p. 302.
b	*ILS* 1011.
c	Halfmann, 1979: pp. 111-112.

TABLE 12:   SENATORIAL ADMINISTRATORS OF A.D. 80/81

GOVERNORS OF IMPERIAL CONSULAR PROVINCES[a]

SENATOR	PROVINCE
Cn. Julius Agricola	Britain
A. Caesennius Gallus	Cappadocia-Galatia
L. Funisulanus Vettonianus	Dalmatia
D. Junius Novius Priscus	Lower Germany
Q. Corellius Rufus	Upper Germany
T. Atilius Rufus	Pannonia
C. Calpetanus Rantius Quirinalis Valerius Festus	Spain
L. Ceionius Commodus	Syria

PROCONSULS OF SENATORIAL CONSULAR PROVINCES[b]

C. Laecanius Bassus Caecina Paetus	Asia

GOVERNORS OF IMPERIAL PRAETORIAN PROVINCES[a]

M. Cornelius Nigrinus Curiatius Maternus	Aquitania
L. [?Antonius Saturninus]	Judaea
T. Tettienus Serenus	Lugdunensis
C. Cornelius Gallicanus	
T. Aurelius Quietus	Lycia-Pamphylia
L. Tettius Julianus	Numidia

IURIDICI OF IMPERIAL PRAETORIAN PROVINCES

?C. Salvius Liberalis Nonius Bassus	Britain[c]
L. Julius Proculeianus	Cappadocia-Galatia[d]

PROCONSULS OF SENATORIAL PRAETORIAN PROVINCES[a]

L. Bruttius Maximus	Cyprus

NOTES TO TABLE 12

a	Eck, 1982: p. 304
b	Eck, 1982: p. 304 but cf. Kreiler, 1975: p. 38 and Devreker, 1976b: p. 182.
c	*ILS* 1011
d	Halfmann, 1979: pp. 110-111

Reign of Titus

TABLE 13:   SENATORIAL ADMINISTRATORS OF A.D. 81/82

GOVERNORS OF IMPERIAL CONSULAR PROVINCES

SENATOR

Cn. Julius Agricola	Britain
A. Caesennius Gallus	Cappadocia-Galatia
L. Funisulanus Vettonianus	Dalmatia
?D. Julius Novius Priscus	Lower Germany
Q. Corellius Rufus	Upper Germany
C. Vettulenus Civica Cerialis	Moesia
T. Atilius Rufus	Pannonia
?L. Ceionius Commodus	Syria

GOVERNORS OF IMPERIAL PRAETORIAN PROVINCES[a]

M. Cornelius Nigrinus Curiatius Maternus	Aquitania
C. Cornelius Gallicanus	Lugdunensis
C. Caristanius Fronto	Lycia-Pamphylia
L. Tettius Julianus	Numidia

IURIDICI OF IMPERIAL PRAETORIAN PROVINCES

| C. Salvius Liberalis Nonius Bassus | Britain[b] |
| C. Antius A. Julius Quadratus | Cappadocia-Galatia[c] |

PROCONSULS OF SENATORIAL PRAETORIAN PROVINCES

| L. Plotius P[egasus?] | Cyprus[d] |
| ?A. Lappius Maximus | Pontus-Bithynia[e] |

NOTES TO TABLE 13

a   Eck, 1982: p. 305
b   *ILS* 1011
c   Halfmann, 1979: pp. 112-115
d   Champlin, 1978: pp. 269 ff.
e   Kreiler, 1975: p. 140

129

uncommon, however.

On the other hand, innovation in administrative policy is suggested by the subordinate officials assigned in the late seventies and early eighties to the new Cappadocia-Galatia complex. Its creation was one of the most significant military developments of Vespasian's reign and the work was continued by Titus, with the vast complex of military roads dating to the governorship of A. Caesennius Gallus whose appointment was almost certainly due to Titus[82]. But the most interesting development of his reign was the policy, possibly initiated by Vespasian, of appointing senators from the Greek east as assistants (*iuridici*) to the consular governors of Cappadocia-Galatia. Three such senators held this post in succession, viz. Ti. Julius Celsus Polemaeanus, L. Julius Proculeianus and C. Antius A. Julius Quadratus[83]. Consistent with this innovatory policy was the employment of senators of similar origin in a number of military commands. Their promotion to significant posts in the early years of the second century has long been noticed. Recently, it has been shown that the tendency was obvious as early as Domitian's reign[84]: C. Antius A. Julius Quadratus, for instance, was the first easterner to govern the vital consular province of Syria (ca. 100-103) and also to hold an ordinary consulship (in 105, as *cos. II ord.*), but he had also been appointed to the imperial praetorian province of Lycia-Pamphylia by Domitian at the time of Saturninus' revolt[85]. Yet, even then, this was not an innovation. The tendency was evident late in Vespasian's reign. Note how elaborately T. Caristanius Calpurnianus Rufus described the award of a legionary command ca. 78 to one of his relatives, C. Caristanius Fronto - "legate of the deified emperor Vespasian Augustus of the legion *IX Hispana* in Britain."[86]. Fronto appears to have been the first senator from the Greek east to be appointed to the command of a legion. Compare the bald description of a similar post held in ca. 80 by the Italian Javolenus Priscus - "legate of the legion *IV Flavia*"[87]. Fronto was then appointed by Titus to the governorship of an imperial praetorian province, Lycia-Pamphylia, again being the first from the east to hold such a post[88]. Admittedly, Fronto's ancestors were Italian, but Titus' policy was shown in his appointment of Ti. Julius Celsus Polemaeanus, a senator from the east and with no Italian connections, to the command of the legion *IV Scythica*[89].

In general, such appointments were restricted to the Greek-speaking eastern provinces. In the west, the standard policy was adopted. Note, *inter alia*, the Spaniard L. Antistius Rusticus in command of the legion *VIII Augusta* in Germany and the Italian C. Salvius Liberalis Nonius Bassus as assistant (*iuridicus*) to Agricola in Britain. Another Spaniard, L. Antonius Saturninus, may well have been appointed by Titus to succeed L. Flavius Silva Nonius Bassus in

Judaea[90], whilst the Italian Javolenus Priscus commanded the
legion *IV Flavia* in Dalmatia. Since comparatively few of
Titus' praetorian governors and legionary legates are
attested, it would be hazardous to draw definite conclusions
in this regard, beyond noting the innovation in two significant areas - Cappadocia-Galatia, a Flavian creation and
cornerstone of Vespasian's eastern policy, saw the appointment
of trusted Corbulonian legates as consular governors together
with eastern senators as their assistants, whilst, for the
first time, easterners lacking Italian ancestors were given
command of legions and imperial provinces.

In some areas, then, Titus' policy was innovatory, though
perhaps the origin of the changes can be discerned late in his
father's reign; but, whilst some of the credit may well be
ascribed to Vespasian, it is not unreasonable to see the hand
of his elder son in these new directions in imperial policy.
Vespasian's health was failing during 79 and Titus' ability
and experience together with the substantial responsibilities
assigned to him throughout the seventies strongly suggest that
it was his insight that promoted the new ideas.

It is possible to discern his influence not only in the
emergence of senators from the Greek east, but also in the
promotion of a group of Italian officials in the period 79-81.
In 62, Titus' uncle by marriage, L. Caesennius Paetus, had
been responsible for the debacle at Rhandeia[91] and recalled to
Rome in disgrace (*Ann.* 15.10-14, 25; Dio, 62.21), a fate
shared by his subordinate legates who included L. Funisulanus
Vettonianus, commander of the legion *IV Scythica* (*Ann.* 15.7).
Not unexpectedly, they did not return to public life during
Nero's reign. With the new regime, however, Paetus prospered,
being recalled to the governorship of Syria, thanks, no doubt,
to his Flavian connections[92]. Funisulanus Vettonianus also
returned to favour, holding a number of praetorian posts
during the seventies and reaching the consulship late in 78,
an honour granted in the following year to Paetus' son, L.
Junius Caesennius Paetus[93]. Clearly, all had been forgiven;
but the reasons are not immediately obvious. Perhaps the
elder Paetus had been able to persuade his brother-in-law that
the former legate of the *IV Scythica* had been unfairly treated
- as indeed he had, for he opposed Paetus' intervention in 62
(*Ann.* 15.10). Recently, it has been suggested that the
explanation for Funisulanus' restoration to imperial favour
should be sought in the influence of Tiberius Julius, Aug.
lib., the father of Claudius Etruscus and highly respected
freedman of Vespasian and Titus[94]. Some evidence can be
adduced in support of such a view.

Subsequent to his consulship, Funisulanus' career was as
distinguished as it had previously been unremarkable. Despite
his lack of recent military experience, he was quickly granted
the *fasces* and moved to the imperial province of Dalmatia,
which he administered so successfully that Domitian promoted

him to Pannonia and, subsequently, to Moesia where he became
the first governor of Upper Moesia (ca. 86/87)[95]. Replaced
there by his relative Tettius Julianus, he returned to Rome
and received numerous honours - *dona militaria*, a second,
highly prestigious priesthood (*sodalis Augustalis*) and the
proconsulship of Africa (ca. 91)[96]. His re-emergence under
Titus coincided with the award of significant posts to two of
his relatives. The equestrian C. Tettius Africanus Cassianus
Priscus, who had held the posts of prefect of the *uigiles* and
the *annona* under Vespasian, was now promoted by Titus to the
prefecture of Egypt (ca. 80)[97]. At the same time, his
senatorial relative Tettius Julianus, who was the brother-in-
law of Tiberius Julius, Aug. lib.[98], emerged from apparent
obscurity under Vespasian to receive the prestigious post of
commander of the legion *III Augusta* together with the
praetorian governorship of Numidia. He too was subsequently
promoted by Domitian - to a consulship in 83 and to the
consular province of Upper Moesia as successor to his relative
Funisulanus Vettonianus[99]. The relationship between these
four Flavian officials may be seen from Table 14.

TABLE 14: THE TETTII AND THEIR RELATIVES

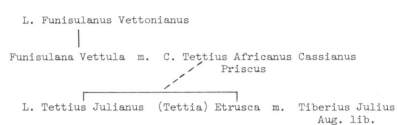

L. Funisulanus Vettonianus

Funisulana Vettula m. C. Tettius Africanus Cassianus
                                    Priscus

L. Tettius Julianus (Tettia) Etrusca m. Tiberius Julius
                                              Aug. lib.

Funisulanus, Tettius Africanus and Tettius Julianus
emerged almost simultaneously in Titus' brief reign. It would
not be unreasonable to ascribe their appointments to the
efforts of their influential relative Tiberius Julius, Aug.
lib., whose financial expertise had long aided the Flavians.
They had rewarded him for his services in administering the
neruos belli (*Hist.* 2.84) during the Flavians' rise to power
by admitting both his sons to the equestrian order (between
69 and 71), by having him appear in the lavish Jewish triumph
in 71 and, in 73, by adlecting him as well to the equestrian
order, despite his origin[100]. Until his dismissal by Domitian
ca. 82/83, he remained *a rationibus* of the three Flavian
emperors[101]. Obviously, he had their confidence. He could
well have persuaded Titus that his relatives were both
capable and trustworthy, and, indeed, this would have been a
correct assessment: Domitian would hardly have been swayed by
Tiberius Julius, Aug. lib., for he dismissed him early in the

reign, yet he retained both Funisulanus and Tettius Julianus
who served him with distinction.
    Of some interest, too, is the fact that Titus appointed
the Tettii to areas of considerable sensitivity in precisely
the same year. The military significance of Egypt and Numidia
was familiar to Titus in view of the history of the past
decade. Late in 69, both Vespasian and Mucianus stressed that
the Flavians could "force the army of Vitellius to its knees
merely by lack of pay and supplies"; they were already in
possession of "the revenues of the richest provinces", i.e.
Asia and Syria, and needed only Egypt "with its control of the
corn supply"[102]. To ensure complete mastery, Vespasian "was
making preparations for a naval and land invasion of the
province of Africa ... and, by withholding the grain supplies,
he aimed at sowing famine and dissension among his enemies"[103].
The lesson was clear: control of Egypt and Africa was
absolutely vital and had always been so. According to
Tacitus:-
> One of the secrets of imperial policy was that senators
> and Roman knights of the higher rank were forbidden to
> enter Egypt, except by permission, and he had especially
> reserved the country, fearing that anyone who held a
> province containing the key of the land and of the sea,
> with ever so small a force against the mightiest army,
> might subject Italy to starvation[104].
As a result, it was administered by an equestrian prefect and
not by a man of senatorial rank, an anomaly rendered all the
more obvious by the fact that the prefect was placed in command of legionary armies. In these circumstances, Titus'
arrangements in 80 were remarkable. No doubt he was influenced by the Tettii's persuasive relative, Tiberius Julius, Aug.
lib., yet it would appear not unreasonable to suggest that it
was a deliberate decision on the part of the new emperor and
represented a policy that was particularly Titus' own, one
that probably would not have won the approval of his more
cautious father. Vespasian seems to have been wary of his
elder son's headstrong qualities as early as the Judaean
campaign; he was prone to take risks, and, even during the
siege of Jerusalem, his legates saw fit to beg and plead with
him to be more careful and remember his position as commander
(*BJ* 5.88)[105]. Thus, Vespasian's rehabilitation of the Tettii's
relative, Funisulanus Vettonianus, was somewhat cautious. The
three praetorian posts accorded to him in the seventies were
prestigious but "well removed from the centres of power"[106].
The absence of a praetorian governorship was significant and
so his subsequent consulship in 78 and promotion to an armed
province[107] (Dalmatia, possibly as early as 79) could perhaps
indicate a sudden change of attitude on the part of the
elderly Vespasian; far more likely, though, in view of the
appointment of the Tettii to Egypt and Africa in 80, the new
direction in Funisulanus' career should be ascribed to Titus

(at the instigation, no doubt, of Tiberius Julius, Aug. lib.).
It represented a departure from his father's more cautious
and predictable policies, whereas his appointment to military
provinces of senators from the Greek east was rather an
extension of them.

The innovatory aspects of Titus' policies apparently
caused little dismay to his successor. Whatever the extent of
Domitian's hostility towards his brother, he retained Funisulanus Vettonianus, Tettius Julianus and the easterners promoted
in 80/81 and granted them further honours and responsibilities,
though the experiment of related governors being simultaneously appointed to Egypt and Africa was not repeated. On the
other hand, Domitian was less kindly disposed towards some of
Titus' freedmen or former freedmen officials, especially those
holding senior domestic posts within the palace. Tiberius
Julius, Aug. lib., was soon dismissed, as was Tiberius
Claudius, Aug. lib. Classicus, Titus' *procurator castrensis* and
a cubiculo - i.e. he was simultaneously in charge of the
imperial domestic arrangements and (more significantly) of the
imperial bedchamber. His recently discovered career inscription has provoked much discussion, but his eminence in the
period 79/81 is beyond dispute[108]: as *a cubiculo*, he was
particularly influential, particularly close to the emperor.
It is not, perhaps, surprising that he was dismissed by
Domitian.

TITUS' AMICI

It has long been admitted that an emperor's *amici* always had
a significant role to play in the administration of the
empire, a fact that was recognised even by contemporary
observers[109]. According to Helvidius Priscus, "good *amici*
were the most valuable instrument of good government", whilst
Suetonius states that Titus' were "indispensable to the
state"[110]. The policy adopted in their selection, however, is
a matter of some dispute and far less easy to determine, since
it is essential to take into account such divergent and
irreconcilable elements as the almost inevitable continuity of
these administrators from one reign to the next, and, on the
other hand, the emperors' not uncommon practice of co-opting
individuals with particular talents on certain occasions
only[111]. Such factors render somewhat hazardous any attempt
to devise the policy adopted by any one emperor in this
regard, and even more so with an emperor whose reign was as
brief as Titus'.

By the time of his accession, and indeed for many years
past, the senate's role in administration was minimal, even
though individual senators acquired considerable power. Their
number included the governors of imperial provinces both
praetorian, and, in particular, consular, but it must be
stressed that such a role involved their absence from the

capital, often for considerable periods of time: Funisulanus
Vettonianus seems to have served for most of the eighties in
Dalmatia, Pannonia and Upper Moesia whilst Agricola was in
Britain from ca. 77/78 to 83/84. Thus important decisions
were taken by those in Rome, by the emperor essentially, in
consultation with a restricted circle of available *amici*.
They were not a recognized constitutional body; there was no
"fixed list" of members, but the same people were probably
called in regularly for consultation[112]. Most were senators,
but prominent equestrians were frequently invited to attend[113]:
Pliny the Elder,perhaps when he was *praefectus classis* or
praefectus uigilum, used to be summoned by Vespasian "before
daybreak" (Pliny, *Ep.* 3.5.9). The *praefectus praetorio* would,
almost certainly, have been present on most occasions[114]. The
senatorial *amici*, apart from those precisely attested as such
in literary, epigraphic or papyrological sources, probably
included the *consules II*, the *praefectus urbi* and the *curator
aquarum*[115]. But, in any reign and especially so in a brief
one, it is difficult to assess precisely the extent of their
power, the policy governing their selection or, indeed, even
to be certain of their identity.

T. Flavius Sabinus (= Sabinus III), Titus' cousin and
father of the *consul ordinarius* of 82 (T. Flavius Sabinus =
Sabinus IV), had held a second consulship in 72 and was
curator aedium sacrarum et operum locorumque publicorum under
Titus[116]. He should be regarded as one of the senior *amici*,
even though very little is known of him. Another Flavian
relative, M. Arrecinus Clemens, would also have been included,
unless he was absent from Rome during part or all of the reign
as consular legate of Hispania Citerior[117]. The ability and
usefulness of A. Didius Gallus Fabricius Veiento, *cos. II* in
80 with Aelius Lamia, would not have escaped Titus' notice;
he assisted in the formulation of imperial policy throughout
the Flavian era[118]. The "bland and elegant" L. Junius Q.
Vibius Crispus, *cos. II* in 74, was another experienced
politician who served all three Flavian emperors; both he
and Veiento held third consulships early in Domitian's reign,
probably in 83[119]. Another Neronian survivor, M. Pompeius
Silvanus Staberius Flavinus, *cos. II* ca. 76 and designated to
a third in 83, so it seems, must have acquired considerable
experience during his lengthy career (his first consulship
occurred early in Claudius' reign); though "torpid and
timorous" during the events of 69/70, he was appointed *curator
aquarum* in 71[120] and could be considered as the third of the
elder statesmen amongst the *amici*. Other members of this
"group" could well have been M. Cocceius Nerva and L. Valerius
Catullus Messallinus. Nerva, the future emperor, had been
rewarded by Nero for his services at the time of the Pisonian
conspiracy. Subsequently, he found favour with the Flavians,
holding two ordinary consulships at critical periods - the
first as early as 71, with Vespasian as colleague, and the

second with Domitian in 90, immediately after the suppression
of Saturninus' revolt; in addition, he was the only non-
member of the family to receive two such awards. Probably,
then, he was an *amicus* of Titus[121]. The blind delator,
Catullus Messallinus, had been appointed *cos. I ord.* in 73
and was a member of Domitian's notorious *rhombus* council
(Juvenal IV); despite his subsequent reputation, there is no
reason to suppose that Titus did not avail himself of his
services - he was certainly regarded as an intimate friend of
Nerva and Fabricius Veiento[122].

Closer to Titus in age and background were Sex. Julius
Frontinus, M. Hirrius Fronto Neratius Pansa and M. Ulpius
Traianus (senior), three loyal, experienced administrators and
military commanders. Frontinus was one of the outstanding
senators of the last quarter of the first century. He probably commanded a legion in the campaign against Civilis,
proceeded to hold the *fasces* early in Vespasian's reign, was
appointed to Britain soon afterwards and subsequently served
Domitian as *comes* in his war against the Chatti and as
proconsul of Asia (ca. 85). In 97, he replaced Acilius Aviola
as *curator aquarum*, was granted a second consulship in 98,
and, in 100, achieved the rare distinction of a third, ordinary
consulship which he held with the emperor Trajan. Whilst
there is no evidence of his activities under Titus, it would
not be unreasonable to assign a place in the *consilium* to a
senator of his ability and loyalty[123]. A close contemporary
of his, Neratius Pansa, had governed two imperial provinces
following his consulship and adlection *inter patricios*,
presumably in 73/74; at the end of Vespasian's reign, he was
serving in the second of these, Cappadocia-Galatia, where he
was replaced by Titus' relative, A. Caesennius Gallus. At
some point in his career, he held the post of *curator aedium
sacrarum et operum locorumque publicorum*; he would have been
an invaluable *amicus* for Titus[124]. Traianus, too, had
recently returned from that area. Another prominent
Vespasianic administrator, he had been granted an extended
tenure of Syria (ca. 73 to 77) and then proceeded to the
proconsulship of Asia (ca. 79). Some have suggested that he
was the architect of Vespasian's eastern arrangements, but,
whilst the evidence for assigning such a role to Traianus is
not compelling, it is obvious that the experience and proven
ability of this eastern specialist would not have escaped
Titus' notice. After all, they had been legates together in
Judaea a decade previously[125]. The fact that these three
senators held the *fasces* early in Vespasian's reign suggests,
but does not guarantee, that they were only some seven to ten
years older than Titus; they were also close to him in background and outlook, much closer in all respects than the
former Neronian counsellors. All four had been legionary
legates at approximately the same time, and Frontinus,
Neratius Pansa and Traianus were quick to realize where their

futures lay. It seems not unreasonable to suggest, then, that these three close contemporaries formed a unit on whose military knowledge and administrative experience Titus could rely heavily.

Another Flavian official, the patrician M'. Acilius Aviola, *curator aquarum* from 74 to 97 (Frontinus, *De Aq.* 102), should also be included amongst his *amici*[126]. The advice of the famous jurist, [Plo]tius Pegasus, appointed *praefectus urbi* by Vespasian, would have been invaluable; his eastern origin would have been no impediment. He and his brother Grypus were prominent administrators during the Flavian period and the L. Plotius P..., proconsul of Cyprus ca. 81/82, was perhaps his son; the family showed consistent loyalty to all the Flavians and served them well[127]. One other senator, a certain Gallicanus, has been attested in a rescript of Titus as one of his *amici*[128]. He could well be the C. Cornelius Gallicanus who served as military tribune in Vespasian's army, was presumably adlected *inter praetorios* in 73/74 and held the proconsulship of Baetica in 79/80. He was granted the *fasces* by Domitian in 84. During most of Titus' reign he was probably absent from Rome, since he had served as governor of the imperial praetorian province of Lugdunensis before his consulship[129]. In these circumstances, it would be hazardous to attempt to assign him any role in the *consilium*, even though he is the only *amicus* whose status is recorded epigraphically.

The most influential *amici* were obviously those consistently in Rome, close to the emperor. So, in this regard, the significance of a serving praetorian or consular legate has to be discounted. Not so with the praetorian prefect; he was the *sacri lateris custos*[130], he rarely left the capital. Unfortunately, no one is definitely attested in the post under Titus. Domitian's early prefects were Cornelius Fuscus and L. Laberius Maximus, both his appointees[131]. If Laberius is the "Maximus" of *P. Berl.* 8334, then his predecessor as guard commander was a certain "Julius"[132], perhaps the L. Julius Ursus already known as *praefectus annonae* and as *praefectus Aegypti*[133]; a promotion from Egypt to the guard was perfectly regular under the Flavians, though the reverse held true in previous reigns. It is also possible that L. Julius Ursus should be identified with the Ursus of Dio, 67.3.1 and 67.4.2, who, in danger of losing his life early in Domitian's reign, was rescued by Titus' daughter Julia and finally granted a consulship (84); this Ursus, whether or not Titus' former prefect, finally held the *fasces* for the third time in 100[134]. Now *P. Berl.* 8334 does indicate that Julius was being moved *in amplissimum ordinem*; still, such a reconstruction is fraught with difficulties, not the least of which being the rapid transition from equestrian to senatorial and consular status within a remarkably brief period. Nonetheless, it is possible that Ursus was Titus' prefect and in high favour, but

Domitian, who was probably planning his German campaign at
this time, may well have been seeking a more aggressive
prefect in the style of Cornelius Fuscus: we know that Fuscus,
but not Ursus, was present amongst the counsellors in
Juvenal's famous Satire IV. At all events, Ursus was moved
into the senate, his transfer being "suitably veiled in bland
and diplomatic phraseology"[135]. Not all of Titus' *amici* found
favour with Domitian.

One could, then, distinguish the following groups within
his *consilium*:-
- (a)   Imperial Relatives: M. Arrecinus Clemens and T.
        Flavius Sabinus;
- (b)   Senior Statesmen: A. Didius Gallus Fabricius Veiento,
        L. Junius Q. Vibius Crispus, M. Pompeius Silvanus
        Staberius Flavinus, M. Cocceius Nerva and L. Valerius
        Catullus Messallinus;
- (c)   Administrators/Generals, Contemporaries of Titus: Sex.
        Julius Frontinus, M. Hirrius Fronto Neratius Pansa and
        M. Ulpius Traianus;
- (d)   Other: M'. Acilius Aviola, [Plo]tius Pegasus,
        Gallicanus and [L. Julius] Ursus.

In general, he appears to have relied heavily on his father's
amici, and not unexpectedly in view of his own rule during
Vespasian's reign: an heir apparent also praetorian prefect
was clearly in an ideal position to assess their capabilities.
But no doubt changes would have occurred had he lived longer.

A slight hint of his intentions may be discerned in some
of his consular appointments (Table 9). Whilst not *amici*,
they seem to have enjoyed his special favour and could well be
considered as indicative of future policy in this regard. Ten
years previously, M. Tittius Frugi had been *legatus* of the *XV
Apollinaris* and had participated in Titus' council of war[136];
but, for some unknown reason, Vespasian did not promote him,
and it was not until his former commander's accession to the
throne that he received his consulship. Yet other legionary
commanders of 68/69 who had displayed loyalty to the new
dynasty received the *fasces* almost at once[137]. Now Titus may
simply have been rewarding an old colleague; on the other
hand, his motives may have been more complex, and, if he was
contemplating a future move away from senators favoured by
Vespasian, one would expect to see promotions such as this.
A legionary legate from the civil war period with a career
similar to that of Tittius Frugi was M. Roscius Coelius,
commander of the *XX Valeria Victrix*; his unit was stationed
in Britain in 69, but it was not until March 81 that he
received his suffect consulship[138]. He had been involved in
a mutiny against the governor of Britain, Trebellius Maximus,
whose policies were very unpopular with the army and were in
no small measure responsible for the revolt. But whereas
Trebellius had fled to Vitellius[139], Coelius apparently
satisfied the new regime, for, if there had been any doubts

about his loyalty, he would never have been promoted. Once again, Titus was promoting a man whom Vespasian seems to have overlooked, with the intention, presumably, of seeking support beyond his father's favourites. Somewhat similar is the case of Tettius Julianus, commander of the *VII Claudia* in 68/69: he was appointed to the imperial province of Numidia by Titus in 80. It has already been noted that he had powerful connections in the senatorial and equestrian hierarchy[140]. The promotion of these three officers is consistent with the theory that he was seeking to build a base of support that was strictly his own.

Of particular significance was the suffect consulship awarded in May/June 81 to Titus Junius Montanus from Alexandria in the Troad where his father, of the same name, had established himself as a colonist in the early years of the first century[141]. As one of the first consuls ever appointed from the Greek east, he was obviously highly esteemed by Titus and for reasons that are not immediately apparent[142]; in fact, his selection is somewhat puzzling. His career[143] had been most promising at the outset, when, under Nero, he served as *triumvir monetalis*, the most prestigious section of the vigintivirate: usually it was reserved for patricians - which Montanus clearly was not, for he later became *tribunus plebis* - or, at least, for the sons of senators with potential military ability. Subsequently, however, his progress was fairly unspectacular - a military tribunate in Moesia with the *V Macedonica*, a quaestorship in Pontus-Bithynia, a tribunate of the people, praetorship and proconsulship of Sicily. When he held these posts is uncertain, but in view of his consulship in 81, his praetorship would have to be assigned to ca. 70/71, or, more probably, somewhat earlier. At the very least, then, his praetorian "career" extended over most of Vespasian's reign and consisted of a solitary post, a praetorian proconsulship, whose holders "seldom came to anything"[144]: here was no hint of future preferment. Yet Titus reverted to Nero's original assessment of Montanus and gave him the *fasces*. Later, so it seems, this "slow, fat"[145] senator appeared in Domitian's *consilium*[146] - despite Dio's comment that Domitian "quite outdid himself in visiting disgrace and ruin upon the friends of his father and brother" (67.1.2). Far more significant, though, was the fact that yet another senator passed over by Vespasian received substantial honours from Titus.

The literary sources are distinctly unhelpful in their assessment of his policy in selecting *amici*. Dio's comment (67.1.2) has already been noted. Suetonius flatly contradicted it, claiming that "Titus chose as his friends men whom succeeding emperors retained as indispensable alike to themselves and to the state and of whose services they made special use"[147]. Their views are irreconcilable. Probably, the majority of Titus' *consilium* consisted of traditional

Flavian supporters, most of whom were retained by his
brother[148]. On the other hand, there are indications that,
had he lived longer, he would have modified or enlarged its
composition.

TITUS' ADMINISTRATION: ECONOMIC POLICY

During Vespasian's reign, Titus was undoubtedly influential in
the formulation of administrative policy, and it was to be
expected that, on his accession, no radical changes would
occur. No record exists of alteration in military displace-
ments or of substantial changes in territorial boundaries;
Vespasian's policies in education and the arts and in the
revision of colonial lands remained unchanged[149]. Titus'
legislation, too, followed the general trend of greater
humanitarianism and efficiency established by his father. In
certain sectors, however, modification of Vespasianic policy
bears the distinct mark of Titus' personality. With a more
complex nature than that of his practical and somewhat blunt
father and a heightened awareness of public opinion, Titus was,
so we are told, intent on administering the empire with
parentis affectus (*Titus* 8.3) - to be interpreted, presumably,
as a move towards a despotic personal regime tempered with
paternalism.
      In the matter of financial administration, the sources
proclaim his generosity (*Titus* 7.3, 8.1). Modern historians,
however, seem to regard his economic policies with the greatest reserve: in fact, most find him incompetent, or, at
best, careless and extravagant[150]. Now, at the outset of
Vespasian's principate, Rome's financial situation was critical, because of the extravagances of Nero's reign together with
the cost of the civil war that had left widespread destruction
as its legacy; not even the city had recovered from the fire
that had devastated it during Nero's rule[151]. As founder of
the new dynasty, Vespasian was obliged to undertake the
restoration of what had been destroyed in the struggle for
power, and such was the state of the treasury that forty
thousand million sesterces were, in his estimation, necessary
to establish financial security[152]. Consequently, taxes once
remitted were again imposed and new ones introduced[153].
According to historians, no source of income was left untapped
(*Vesp*. 23.3; Dio, 66.14.5), and although Vespasian acquired
thereby a reputation for parsimony, he was undoubtedly
successful in restoring financial stability. So it is not
unreasonable to assume that Titus began his principate with at
least sufficient funds in the treasury.
      A brief analysis of the financial position in the early
years of Domitian's reign reveals a not dissimilar situation.
Shortly after his accession, he was able to cancel debts outstanding to the treasury for more than five years (*Dom*. 9.2)
and he also decided to refuse inheritances when the testator

had surviving children (*Dom.* 9.2). In 82, he decreed that
those squatting on the *subsiciua* should be confirmed in their
possession of them (*Dom.* 9.3)[154]. Again, he granted a
substantial pay increase to the troops (*Dom.* 7.3; Dio, 67.3.
5), presumably in 84[155]. Significant, too, is his reversal of
previous Flavian policy by increasing the gold and silver
content in his coins. The gold aureus was increased in weight
slightly, while the silver denarius averaged at least 90.8%
purity, as compared with 85% for the same coins under Vespasian and Titus[156]. Immediately on his accession, he had to
find money for both the regular *congiarum* and the donative,
only two years after the preceding one. Finally, there were a
number of works left incomplete when Titus died - the Flavian
amphitheatre, the temple of Vespasian and Titus, the baths of
Titus and the arch of Titus, and he had also to see to the
rebuilding of the Capitol and the restoration of a number of
edifices on the Campus Martius (the Pantheon, the Odeum and
the Serapeum) that had suffered in the fire of 80[157]. In
these circumstances, it is clear that Domitian had substantial
sums of money available for distribution early in his reign;
possibly his eagerness to spend aroused the opposition of the
careful Tiberius Julius, Aug. lib., leading to his dismissal[158]. But he did have the money to spend; at the very
least, he was left a balanced budget. Therefore, Titus'
financial acumen must be recognized; the economy did not
suffer during his reign. His much-proclaimed generosity
(*Titus* 7.3, 8.1) should not obscure the force of Dio's comment
that "in money matters Titus was frugal and made no unnecessary expenditures" (66.19.3).

Ample scope for his generosity was soon provided by the
natural disasters of his reign. The eruption of Vesuvius, the
most serious of these catastrophes, occurred on August 24,
79[159]. It resulted in the destruction of Pompeii, Herculaneum
and Stabiae; according to Dio (66.23), volcanic ash spread
even as far as Syria, Egypt and Africa, causing various
injuries to men, farms and cattle and destroying all fish and
birds. For areas with essentially pastoral and agricultural
industries, the consequences were far reaching. The resulting
shortage of food was aggravated by the outbreak of a serious
epidemic, described by Suetonius as the worst ever known
(*Titus* 8.3). The eruption also caused the death of the elder
Pliny, who, as prefect of the fleet at Misenum, had sailed up
to the scene of the disaster[160]. Titus reacted promptly. He
visited the area at once and again in the following year. To
expedite the work of reconstruction, he undertook the appointment of two *curatores restituendae Campaniae* who were to be
drawn by lot from senators of consular rank (*Titus* 8.4; Dio,
66.24.3). There is also epigraphic evidence of his activity
in repairing the damage at Naples caused by the earthquake
accompanying the eruption[161]. He provided some of the money
needed from his own resources, and, as well, made immediate

use of the property of those who had died without heirs (*Titus* 8.4): in view of the unexpected nature of the disaster, this was no doubt considerable. Now, legally, such property was *uacantia* and so belonged to the treasury[162]; but Titus simply assigned the proceeds to the rebuilding programme. Whilst, then, the total cost of the reconstruction was no doubt considerable, it must be stressed that this is not necessarily to be interpreted merely as evidence of the new emperor's generosity; his use of the *bona uacantia* indicates that his *parentis affectus* (*Titus* 8.3) was tempered by an almost Vespasianic financial acumen and that his generosity was balanced by a desire to avoid unnecessary expenditure (Dio, 66.19.3; cf. *Titus* 7.3, 8.1).

In 80, whilst he was in Campania on his second visit to the disaster area, Rome faced a further crisis when a fire ravaged the city for three days and nights, spreading over large sections and destroying the temple of Jupiter Capitolinus, the Pantheon, the porticus of Octavia and its library, the temples of Neptune, Isis and Serapis, the theatre of Balbus, the baths of Agrippa and many others (Dio, 66.24.1-2): in particular, the area around the Campus Martius and the Circus Flaminius, to the north-west of the city, suffered most[163]. Titus assumed responsibility for the cost of reconstruction; he is even said to have stripped his own villas of their decorations, distributing them amongst the ruined temples and public buildings (*Titus* 8.4). More importantly, he appointed a commission of knights to assist with the work of restoration. Suetonius, however, stresses the cost involved: "he was more generous than any of his predecessors" (*Titus* 7.3), his staff felt that he was "promising more than he could perform" (8.1). Yet, despite the huge sums that must have been involved, he still managed to leave his brother a well-filled treasury.

The references in the literary sources to Titus' generosity are supported by more concrete examples. Taxes were remitted, notably those imposed by Vespasian in Rhodes and Cos[164]. The provincial tax on Caesarea was abolished by the gift of *ius Italicum*, whilst Aventicum in Helvetia may also have received benefits[165]. But it would be unwise to read too much into what may well have been isolated examples of tax-remissions. Despite his reputation, officially fostered, for open-handed liberality, he was no doubt aware of the problems such a policy would pose. Indeed, an examination of his financial measures in Egypt, the one province with something like detailed evidence, suggests that his generosity to Rhodes, Cos and Caesarea was balanced by substantially increased revenues from the Nile Valley.

He turned his attention, as his father had done, to the problem of private estates in the area. It was not so much that Vespasian and Titus ceased to favour the formation of new private estates; rather, they insisted that the buyers be residents in the country, not members of the imperial house

nor of the senatorial or equestrian aristocracy, nor imperial
freedmen, nor even wealthy Alexandrians. Apparently, the
local administrators of Egypt, including even the prefects,
had found it a far from easy task to force noble landowners to
fulfil their financial obligations and so vast amounts of
highly taxed land were financially unproductive; they represented a loss to the crown. The new policy involved the
liquidation of many of these vast estates and the suppression
of absentee ownership. The appropriated tracts of fertile
land were either sold or let to anyone who wished to become a
small landholder, thus increasing the number of landowners and
the amount of crown revenue[166]. Further impetus was probably
provided by the events of 69/70. Possession of Egypt had been
vital and it remained a most favourable base of operations for
any rival claimant to the throne. Liquidation of the large
estates was consistent with such a fear. One should not, then,
be confused by Titus' official propaganda which stressed his
liberality rather than his financial acumen. The latter he
had inherited from his father, grandfather and great-
grandfather; as well, he had had the advantage of a court
education, and, more recently, of assistance from Tiberius
Julius, Aug. lib.[167]. He was well aware of the need to
observe the formalities and appear to be generous, and at the
same time ensure that he had the funds to be so.

PUBLIC WORKS

So Titus was able to pour vast amounts of capital into
extensive building schemes in Rome, Italy and the provinces.
In honour of his deified father, he proposed to erect a
temple on a site south of the temple of Concord. Although the
interior work was completed under Domitian, the foundations
and the core of the podium, at least, were almost certainly
built during Titus' reign: later, it was named the *templum
Vespasiani et Titi*[168]. He also continued the construction of
the Flavian amphitheatre, possibly adding the third and fourth
levels, together with some rows of seating, to the first two
tiers already built by Vespasian; this, at any rate, is
suggested by the depiction of the amphitheatre on a coin of
his reign where the external view of four tiers and the
internal view of the seating is represented[169]. In the same
district, he appropriated land to the west of the *domus aurea*
and arranged for the construction of the relatively modest
baths which the space permitted. Suetonius comments that they
were built in great haste (*Titus* 7.3), presumably for the
opening of the amphitheatre, but they seem to have been
finished by his brother, since the Chronographer of A.D. 354
lists them under the works of that emperor[170]. The completion
of his additions to the Flavian amphitheatre was celebrated by
a spectacular hundred-day festival, with seafights staged on
an artificial lake, infantry battles, wild beast hunts and

other similar activities (Dio, 66.25). It would not be
appropriate to regard these celebrations associated with the
dedication simply as an example of frivolous spending.
According to Suetonius (*Titus* 7.3), they were "most magnificent and costly". But, with the recent natural disasters - the
eruption of Vesuvius, the accompanying shortage of food, the
severe epidemic and the fire that ravaged parts of Rome -
civilian morale must have been at a low ebb, a factor that
Titus was too wise to neglect. In these circumstances,
liberality and munificence would hardly have seemed out of
place.

Within Rome, a number of aqueducts were repaired, notably
the *aqua Marcia* and the *aqua Claudia*[171]. He organized the
reconstruction of the temple to Jupiter Capitolinus after its
destruction in the fire of 80[172]; also attributed to him is
an arch, the ground plan of which was uncovered within the
Circus Maximus. It could well be the remains of the arch
voted to Titus by the senate during his reign in honour of the
capture of Jerusalem, while the famous arch of Titus on the
Sacra Via may have been commenced in his reign for another
purpose and only later became a monument in honour of his
deification[173].

The substantial construction in Rome was matched in Italy
and the provinces, and though private individuals were no
doubt responsible for part of the cost, the greater proportion
of the work was almost certainly undertaken with treasury
funds. The ruins of baths uncovered north of the Via dell'
Annunziata are probably the remains of those build by him in
81[174]; a temple was constructed at Borussia Rhenana; in
Laodicia in Phrygia, an amphitheatre and a stadium were
erected, the former being dedicated to him[175]; the *aqua
Curtia* and the *aqua Caerulea*, supplying water to the *aqua
Claudia*, were renovated, though they had been repaired by
Vespasian a decade earlier; an aqueduct was also added to the
temple of Zeus at Smyrna[176]. There is evidence, too, of his
concern for the maintenance of canals in Egypt, for the
construction of a temple to Aphrodite Cypria and himself as a
god in Cyprus, for the baths and a porch at Aperle in Lycia,
for the restoration of an Augusteum at Ephesus, and for a
variety of other works at Smyrna, Ephesus, Cyprus, Moesia,
Karnak and Hippo[177]. In Britain, the completion of the
basilica at Verulamium was commemorated by the erection of a
huge inscription some fourteen feet by two. Apparently, the
devastation caused by Boudicca's rebellion had been
repaired[178].

Substantial sums of money were devoted to an extensive
programme of road construction and maintenance. Within Italy,
inscriptions attest to the completion of the Via Flavia from
Trieste to Polla, and to the reconstruction of the Via Aurelia
and of the Via Flaminia[179]. In the provinces, roadwork was
continued in Cyprus and Numidia[180], whilst the Via Nova in

Spain, already begun by Vespasian, was of particular concern
to Titus and virtually completed by him, as a number of
recently discovered milestones indicate[181]. Most significantly, he concentrated on the Cappadocia-Galatia area, the new
province of the early seventies. Its governors were senators
of proven loyalty and competence who had served the regime with
distinction in the civil war period. Under Vespasian and
Titus, a vast network of military roads was developed, extending from Lycaonia in the south and Pisidia in the west to the
Euphrates frontier and the Pontic coast[182]. Titus gave
considerable impetus to the programme initiated by his father,
with the appointment of his relative A. Caesennius Gallus as
governor; his term (80-82) was in fact the most active in the
development of this complex network of strategic roads[183].
That the programme was expensive is beyond doubt, but subsequent events justified the cost and testify to the foresight
of Vespasian and Titus; the Parthian frontier was secure and
peaceful, and the way open for a future policy of expansion
under Trajan.

In short, Vespasian had left his son a large reserve in
the treasury, enabling him to provide for the demands on the
public purse traditionally made in the first months of a new
emperor's reign, and, whilst the unpredictable disasters of 79
and 80 were enormously costly, he was still able to make
considerable progress in alleviating the immediate distress,
for he had retained his father's financial adviser, and was
not himself lacking in economic skills. His early experience
in Nero's court,and later in Vespasian's, served him well.
He could be the charming and affable diplomat, and, at the
same time, display the shrewdness and practicality of his
immediate ancestors[184]; unlike them, he knew that it was
advisable to disguise such talents. He made much of his
liberality and generosity, for words were less expensive than
deeds: his famous comment, "I have wasted a day" (*Titus* 8.1),
reportedly made when a day passed without a benefit being
conferred on anyone, should be regarded as little more than a
reflection of the historical tradition he himself imposed. The
fact that he broke with custom by ratifying in a single edict
all the *beneficia* conferred by previous emperors attracted the
attention of both Suetonius (*Titus* 8.1) and Dio (66.19.3);
for Suetonius, it was consistent with his overwhelming
generosity and hence the anecdote serves to introduce a series
of items in the same vein. Yet the *beneficia* in question had
already passed his father's scrutiny. Titus' generosity was
illusory. Again, it is possible to discern in a number of
items that his publicly acclaimed liberality was tempered with
thinly disguised efficiency and administrative common sense.
After the eruption of Vesuvius, the work of restoration was
thoroughly organized by the commission of *curatores restituendae Campaniae*; even more valuable was his appropriation of
the property that passed to the state as a result of persons

dying without heirs. His retention of the proceeds of the
subsiciua and the more efficient collection of taxes from
Egypt conferred immense advantages. The same trait is evident
in the recently discovered letter to the Muniguenses, pro-
claiming his generosity *(malui cum indulgentia...loqui)* but
nonetheless rejecting their appeal against having to pay a sum
of money to a certain Servilius Pollio:-

> The emperor Titus Caesar Vespasian Augustus, pontifex
> maximus, of tribunician power for the eighth time,
> saluted as victorious commander fourteen times, consul
> seven times, father of his country, sends greetings to
> the *quattuoruiri* and decurions of Munigua. Since you
> have appealed against having to pay the sum of money
> which, according to the decision of Sempronius Fuscus,
> you owed Servilius Pollio, the penalty for an improper
> appeal should have been exacted from you. But I have
> preferred to speak with my accustomed generosity rather
> than with your temerity and have remitted 50,000
> sesterces on the grounds of the poverty which you have
> claimed on behalf of your community. I have written to
> my friend the proconsul Gallicanus that you should have
> paid Pollio the sum awarded but that he is to release you
> from the interest, calculated from the day that the
> decision was made. It would be fair to take into account
> the profits from your own revenues which you said were
> leased by Pollio so that your community incurs no loss
> from this transaction. Farewell. Given on September
> 7[185].

Ultimately, the success of his economic policy was demonstrated by the substantial sums available to his brother in
the early years of his reign. He could not have spent as he
did if he had inherited a depleted treasury. Titus' reputation for generosity and liberality, then, was the deliberate
result of his own propaganda, and experience had taught him
the virtue of disguising his financial acumen. Dio provides
the fairest summary of his economic policy: "In money matters,
Titus was frugal and made no unnecessary expenditure" (66.19.
3).

LEGISLATIVE ACTIVITY

Recorded evidence for legislative activity in Titus' reign is
slight and what survives represents for the most part minor
modifications to existing laws to ensure more efficient
administration. In general, popular social measures were his
focal point and the major beneficiary of his reforms was the
army, notably in the areas of land ownership, marriage and
testamentary freedom.

Five military diplomas survive from the period 79-81 -
one records privileges to veterans (right of marriage and
exemption from taxes on land allotted to them)[186], whilst the

others refer to grants of *ciuitas* and *conubium* for soldiers in Pannonia and Germany and for *classiarii* in Egypt[187]. These documents have recently received attention in an attempt to find some pattern in the ever-changing format of military diplomas during the period from 54 to 100[188]. An examination of all the relevant documents has led to a broad division into three main types, viz. I, issued to serving soldiers only; II, issued to both serving soldiers and veterans; and III, issued to veterans only. Types I and III had been in use since the reign of Claudius[189], but the first known instance of II belongs to Titus' reign[190]. Apparently, the intention was to unify the system of granting diplomas; whether discharged or not, soldiers were to be granted a diploma after twenty-five years of service, and so the change of format under Titus was an attempt at administrative reorganization aimed at greater systematization and improved efficiency.

Further military reform under Titus is referred to in the *Digest*:-

The deified Julius Caesar was the first who granted soldiers the free power to make a will, but this concession was only temporary. The first after him to confer this power was the deified Titus[191].

According to the *Digest*, the bill was based on the analogy of Julius Caesar's temporary law[192], a reading rejected by some scholars[193] who regard the reference to Caesar's concession as an interpolation and hold that testamentary freedom for soldiers within Roman law should be attributed to Titus.

With regard to the civil sphere, a bill was introduced by Titus which reduced to one the number of praetors appointed to supervise and control the powers of trustees appointed under wills:-

The deified Claudius added two praetors who administered justice in matters of trust, one of whom the deified Titus dispensed with[194].

Prior to this, in accordance with an innovation of Claudius, there were two *praetores fideicommissarii*[195], and the reduction under Titus was consistent with the stricter interpretation of the law of property throughout the principate, when testamentary bequests (trusts) passed from the field of moral to that of legal obligation[196]. Another passage from the *Digest* records a law introduced by Titus concerning the "prescription of twenty years" (*praescriptio uiginti annorum*) that was required before ownership of the property of an intestate deceased (*bona uacantia*) could be established:-

The deified Pius stated in a rescript to Coelius Amarantus that notice to the treasury (i.e. *fiscus*) of an estate without an owner was prescribed after four years and that this time should be calculated from the day when it began to be certain that there was no heir and no possessor under praetorian law. The prescription of twenty years, however, which is observed with reference

to the property of persons who have been notified, and do
not institute proceedings to recover it, is, according to
a constitution of the deified Titus, usually calculated
from the day on which anything could begin to belong to
the treasury (i.e. *fiscus*)197.
Titus' law, together with the modification of Antoninus Pius,
provided that the property of an intestate deceased could
legally belong to a squatter only so long as he could prove
that he had been in possession of it for a period of twenty
years and so long as he made some effort to undermine the
testator's status within four years of his death; it is also
of some interest in that it assists in determining the precise
function of the imperial treasuries (*aerarium* and *fiscus*).
Now, under Augustus' *Lex Julia de maritandis ordinibus*, the
property of an intestate deceased passed to the *aerarium*, and,
according to Tacitus (*Ann*. 3.25; 28), the *Lex Papia Poppaea*
had similar provisions. However, the *fiscus'* claim to such
bona uacantia is first attested in the reign of Tiberius and
was thereafter well established (*Ann*. 2.48.1; Pliny, *Ep*.
10.84); indeed, by the middle of the second century, a
procedure had been established whereby the *bona* were turned
over directly to the *fiscus*. So, in 79, when Titus used "for
the rebuilding of the buried cities the property of those who
lost their lives in Vesuvius and had left no heirs alive"
(*Titus* 8.4), it would seem that, by law, such *bona uacantia*
should have been claimed by the *aerarium*. However, as the
rescript of Antoninus Pius indicates, Titus must have legal-
ized what had been the practice for some time and so affirmed
the *fiscus'* claims. This was hardly an act of usurpation;
the distinction between public (*aerarium*) and imperial
(*fiscus*) revenues had surely been blurred for decades. The
emperor controlled both and any transference of jurisdiction
did not involve conflict between imperial and senatorial
powers. Titus' legislation, then, may be viewed as essentially a matter of administrative convenience198.

Finally, there is Pliny's reference to letters from Titus
to the Lacedaemonians and the Achaeans concerning the position
of children born free but abandoned and subsequently sold into
slavery (*Ep*. 10.65.1-3). Unfortunately, no other details on
Titus' legislation with regard to foundlings have come to
light, and Pliny's reference is too brief to provide an
accurate idea of the contents of Titus' correspondence.

Whilst, to some extent, these legislative changes were
purely administrative and to be expected in the normal development of the empire, they are not inconsistent with his
policy of widely advertised generosity coupled with a drive
for greater efficiency and firm financial control.

PROVINCIAL POLICY

In Titus' brief reign, it is difficult to detect any diverg-
ence from his father's provincial and foreign policies. For
both of these skilled and experienced commanders, enduring
stability implied further conquests, where necessary, together
with a reorganization of existing territory to provide for
future expansion as well as for immediate consolidation. It
would be quite erroneous to stress the defensive nature of
their foreign policy, for it was essentially aggressive -
though any territorial advances were carefully and thoroughly
prepared. Whilst the legions became more and more sedentary,
with forts rebuilt in stone, it was not unusual to find
legionary detachments sent and established further afield.
Thus in 81, Titus established a new permanent camp in stone
for a detachment of the *III Augusta*[199] at Lambaesis in
Numidia to thwart the incursion of tribes on the empire's
frontiers. Likewise in the east, Vespasian's policy was
continued. The extensive programme of road-building undertak-
en in the seventies was expanded by Titus and a network of
military roads developed, and though the reorganization was
not put to the test for another forty years, Trajan's rapid
advances in Armenia and Mesopotamia were prepared and
facilitated by the forethought of Vespasian and Titus[200].
Their programme was virtually completed during A. Caesennius
Gallus' term as governor of Cappadocia-Galatia (80-82); his
activity is attested by inscriptions from a number of different roads and the dedication from the fort at Dascusa on the
Euphrates[201].
    In the northern provinces too, Titus persisted with his
father's objective of connecting the Rhine and Danube legions
by establishing a continuous chain of military posts between
them. Forts and strategic roads were built or rebuilt[202]
with the aim of closing the gap in the fort system between
Oberstimm and Linz in Upper Austria. As part of this
programme, a road was constructed on the northern bank of the
Danube, starting somewhere near Neuburg and crossing to the
south bank near the newly established fort at Eining. An
inscription from 80 found at Kösching[203] indicates that
activity continued in the region during Titus' reign, but it
would be hazardous to speculate on what further plans, if any,
he had formed to deal with the problems in this area.
Presumably, Vespasian's strategy was to be followed closely.
    In the main, our knowledge of his frontier policy depends
on archaeological and epigraphic evidence alone, and in view
of the brevity of his reign, any assessment of his intentions
must be regarded with caution. Tacitus' *Agricola*, of course,
represents something of an exception, yet difficulties are
encountered in evaluating this invaluable source of information. The chronology of Agricola's tenure has been hotly
disputed, but it seems most likely that his governorship began

in 77 and ended in 83/84[204]. On this basis, the campaigns undertaken in Titus' reign were those of the fourth and fifth seasons, with a policy of continued expansion together with the consolidation of previous gains to prepare the way for the subjugation of further territory. His third year in Britain (79) had seen the conquest of virtually the entire area of the Scottish lowlands between the Tyne-Solway and Forth-Clyde isthmuses; at the same time, the gains were secured by the construction of a series of forts throughout the entire area[205]. It would not be unreasonable to assume that in this, the last year of Vespasian's reign, Titus was even more closely involved with military planning and had fully approved of Agricola's plans. With the accession of Titus, however, his activities were more restrained and the fourth season (80) saw the establishment of a chain of forts along the Forth-Clyde isthmus and the consolidation of the area behind it[206]. There is no reason whatsoever to interpret this as an indication of the new emperor's supposedly conservative foreign policy or as evidence of conflict between Agricola and Titus; after all, it was not Titus who ordered the closure of Inchtuthil[207]. Quite the contrary - this was the necessary prelude to a period of future expansion. Agricola may well have expected to be replaced after having served the more or less regular three terms in office, but his spectacular successes had earned the enthusiastic support of both Vespasian and Titus. Thus, in the following season (his fifth, in 81), the advance began again. He crossed the Clyde, "subdued in a series of successful actions tribes hitherto unknown and drew up his troops on the side of Britain facing Ireland"[208]. The conquest of the entire south-west was all but complete.

Apart from hostilities in Britain, the only recorded disturbance occurred in the east and involved the Parthians. The details of their relationship with Titus remain obscure. It would seem that the power struggle between Pacorus and Vologaeses[209] (I, II or possibly both) prevented any chance of contact, but, so far as is known, Titus failed to make any real attempt to exploit the situation. Dio, however, does refer (66.19.3) to the appearance of a certain Terentius Maximus who attempted to impersonate Nero[210]. He was an Asian by birth, but bore a striking resemblance to Nero in appearance, voice and musical talent. The somewhat hazy details of Nero's death combined with his popularity in the east gave rise to hopes that he was still alive[211]. Some indication of the influence of such a pretender and of his reception by local and imperial officials emerges from Dio's account of the appearance of a pseudo-Alexander in 221:-

A *daemon* calling himself Alexander of Macedon and resembling him in appearance and dress set off from the region of the Danube... and travelled through Moesia and Thrace... All those who were with him in Thrace attest that accommodation and provisions were provided for him at public expense. Not a soul, neither governor nor soldier nor procurator, not the magistrates of the local communities, dared to withstand him or say anything against him (79.18.1-3).

Such pretenders, then, were potentially dangerous. Terentius, it seems, gained a few followers in Asia, acquired more supporters as he advanced to the Euphrates and finally sought refuge with Artabanus IV, the Parthian *archegos* (Dio, 66.19.3). The Parthian king (*basileus*), Pacorus II, had been challenged by Artabanus IV, whose brief period of influence can be dated from his coins to Oct. 80 - Oct. 81[212], and presumably Titus refused to recognize the legitimacy of his claim[213]. Relations between them became strained. As a result, "Artabanus, because of his anger against Titus, received Terentius and set about making preparations to restore him to Rome" (Dio, 66.19.3). Dio, it should be noted, describes Artabanus as *archegos* (leader) but not as *basileus*. John of Antioch provides further details: "Terentius fled to the Parthians, claiming that they owed him some recompense for the return of Armenia. He accomplished nothing worthwhile, his identity was discovered and he soon perished"[214]. It would seem that Terentius claimed support from the Parthians in return for the Neronian settlement of Armenia, but was unable to persuade them to assist him. The likeliest interpretation is that Pacorus himself removed both Terentius and Artabanus. On the other hand, it is just possible that Titus had to use force to suppress Terentius, receiving thereby his sixteenth imperial salutation[215]. In this case, either Terentius must have received military assistance from the Parthians and crossed the Euphrates again to meet the Romans - both Dio and John of Antioch emphasize that he had crossed the river and fled to the Parthians - or else, the governor of Syria led an expeditionary force across the river's eastern bank and overwhelmed the opposition[216]. Clearly, the sources are too vague to permit an accurate assessment. At all events, the Flavian arrangements in the east easily withstood the challenge, such as it was, and proved to be more than adequate to deal with any trouble.

Associated directly with his foreign policy were a number of specific measures designed to consolidate the empire. He persisted with his father's practice of founding colonies and extending the citizenship. Turning from Spain to other areas, he saw to the completion of Vespasian's colony of Aventicum[217] and undertook the foundation of a similar establishment at Doclea in Dalmatia. Since a substantial proportion of the ruling class there bore the name Flavius and belonged to the Quirina tribe, it would seem that a wholesale grant of citizenship coincided with the foundation of the *municipium*, almost certainly in Titus' reign[218]. Doclea soon became the most important centre in the south-east of the country, overshadowing the coastal foundations of earlier periods.

Consistent with this attitude was the advancement of senators from the Greek east, who, as has been seen, were appointed to the command of imperial praetorian provinces (Ti. Julius Celsus Polemaeanus to Lycia-Pamphylia) and granted the *fasces* (T. Junius Montanus) during his reign[219].

IMPERIAL CULT

Of some considerable interest is Titus' view of the imperial cult, and, in particular, of the deification of the first non-Julio-Claudian emperor. The precise date of Vespasian's *consecratio* has long puzzled scholars and it has often been argued that it must have occurred not long after July 79[220]. Augustus and Claudius were deified within a month or so of their deaths, as were Titus and most of Domitian's success- ors[221]. Again, Vespasian had been well aware that the Flavian *gens* had no strong claims to provide an enduring dynasty[222], and therefore he made consistent efforts to remedy the defect. What he could not do, though, was to have a *domus diuina*, a *Flauiae templum gentis* (*Dom.* 5, 15.2, 17.3), a college of *Flauiales* (*Dom.* 4.4) and divine filiation for his sons. It was up to Titus to make good these deficiencies and as soon as possible. He should, so it is argued, have done so at once. The evidence, however, is clear. Vespasian was not deified until more than six months after his death; more precisely, the *consecratio* is to be assigned to the first months of 80 and before May at the latest[223].

The reasons for the delay are not immediately obvious. Hostility between father and son following the deaths of Eprius Marcellus and Caecina Alienus has, not very convincing- ly, been suggested as a reason for the postponement[224]: but the existence of such hostility is highly unlikely. The sources would surely have alluded to it in the context of his evil reputation at the time of his accession, and, in any case, it was so clearly to Titus' advantage to have his father deified that their personal relationship and his real attitude to his father's memory would have been utterly irrelevant in this situation. The eruption of Vesuvius some two months after Vespasian's death[225] may perhaps have rendered inapprop- riate and unseasonable the public celebration[226] of a *consecratio*, but such an explanation also lacks plausibility.

On the other hand, the deification of an emperor not connected with the Julio-Claudians was without precedent and posed a number of practical problems. No doubt Vespasian could be presented as having earned a *consecratio* by his impressive array of honours and by his truly Augustan image, the successor not so much of Otho and Vitellius but rather of Galba: his apotheosis was hardly likely to be met with the sort of opposition that Antoninus Pius faced fifty years later at the proposed deification of Hadrian[227]. But it was an innovation, and, as well, the very nature of the imperial

cult required a certain amount of preparation.
Religious emotion was not automatically connected with
the cult. On the contrary, there is not the slightest
evidence of any such displays. No *ex uoto* offerings have
survived to attest to the piety of the worshippers. No
person in the empire, so far as is known, ever addressed a
prayer to an emperor living or dead. They were, of course,
venerated - but so were the legionary standards, and no one
prayed to them[228]. Participation in the cult in the
provinces was essentially a political and social matter. For
persons of wealth and ambition, provincial priesthoods
provided access to greater honours[229]. So the problem facing
Titus in the extension of the existing imperial cult was
essentially administrative. A new municipal and provincial
flaminate was required together with the erection of a
suitable temple in Rome and the careful presentation of the
consecratio on the coinage. Once adequate preparations were
in train, the ceremony could proceed, but haste was not
essential, for Titus clearly did not feel any immediate need
for the support of a deified parent.

In 80, then, he set about the institution of a cult. He
chose the space to the south of the temple of Concord as the
site for a temple in honour of his father; ultimately, it was
called the *templum Vespasiani et Titi* and completed by
Domitian[230]. The *consecratio* was widely portrayed on the
coins, with Vespasian appearing togate and radiate[231], whilst,
in many cities of the empire, *flamines* for the cult of the
deified Vespasian were appointed either by decree of the
local decurions or else by imperial nomination[232]. Since the
official creation of a *diuus* by senatorial decree was a
particularly Roman practice, *flamines* are found in the western
provinces rather than in the Greek east. He also secured the
deification of Domitilla; though her identity has not been
definitely established, she was almost certainly his sister
and not his mother[233]. His daughter Julia also received the
title *Augusta* and was associated on coins with Venus and
Vesta[234].

In most of his administrative activities, the imprint of
his personality is clear, even though many of his measures
differed but little in their essentials from the Vespasianic
model. To some extent, the brevity of his reign limited
opportunities for innovation and enforced the apparent
similarity of policies. However, he knew well that, to
ensure good government in the long term, he had to improve his
public image, so damaged by his actions in the seventies,
especially the executions of Eprius Marcellus and Caecina
Alienus in 79. Hence he was liberal and generous; he
proclaimed his own *clementia*. Yet this quality was never
regarded as one of the Republican virtues, but, rather, as one
of the privileges of an autocrat[235]. Indeed, Titus' *clementia*
represented the liberality and generosity to be expected from

an emperor who was essentially a shrewd financier, an
experienced politician and an able diplomat. Speculation as
to whether his supposed lavishness would finally have ruined
the empire had he lived longer is obviously pointless; we can
but note that Domitian began his reign with a surplus. Titus
deliberately chose to portray himself as generous, just as his
father had preferred to be seen as parsimonious. It was a
shrewd manoeuvre, for it tended to disarm opposition.
Objections from the recipients of governmental liberality tend
to be few, and premature death served only to reinforce the
official image that was widely accepted and believed by subsequent writers.

DEATH AND DEIFICATION

Titus' benevolent reign did not have to face the test of time,
for, at the age of forty-one, after twenty-six months and
twenty days as emperor, he died on September 13, 81[236].
Subsequently, the circumstances surrounding his death were
held to have been suspicious, and so persistently was Domitian
implicated in the rumours that Titus' unidentified final
regret[237] (*Titus* 10.1) was popularly attributed to his failure
to eliminate his brother (Dio, 66.26.2-3). The accusations
against Domitian, however, appear to have been unjustified and
an examination of the evidence suggests strongly that he died
of natural causes, though there is also the possibility that,
during the last months of his life, he was aware that death
was near.
     According to Suetonius (*Titus* 10.1), he became so
despondent, presumably during the final celebrations for the
dedication of the Flavian amphitheatre, that he wept publicly
and became even more depressed "because a victim had escaped
as he was sacrificing and because there had been thunder from
a clear sky". In this state of mind, he set out for the
Sabine country of his ancestors, but, at the first resting
point on the journey, he contracted a fever which proved
fatal; he died in the same villa as his father[238]. Such is
the version outlined by Suetonius, followed by the anonymous
epitomator of Aurelius Victor's *De Caesaribus* and frequently
accepted in modern literature, even though other ancient
authors provide widely contrasting accounts. The difference
between the Epitome of the *De Caesaribus* and the original is
remarkable, for, in the latter, Titus is said to have been
poisoned (*De Caes.* 10.11)[239]. This version, often repeated
by mediaeval writers, was also favoured by the notoriously
unreliable Philostratus; according to him, Titus died after
eating the poisonous fish known as the sea-hare that had been
introduced into his food by Domitian:-

> The sea-hare produces a peculiar liquid, more poisonous
> than any other creature on land or sea. Nero used to mix
> it into his dishes to dispose of his greatest enemies,

and Domitian used it to dispose of his brother Titus, not because he dreaded sharing power with his brother so much as doing so with a kind and honest man (*Vita Apoll.* 6.32). Other writers implicate the younger brother[240]. Suetonius believes that, when Titus was dangerously ill, Domitian ordered him to be left for dead (*Dom.* 2.3), whereas, according to Dio, Domitian plunged him into a vessel packed with snow while he was still breathing so as to hasten his end (66.26. 2-3). On the other hand, Plutarch (*De Sanitate Tuenda* 3) claims that he died through unwise use of the baths when ill; and, for the Jews, his early death represented vengeance from heaven for the destruction of Jerusalem - in their tradition, he was supposed to have been tormented day and night by the noise of a gnat which had lodged in his brain for seven years and which grew as large as a dove, finally causing death[241]. More recently, it has been argued that he died of malignant malaria, contracted in the Sabine country[242]. The symptoms evident at his death were similar to those of malaria, but since Roman writers were quite familiar with the type of fever normally associated with such a disease, and since his contemporaries were puzzled over the cause of his death, it would seem possible that a less common, but more malignant form of malaria was responsible. Finally, it could well be that, for some time prior to his death, Titus was aware that he was suffering from a terminal illness - hence the reference in Suetonius (*Titus* 10.1) to his fits of depression, presumably at the dedication of the Flavian amphitheatre, and his departure, in that state of mind, for the Sabine country of his ancestors. But the details provided are not fully consistent with such a theory. The spectacles which Titus gave at the opening in 80 (*Titus* 7.3) lasted one hundred days (Dio, 66.25), but it was not until the summer of the following year that he left for the Sabine country; he was still in Rome on May 19, 81, attending a meeting of the Arval Brethren[243]. Suetonius may be referring to some other *spectacula* or perhaps the public shedding of tears was intended to reflect his concern for the victims of the various natural catastrophes of the year rather than his fear of imminent death, though, in this case, one would have expected the compliant sources to have recorded such an explanation. The theory that he was suffering from a terminal illness should, then, be rejected, and in view of the plethora of inconsistent explanations provided by the ancient sources, it seems probable that he died unexpectedly of natural causes and that the rumours of foul play should be regarded as unfounded.

Despite the animosity between them, Domitian delivered the funeral eulogy himself (Dio, 67.2.6) and had Titus deified. The apotheosis took place some time after Oct. 1, 81, for, on that date, the minutes of the Arval Brethren refer to Julia as *T. imp. f.*, not *diui Titi f.*[244]; the only other indication in the sources is Dio's brief statement (67.2.6)

implying that Domitian deified his brother without delay[245].
According to the ancient sources, Domitian's honours for Titus
were minimal, the *consecratio* being the only mark of respect
given him (*Dom.* 2.3). The inaccuracy of such statements can
easily be demonstrated. At Rome, Domitian undertook the
construction of several monuments in honour of Titus. The
temple of Vespasian begun by Titus was completed under
Domitian, who included the cult statue of his brother as well
as that of his father, and changed the building's name to the
templum Vespasiani et Titi[246]. On the Campus Martius, the
porticus diuorum was erected; its three temples suggest that
the worship of the three Flavians was intended[247]. A further
indication that the cult of Titus was included is provided by
the *Lex Collegi Aesculapi et Hygiae* of 153, for we are told
that the members of this *collegium* met at the porticus, in the
aede diui Titi[248]. Titus also shared in the honour of the
templum gentis Flauiae, which was built on the site of
Domitian's birthplace and loudly acclaimed by the poets
Statius and Martial[249]. He also received honours independent-
ly of his father and brother. An arch now generally known as
the arch of Titus was erected on the Sacra Via. It used to be
thought that it had been built by later emperors, but the
principal objection to accepting a Domitianic date, that of
ill-feeling between the two brothers, does not provide an
adequate reason for rejecting the clear evidence of archi-
tectural styles[250]. The arch celebrates Titus' *consecratio*
and his early victory over the Jews. The former is symbolized
on the ceiling of the vault, with Titus astride an eagle being
carried upwards[251], whilst, in other scenes on the inner walls
of the arch, the spoils from the Temple of Jerusalem are shown
being carried into Rome, and Titus in triumphal garb appears
riding a chariot, surrounded by attendants, crowned by a
winged figure of Victory and about to pass through a triumphal
arch with Roma guiding his horses.

Furthermore, on his death, there appeared a college or
number of colleges with members responsible for the cult of
the deceased Flavian emperors. The names assigned to the new
college suggest that the original priesthood of Vespasian,
the *sodales Flauiales*, was given the additional responsibility
for the cult of Titus, since the college came to be known as
the *sodales Flauiales Titiales* or the *sodales Titiales
Flauiales*[252]. The appearance of the term *sodales Titiales*
possibly resulted from a shortening of the longer form when
the memory of Titus' benevolent rule had overshadowed that of
his father. In the municipalities, the cult of Titus was
served by *flamines*; epigraphic evidence of their existence is
widespread throughout the empire[253].

Titus was endowed with considerable natural charm, talent
and intelligence. He had an excellent memory and an ability
to learn all the skills of peace and war. He handled weapons
and rode like an expert; he could compose poetry and speeches

both in Latin and Greek, and was a competent singer and harpist. Furthermore, he had had the advantage of excellent tutors at court during the fifties, in Judaea in the sixties, and, of course, during his father's principate in the following decade. His success as emperor can then be attributed to his personal qualities and the thorough preparation he had received for his task. Essentially, his reputation was deserved. In his brief reign, the new dynasty was firmly established. There is no reason to doubt that he maintained the high standard of administrative competence in Italy and throughout the empire. Suggestions of a forthcoming economic disaster should be treated with extreme caution and care taken not to be misled by Titus' own propaganda; for his *clementia*, that much-proclaimed virtue of an autocrat, was widely advertised but less widely practised. It was consistent with his view of the emperor's role, accurately summarized by Suetonius as *parentis affectus* (*Titus* 8.3). Benevolent, paternalistic autocracy had now emerged, power had become increasingly centralized in his hands, the senate was honoured but rendered ineffective. Titus was the model for Trajan and his successors.

To some extent, his reputation was enhanced by his early death, but there is no substantial reason to assume that disaster would have overtaken him had he lived longer. One can but lament the fact that his wise initiatives in administrative policy were, inevitably, so few.

NOTES

1. The precise date of his death is in dispute. According to Suetonius (*Vesp.* 24), it occurred on *viiii Kal. Iul.*, i.e. June 23, but most recent scholars accept June 24, on the basis of the length of his reign given in Dio, 66.17.3, e.g. Weynand, *RE* 6.2674; Hammond, 1938: p. 36; Homo, 1949: p. 383; Buttrey, 1980: pp. 7, 20. On the other hand, Braithwaite, 1927: p. 68; McCrum and Woodhead, 1966: p. 6; Garzetti, 1974: p. 257 prefer the 23rd. Holzapfel, 1921: p. 76, adopts the view that he died on the night of the 23rd/24th.

2. The extreme coldness and the curative powers of the springs at Cutiliae are noted by the elder Pliny:- *sed Cutiliae in Sabinis gelidissimae suctu quodam corpora inuadunt ut prope morsus uideri possit, aptissimae stomacho, neruis, uniuerso corpori*: *NH* 31.10. Similarly, Vitruvius 8.3; Celsus 4.5.

3. Most scholars reject the rumour, e.g. Homo, 1949: p. 382:- "un commérage sans plus" and Fortina, 1955a: p. 98:- "inverosimile". Garzetti, 1974: p. 259, notes that Titus was "the target of the persistent accusation...that he had poisoned his father as the crowning touch to behaviour that had long been disloyal... (but there is) much ampler and more explicit testimony to his complete loyalty".

4. It is difficult to assess the extent of his unpopularity. Suetonius, though, comments that he came to the throne *omnibus inuitis* (*Titus* 6.2).
5. Suetonius accuses him of *saeuitia, luxuria* and *libido* (*Titus* 7.1). The youthful Nero was similarly charged with *petulantia, libido, luxuria, auaritia* and *crudelitas* (*Nero* 26.1). Tacitus comments that *laetam uoluptatibus adulescentiam* (*Titus*) *egit*, but as well was *suo quam patris imperio moderatior*: *Hist*. 2.2. See Price, 1919: p. 39; Mooney, 1930: p. 484; Martinet, 1981: p. 66.
6. Suetonius' schematic arrangement focused attention on such changes. Chapters seven and eight of his *Titus* open as follows:- *praeter saeuitiam...* (7.1); *natura autem beneuolentissimus...* (8.1). More dramatic is the change in Gaius: *hactenus quasi de principe, reliqua ut de monstro narranda sunt* (22.1). In his *Domitian*, the opening lines of chapters eight to eleven illustrate the same technique:- *ius diligenter et industrie dixit...* (8.1); *inter initia usque adeo ab omni caede abhorrebat...* (9.1); *sed neque in clementiae neque in abstinentiae tenore permansit...* (10.1); *erat autem non solum magnae sed etiam callidae inopinantaeque saeuitiae...* (11.1). Dio, on the other hand, in discussing Titus' excellent character after his accession, offers an explanation: "This may have been because he had really undergone a change; indeed, for men to wield power as assistants to another is a very different thing from exercising independent authority themselves" (66.18.1).
7. There can be no doubt about her influence on Titus and its effect on his reputation: the sources (with the notable exception of Josephus) consistently refer to it, e.g. *Titus* 1; *Hist*. 2.2; Dio, 66.15.4; *Epit. de Caes*. 10.5.
8. Garzetti, 1974: p. 258.
9. See Waters, 1964: p. 49.
10. Vittinghoff, 1936: pp. 12-51.
11. *saeuitia* is the standard term to describe a tyrant: see Dunkle, 1971: pp. 12-20; Martinet, 1981: p. 66. Suetonius uses it at least once of Tiberius (61.2), Gaius (32.1), Claudius (15.4), Nero (33.1), Galba (12.1), Vitellius (13.1), Titus (7.1) and Domitian (10.1) - the *saeuitia* of *Vesp*. 1.1 refers to Domitian. In contrast is *clementia*, which Suetonius uses more rarely, e.g. of Augustus (51.1), Tiberius (53.2: but sarcastically, for not having had Agrippina strangled), Nero (10.1: Nero's declaration of his own good intentions early in his reign), Vitellius (14.2: again sarcastically, at the time of an execution), and Domitian (10.1: he was no longer *clemens*).
12. Levi, 1954: pp. 288-293.
13. Hammond, 1956: pp. 82-83; Garzetti, 1974: p. 258. For his post as *pontifex maximus*, see McGuire, 1980: pp. 147-149; Martinet, 1981: p. 98. Hammond, 1959: p. 97 and Blamberg, 1976: p. 133 n. 16, comment on the absence of the

post on Titus' early gold and silver coins, but see Mattingly, 1930: pp. 432, 223 (note) where he lists a coin with the legend *cos VII tr. p. VIII p. m.*, i.e. from July 79. On the other hand, Mattingly's reported denarius (p. 223) with the legend *cos VII tr. p. IX* (but no *p. m.*) has no authority: see Buttrey, 1980: p. 25. The title *pater patriae* did not appear on coins until later in 79: see Mattingly, p. lxxi; Hammond, 1959: p. 124. His consulships will be considered later; it is clear, however, that he was designated to his eighth consulship by Vespasian (*IGRR* 3.223: Titus is *cos. (VII) des. VIII* during his father's lifetime), despite Hammond, 1959: pp. 83, 118 ns. 162, 164, who argues that the designation did not occur until the very end of 79.

    14. *imp. XV* occurred later in 79 and is specifically attributed by Dio to the victory of Agricola in Britain (66.20.3). He was already *imp. XIV* in 78 (Buttrey, 1980: p. 19).

    15. Brunt, 1975b: p. 30.

    16. *imperaturus omnibus eligi debet ex omnibus*: Pan. 7.6

    17. *an senatum populumque Romanum, exercitus prouincias socios transmissurus uni successorem e sinu uxoris accipias, summaeque potestatis heredem tantum intra domum tuam quaeras? non totam per ciuitatem circumferas oculos et hunc tibi proximum, hunc coniunctissimum existimes, quem optimum quem dis simillimum inueneris?*: Pan. 7.5.

    18. *ad hoc audiebas senatus populique consensum: non unius Neruae iudicium illud, illa electio fuit...ille tantum iure principis occupauit, primusque fecit quod facturi omnes erant*: Pan. 10.2.

    19. See *PIR*² H 59. He served as quaestor under Claudius, as *legatus cum legione quaestorius* in Syria (*Ann.* 12.49), as tribune of the people under Nero (*Ann.* 13.28) and as praetor in 70 (*Hist.* 4.53).

    20. This could perhaps have seemed ominous in view of Caecina's fate in similar circumstances (*Titus* 6.2).

    21. For the conspiracy, see Price, 1919: p. 64; Mooney, 1930: p. 483; McGuire, 1980: pp. 152-159; Martinet, 1981: pp. 100-101. The *prouidentia* coins (see Mattingly, 1930: p. 259, Nos. 178-181) might have been issued to mark his escape; compare *ILS* 157, with its reference to Tiberius' escape from Sejanus:- ...*prouidentiae Ti. Caesaris Augusti nati ad aeternitatem Romani nominis, sublato hoste perniciosissimo p. R...*

    22. Most of these allegations against Domitian are accepted by, for example, Sutherland, 1935: pp. 155-156 and Morford, 1968: pp. 69-71, but rejected by Waters, 1964: pp. 56 ff. and Urban, 1971: pp. 76 ff., pp. 100-102.

    23. To this list one could perhaps add his refusal to marry his niece Julia, daughter of Titus (*Dom.* 22: accepted by Morford, 1968: p. 71 but rejected by Waters, 1963: p. 216)

and the allegation that he murdered Titus (Dio, 66.26.2; but see Bastomsky, 1967: pp. 22-23).

24. This is stressed by Urban, 1971: pp. 107 ff., who argues that Tacitus regarded Titus purely as a foil for Domitian; with Luck, 1964: pp. 73-75, he sees a parallel between Tiberius/Germanicus on the one hand, and Domitian/ Titus on the other. But without Tacitus' account of the reigns of Titus and Domitian, any attempt to assess accurately the role he assigned to Titus seems particularly hazardous.

25. e.g. Pliny, *Pan.* 48.4; *Dom.* 18.1; *Hist.* 4.40; *Agr.* 45.3.

26. Note, in particular, Syme, 1930: pp. 55-70; Rogers, 1960: pp. 19-23 (but compare Bauman, 1974: pp. 159-169); Pleket, 1961: pp. 296-315; Waters, 1963: pp. 198-218 and 1964: pp. 49-77; B.W. Jones, 1973: pp. 79-91; Devreker, 1977: pp. 223-243.

27. See Gallivan, 1981: pp. 189, 196, 199: it was not unknown, of course, for members of the Flavian family them-selves to hold ordinary consulships for six months, e.g. Vespasian and Titus in 70 (*ibid.*, p. 195).

28. See B.W. Jones, 1971: p. 270. Waters, 1963: p. 63, argues that Domitian was treated just as "the heir might have anticipated, unless he had formed the notion that Titus' special prerogatives under his father would now fall to him". It is quite likely, though, that Domitian had indeed formed such a notion: the difficulty is rather to determine the steps he took to achieve what he saw as his "rights". Evans, 1978: p. 113, describes his position in Titus' reign as "humiliating".

29. For Vespasian's status and financial position at various times, see Waters, 1964: pp. 52-65, and pp. 53-54 for the education of his sons; Morford, 1968: pp. 65-71, discuss-es the latter problem in more detail and stresses the dispar-ity of their early opportunities; for a more sceptical view of Vespasian's finances, see McGuire, 1980: pp. 109-193.

30. For general discussions on his status under Vespasian, see Gsell, 1894: pp. 6-31; *RE* 6.2544-2549; Kornemann, 1930: p. 62; Hammond, 1956: pp. 82-83; Waters, 1964: pp. 55-63; Morford, 1968: pp. 69-71; B.W. Jones, 1971: pp. 264-270. Apart from his lack of tribunician power and *imperium*, his inferior status was immediately obvious from the numeration of his consulships, which was always one below his brother's, e.g. in 76, Titus was *cos. V ord.* and Domitian *cos. IV suff.* (Gallivan, 1981: p. 214).

31. *e sex consulatibus non nisi unum ordinarium gessit*: *Dom.* 2.1. He is attested as *cos. suff.* in April 71 (with Cn. Pedius Cascus as colleague) and in June (with C. Capetanus Rantius Quirinalis Valerius Festus: Gallivan, 1981: p. 187), as *cos. II ord.* in 73 (with L. Valerius Catullus Messallinus: *ibid.*, p. 188), as *cos. III suff.* in March and April 75 (with L. Pasidienus Firmus: *ibid.*, p. 188), as *cos. IV suff.*

in 76 (replacing either Vespasian or Titus, but his colleague
is unknown: *ibid*.), as *cos. V suff*. in June or July 77 (but
again his colleague is unknown: *ibid*., p. 189) and as *cos. VI
suff*. early in 79 (possibly replacing his father: *ibid*.).
The evidence for each is discussed by Gallivan, *loc. cit*. and
by Buttrey, 1980: pp. 32-34. Suetonius maintains that his
ordinary consulship (in 73) was received *cedente ac
suffragante fratre* (*Dom*. 2.1). Buttrey, p. 33, discusses the
story and dismisses it as "malicious".

    32. His first salutation occurred on his accession: see
RE 6.2550; Buttrey, 1980: p. 30. For Domitian as *Caesar*,
presumably as early as Dec. 69 and then frequently under
Vespasian, see Blamberg, 1976: p. 89; Buttrey, p. 32.
Mattingly, 1930: p. xxxii, considers that *Caesar* indicates his
position as heir, whereas Hammond, 1956: p. 83 and 1959: p.
60, argues that it was the *nomen* of the ruling family:-
"*Caesar* alone after the personal name (as) the regular style
for a subordinate heir...can be demonstrated only for Lucius
Aelius as adopted successor to Hadrian in 137; it may also
have been the style of Trajan and Hadrian during their brief
terms as heirs" (1959: pp. 60-61). For Domitian as *princeps
iuuentutis*, again as early as Dec. 69, so it seems, and then
frequently under Vespasian, see Blamberg, 1976: p. 89 and
Buttrey, 1980: p. 32; its significance is discussed in
detail by Hammond, 1959: pp. 148-149.

    33. For these titles under Titus, see Buttrey, 1980: p.
35 (*Caesar*);Mattingly, 1930: p. 273 n. 1 (*princeps iuuentutis*).
An inscription from the reign of Titus clearly indicates his
brother's status:- *Caesar diui f. Domitianus consul VII
princeps iuuentutis* (*CIL* 3.318, to be assigned to 80 or 81,
not merely 80 as in *CIL*: see Buttrey, p. 3).

    34. Despite Hammond, 1959: p. 83, *IGRR* 3.223 shows
clearly that, before Titus' accession, he was designated as
ordinary consul for 80 with his brother as suffect; on
Vespasian's death, Domitian assumed the vacant ordinary
consulship (Buttrey, 1980: p. 34).

    35. His first *tribunicia potestas* is attested on Sept.
30, 81, when the Arval Brethren sacrificed *ob comitia
tribunicia Caesaris diui f. Domitiani Aug*. (McCrum and Woodhead, 1966: No. 12); that he held it before the 30th is
indicated by *CIL* 16.28 of Sept. 20, 82, where he is already
trib. pot. II (for the problems involved in dating this
diploma, see Buttrey, 1980: pp. 36-37). The precise date is
usually assumed to be Sept. 14 (Buttrey, 1980: p. 30).

    36. It used to be thought that he was not designated to
his eighth consulship until after the death of Titus on Sept.
13, 81 (*RE* 6.2551; *DE* 2.2033). The evidence adduced was
essentially the absence of designation on some of Domitian's
early coins (e.g. Mattingly, 1930: pp. 297-299, Nos. 1-7,
where he appears as *cos. VII* on his first issue but as *cos.
VII des. VIII* on the second); but designation is frequently

omitted on Flavian coins (see Buttrey, 1980: p. 35). To this was added Pliny's reference (*Pan.* 57.1) to emperors who stole consulships which had been designated for others. *CIL* 3.12218, however, which is to be assigned to Titus' reign (81 and not 80 as in *CIL*: Buttrey, 1980: p. 25), clearly shows the designation. For a detailed treatment of the problem, see Eck, 1970: pp. 48-54. He received no other honours from Titus. He remained *sacerdos omnium collegiorum*: attested in 73-76 (*ILS* 267) and in 80-81 (*CIL* 3.12218: see above for the date).

37. ·Augustus died at the age of seventy-five (Suet., *Aug.* 100.1), Tiberius at seventy-seven (*Tib.* 73.1) and Vespasian at sixty-nine (*Vesp.* 24).

38. Suetonius believes that he did:- *patre defuncto...* *numquam iactare dubitauit relictum se participem imperii, sed fraudem testamento adhibitam*: *Dom.* 2.3. Kornemann, 1930: pp. 65-66, accepts Suetonius' charge as justified, and holds that Domitian did in fact try to secure a more substantial position by force. Suetonius also claims that, as a result of his dissatisfaction, *neque cessauit ex eo insidias struere fratri clam palamque*: *Dom.* 2.3. Hammond, 1956: pp. 83-84 n. 120, suggests that the charge may refer to Titus' assuming a greater portion of the private inheritance than was his due.

39. See *PIR*[1] V 161 (Valeria Messallina) for Claudius' age at the birth of his son.

40. Note that Vespasian had arranged a number of dynastic marriages. His two grand-nephews Sabinus IV and Clemens (grandsons of his brother, Sabinus II) married two imperial granddaughters (Julia, daughter of Titus, and Domitilla III, daughter of Titus' sister, Domitilla II). Later, two of Clemens' sons were designated by Domitian as his successors.

41. Mattingly, 1930: p. 260, No. 188.

42. For coins showing Vespasian raising up a kneeling Roma, see *ibid.*, p. 121, Nos. 565, 566 - *Roma Resurges s._c.* (A.D. 71: Vespasian *cos. III*).

43. *ibid.*, p. 259, Nos. 178-181.

44. *ibid.*, p. 140, No. 634 (A.D. 72: Titus, on horseback, about to transfix a prostrate foe); p. 147, No. 652 (72-73: Titus in military dress, a vertical spear in his left hand, Jew kneeling, Jewess running and holding out hands); cast, p. 263 (80-81: Titus, seated on platform, presiding over a distribution); p. 258, No. 177 (80-81: Titus and Domitian, togate, clasping right hands, with legend *Pietas*).

45. For this, see Gagé, 1931: pp. 11-41; Hammond, 1959: pp. 59-60.

46. Mattingly, 1930: pp. xxi-xlii, xlvi-lxix, discusses Vespasian's use of Augustan coin legends; for a more recent examination, see Bianco, 1968: pp. 168-184.

47. For these coins, see Mattingly, 1930: pp. 281 ff., Nos. 261-280 (*Diuus Augustus Pater*, though the types reproduced were not Augustus' but Tiberius' - Buttrey, 1976: p. 455), 281 (Agrippa), 282-285 (Tiberius), 286-288 (Drusus),

289-291 (Livia), 293-295 (Germanicus), 296 (Agrippina the
Elder), 297-302 (Claudius), 305 with five variants (Galba).
    48. Mattingly, 1930: p. 281, No. 261.
    49. *ibid.*, p. 292, No. 305#.
    50. *ibid.*, p. 128, No. 590 (Vespasian, A.D. 71);
Mattingly, 1923: p. 360, No. 261 (Augustus).
    51. For the *Diuus Augustus Vespasianus* sestertii, see
Mattingly, 1930: pp. 269 ff., Nos. 221-225, and, for the
attributes of the two deified emperors, compare the descrip-
tions on p. 269 (Vespasian) and p. 281 (Augustus).
    52. *Moesiae ita praefuit, ut non debuerit in me differri
honor triumphalium eius ornamentorum*: *ILS* 986 = McCrum and
Woodhead, 1966: No. 261.
    53. Gallivan, 1981: pp. 187-189 (Vespasian), 187 (Nerva),
188 (Catullus Messallinus), 189 (Junius Novius Priscus and
Ceionius Commodus, Titus and Domitian).
    54. Buttrey, 1980: p. 34.
    55. Gallivan, 1981: p. 189; Eck, 1980: p. 53.
    56. *ibid.*, pp. 190-191.
    57. *PIR*[2] A 1243.
    58. For the Asinii, see Oliver, 1947: pp. 147-160, and
especially p. 157 for the connection with Germanicus.
    59. Nicols, 1978: p. 17.
    60. e.g. L. Nonius Calpurnius Asprenas (Africa, 82/83:
Eck, 1982: p. 306), P. Nonius Asprenas Caesius Cassianus (Asia,
between 87/88 and 95/96: *ibid.*, p. 87) and Asprenas (Africa,
ca. 92/93: Eck, 1982: p. 320).
    61. For a list of the proconsuls of Africa at this
period, see Eck, 1970: p. 234, who shows that no proconsuls
are attested for the years 93/94 - 96/97 inclusive. There was
normally an interval of at least thirteen years between the
consulship and proconsulship of Africa or Asia around this
time - C. Octavius Tidius Tossianus L. Javolenus Priscus held
the *fasces* in 86 and the African proconsulate ca. 101 (*ibid.*,
p. 234). Pollio would then have been eligible for the
sortitio in the early nineties.
    62. For him, see *PIR*[2] F 368; Houston, 1971: p. 94;
McDermott, 1973: pp. 335-351. His adlection has been
discussed by Eck, 1970: pp. 93-111; McDermott, 1973: p. 337.
    63. Groag, 1929: p. 144 n. 6.
    64. Tacitus names the legates of all the Rhine legions
during the civil war except the commander of the *XXI Rapax*,
even though that legion itself is frequently mentioned, e.g.
Hist. 1.61, 67: 2.43, 100; 3.14, 18, 22, 25. As Syme points
out (1978: p. 15), "Tacitus omitted the legate whose identity
and comportment should have been of some relevance. The
person, it might be conjectured, was reserved for unfriendly
notice in the sequel. Not, perhaps, Flavius Silva. It will
be preferable to assign his command of *XXI Rapax* to the
following years".
    65. For a description of Masada's fall, see Schürer,

1973: pp. 511-512, 515; Furneaux, 1973: pp. 181-191. The
precise date of the conclusion of the siege has been discussed
by Eck, 1970: pp. 99-101 and McDermott, 1973: pp. 337-338 who
favour 74; but note the objections of Evans, 1979: p. 200 n.
1.
    66. Eck, 1970: p. 94.
    67. According to Sherwin-White, 1966: p. 273, "(he was)
apparently out of favour under Domitian".
    68. Eck, 1970: pp. 77-93, assigns the post to 86, but
C.P. Jones, 1973: pp. 689-690, argues convincingly for 85.
According to Devreker, 1977: pp. 226-228, he was an *amicus* of
Domitian as well as of Vespasian and Titus.
    69. See Alföldy and Halfmann, 1973: pp. 331-373.
    70. For some illuminating comments on this topic, see
Syme, 1981: pp. 125-144.
    71. Gallivan, 1981: p. 198.
    72. *ibid.*, p. 195.
    73. *AE* 1948, 56 (Jan. 14); *CIL* 16.26.
    74. *CIL* 6.2059 (with Pactumeius Fronto); for Veiento
and Marius Marcellus, see preceding note.
    75. For the suggestion, see Houston, 1971: pp. 5-6.
    76. For his ancestors, see Taylor, 1956: pp. 9-30 and
Houston, 1971: pp. 5-6. His descendants seem to have included
a son, L. Lamia Aelianus, *cos. ord.* 116, a grandson, Lamia
Silvanus, betrothed to Aurelia Fadilla (daughter of T.
Aurelius Fulvus, later the emperor Antoninus Pius) and a
daughter, Plautia, whose husbands were L. Ceionius Commodus
(*cos. ord.* 106), C. Avidius Nigrinus (*cos. suff.* 110) and Sex.
Vettulenus Civica Cerialis (*cos. ord.* 106) - see Syme, 1957:
pp. 307-312.
    77. For the evidence, see Eck, 1982: pp. 300 ff.
    78. Corellius Rufus' tenure of Upper Germany is assigned
to the period 79/80 - 82/83 by Eck, 1982: pp. 302 (with n.
83) - 306: he is attested there on Sept. 20, 82, but the
fasti of that province are incomplete - apart from Corellius,
no governor is known between Cn. Pinarius Cornelius Clemens
(May 21, 74: *CIL* 16.20) and L. Antonius Saturninus (Jan. 89).
L. Funisulanus Vettonianus is attested in Moesia on Sept. 3,
84 (*CIL* 16.30) and is known to have governed Dalmatia before
that (*ILS* 1005). For their consular year, see Gallivan, 1981:
p. 203.
    79. C. Vettulenus Civica Cerialis is attested in Moesia
on Sept. 20, 82 (*CIL* 16.28); his brother is attested there on
April 28, 74 (or 75) - see Gallivan, 1981: p. 203.
    80. *ILS* 263 = McCrum and Woodhead, 1966: No. 105; for
the date, see Eck, 1982: p. 304 n. 90.
    81. For Pompeius Collega and Neratius Pansa, see Eck,
1982: pp. 293-302, and, for the possibility that A. Caesennius
Gallus proceeded from Cappadocia-Galatia to Syria, see Syme,
1981: p. 135.
    82. For the creation of the new Cappadocia-Galatia

complex and its significance, see Bosworth, 1976: pp. 63 ff.;
Dabrowa, 1980: pp. 385-386; Sherk, 1980: pp. 996 ff.;
Mitford, 1980: pp. 1180-1187; and, for the work of Caesennius
Gallus, Bosworth, 1976: p. 72 n. 65; Dabrowa, 1980: p. 383.
     83. Ti. Julius Celsus Polemaeanus was *iuridicus* there
from ca. 77 to 79, L. Julius Proculeianus followed him and was
replaced by C. Antius A. Julius Quadratus in 81/82: for the
evidence, see Halfmann, 1979: pp. 111-112 (Celsus Polemaeanus),
110-111 (Proculeianus) and 112-114 (Julius Quadratus) and
Sherk, 1980: pp. 1006-1010.
     84. Devreker, 1980: p. 87.
     85. For Quadratus' consular posts, see Halfmann, 1979:
pp. 112-115, and, for his praetorian governorship, Syme,
1980: p. 88.
     86. *ILS* 9485 (= McCrum and Woodhead, 1966: No. 315):-
...*leg. imp. diui Vespasian. Aug. leg. IX Hispanae in Britann.*
... The most recent discussion of Fronto's career is that of
Halfmann, 1979: p. 109.
     87. *ILS* 1015 (= McCrum and Woodhead, 1966: No. 309):-
... *leg. leg. IV Flau*... For Javolenus, see Alföldy, 1968a:
pp. 108-116 together with the comments of Syme, 1971: p. 119.
     88. Halfmann, 1979: p. 109.
     89. *ibid.*, p. 111.
     90. For Rusticus, see *AE* 1925, 126; *AE* 1926, 1 together
with the comments of Alföldy, 1967: pp. 13-15 and 1969: pp.
160-161; Houston, 1971: pp. 14-17; Sherk, 1980: pp. 1012-
1014. For Salvius Liberalis, see *ILS* 1011 with the comments
of Petersen, 1962: pp. 32-33; Houston, 1971: pp. 233-235;
McDermott, 1973: pp. 335-351. For Antonius Saturninus, see
Houston, 1971: pp. 337-338; Syme, 1978: pp. 12-21.
     91. For the details, see Warmington, 1969: pp. 94 ff.;
Garzetti, 1974: p. 176.
     92. The *Flauia T. f. Sabina* of *ILS* 995 was almost
certainly married to Paetus - see Townend, 1961: p. 56 n. 6.
Garzetti, 1966: p. 788, argues that Paetus was sent to Syria
because of his eastern experience, but "capitulation to the
Parthians hardly constituted the kind of experience that
Vespasian would have sought" (Evans, 1978: p. 119 n. 69).
     93. Gallivan, 1981: p. 203.
     94. Evans, 1978: pp. 102-128. His precise name is not
certain but, for the version in the text, see Evans, p. 107.
Much of his career can be recovered from Statius' *laudatio*
(*Siluae* 3.3), commissioned by the freedman's son Claudius
Etruscus to commemorate his father's death. It is clear that
he married a woman of high birth whose *cognomen* was Etrusca
and whose brother obtained the *fasces* and fought victoriously
against the Dacians during Domitian's reign. Etrusca and her
freedman-husband had two sons, Claudius Etruscus and another
whose name has not survived; both sons as well as the father
were adlected into the equestrian order by Vespasian. For a
full discussion of the freedman, see also Weaver, 1965: pp.

145-154 and 1972: pp. 284-294.
   95. For a discussion of his career, see *PIR*² F 570;
Stein, 1940a: pp. 35-37; Jagenteufel, 1958: pp. 45-48;
Thomasson, 1960: pp. 50-51; Houston, 1971: pp. 98-103 and
1976b: pp. 25-26; Evans, 1978: pp. 117-120. It is not clear
when he was appointed to Dalmatia. Eck, 1982: p. 302, argues
that he was there in 79/80, but this is far from certain,
since the only consular post that can be dated with some
security is his governorship of Pannonia where he is attested
on Sept. 3, 84 (*CIL* 16.30) and on Sept. 5, 85 (*CIL* 16.31). If
he served three years in each province, he could well have
been sent to Dalmatia in 80/81 and moved in 82/83.
   96. This is the date suggested by Eck, 1970: p. 90 and
also retained by him in 1982: p. 319; Houston, 1971: p. 103
prefers 90.
   97. His first posts are discussed by Pavis d'Escurac,
1976: pp. 67, 324; for his prefecture of Egypt, see Brunt,
1975a: p. 144.
   98. On the relationship between Tettius Julianus and Ti.
Julius, Aug. lib., see Evans, 1978: pp. 104-105.
   99. For his post in Numidia, see Leschi, 1953: pp. 189-
198 = *AE* 1954, 137; for the consulship, see Gallivan, 1981:
p. 216, and, for the post in Upper Moesia, Eck, 1982: p. 315.
   100. Statius, *Siluae* 3.3.143.
   101. The reason for his dismissal has not been recorded.
Domitian's alleged antipathy for his brother's *amici* is not
well documented (see note 111); on the other hand, Tiberius
Julius may simply have expressed his disapproval of some of
Domitian's financial measures - his cancellation of debts
outstanding to the *aerarium Saturni* for more than five years,
his refusal of inheritances when the testator had children and
his substantial pay increase to the army. Any or all of these
could well have offended the more cautious Tiberius Julius and
his reaction provoked his dismissal.
   102. *quando Aegyptus, claustra annonae, uectigalia
opulentissimarum prouinciarum obtinerentur, posse Vitellii
exercitum egestate stipendii frumentique ad deditionem subigi:
Hist.* 3.8.
   103. *namque et Africam ... terra marique inuadere
parabat, clausis annonae subsidiis inopiam ac discordiam
hosti facturus: Hist.* 3.48.
   104. *nam Augustus inter alia dominationis arcana,
uetitis nisi permissu ingredi senatoribus aut equitibus
Romanis inlustribus, seposuit Aegyptum ne fame urgeret
Italiam quisquis eam prouinciam claustraque terrae ac maris
quamuis leui praesidio aduersum ingentis exercitus insedisset:
Ann.* 2.59.
   105. No doubt Vespasian intended Ti. Julius Alexander
to be a moderating influence on Titus during his campaign.
   106. Evans, 1978: p. 124.
   107. According to Syme, 1958a: p. 649, an appointment as

legatus Augusti of a praetorian province was "vital, carrying
the clear promise of the consulate". Tacitus refers to
Agricola's praetorian governorship of Aquitania as *splendidae
inprimis dignitatis administratione ac spe consulatus, cui
(Vespasianus) destinarat*: *Agr.* 9.1. It was extremely unusual
for a senator who had not governed a military province during
his praetorian career to be appointed to a province of that
nature after his consulship.

108. For the dismissal of Tiberius Julius, Aug. lib.,
see note 158, and, for Classicus' career, *AE* 1972, 574
(discussed by Burton, 1977: p. 163; Weaver, 1980: pp. 150-156;
Boulvert, 1981: pp. 31-41). The Latin section of *AE* 1972,
574, a bilingual inscription, runs as follows:-

> *Ti(berio) Claudio Aug(usti) lib(erto) Classico, diui*
> *T(iti) a cubiculo et proc(uratori) castrensi, diui*
> *Neruae proc(uratori) a uoluptatibus, Imp(eratoris) Neruae*
> *Traiani Caesaris Aug(usti) Germanici Dacici proc(uratori)*
> *a uoluptatibus et ad ludum matutinum et proc(uratori)*
> *Alexandreae, C(aius) Iulius Photinus Celer adiutor in*
> *procuratione Alexandreae ob merita eius.*

Its interpretation has provoked much discussion, since, as
Weaver (1980: p. 152) points out,

> Here we have a career chronologically documented in every
> ascending detail which in fact turns out to be almost
> precisely the same as the supposedly *descending* career of
> Paean Aug. lib (i.e. *ILS* 1569)... In other words,
> apparently the same offices are held by each man during
> his career, but in exactly the reverse order.

His solution is convincing - Classicus was granted equestrian
status by Nerva. His discussion of the career is particularly
interesting; he notes that,

> the combination of the two posts in the one person seems
> unique. Of the two, the *a cubiculo* is the more indicat-
> ive of patronage..(he) had close, perhaps daily, personal
> contact with the emperor. He remained outside the
> administrative service and indeed had no clearly defined
> place in the domestic hierarchy either, except that
> measured by his personal and unofficial influence over
> particular emperors (p. 153).

109. For a list of Titus' *amici*, see Devreker, 1977: p.
227 (revising Crook, 1955: pp. 148 ff.); McGuire, 1980: pp.
103-105.

110. *nullum maius boni imperii instrumentum quam bonos
amicos esse* (*Hist.* 4.7); *rei publicae necessarii(s)* (*Titus*
7.2). Trajan is supposed to have justified Domitian's
efficient administration as follows:- *Domitianum pessimum
fuisse, amicos autem bonos habuisse*: HA *Alex.* 65.5. Of
course, he was probably one of the *boni amici* - see Syme,
1956: p. 268 and 1958a: p. 33; Devreker, 1977: p. 228.
According to Tacitus, Vespasian's *amici* Vibius Crispus and
Eprius Marcellus exercised overwhelming power and influence:-

principes in Caesaris amicitia agunt feruntque cuncta: *Dial.*
8.3.
    111. According to Devreker, 1977: pp. 226-228, eleven of
the twelve *amici* assigned to Titus had also served Vespasian
and nine of them retained their position under Domitian. But
some were summoned only when their particular talents were
required, e.g. the younger Pliny, who was *euocatus in consilium* (*Ep.* 6.31.1) and *in consilium adsumptus* (*Ep.* 4.22.1).
    112. Crook, 1955: p. 26. For a detailed discussion of
their role, see his pp. 21-55 and also the briefer treatment
of Devreker, 1977: pp. 223-225.
    113. Crook, 1955: pp. 23-24. See also the discussion of
Crispinus by White, 1974: pp. 377-382, especially p. 381.
    114. Note, *inter alia*, Naevius Sertorius Macro (Crook,
1955: p. 233, No. 175), Sex. Afranius Burrus (p. 150, No. 17),
M. Arrecinus Clemens (p. 151, No. 31) and P. Acilius Attianus
(p. 148, No. 1).
    115. For these qualifications, see Devreker, 1977: p.
225.
    116. Crook, 1955: p. 165, No. 151a, and *CIL* 6.814 for
the curatorship under Titus.
    117. Crook, 1955: p. 151, No. 31, and Eck, 1970: p. 130,
for the post in Spain (but cf. Eck, 1982: pp. 304-305).
    118. Crook, 1955: p. 164, No. 148. His significance has
been discussed by McDermott, 1970: pp. 124-148.
    119. Crook, 1955: p. 188, No. 340. For the description,
see Syme, 1958a: p. 333, and, for the consulships, see
Gallivan, 1981: pp. 209-210.
    120. Devreker, 1977: p. 227. For the details of his
career, including the possibility that he was designated to a
third consulship for 83, see Eck, 1972b: pp. 259-276, and, for
the description, see Syme, 1958a: p. 593.
    121. Crook, 1955: p. 160, No. 108.
    122. *ibid.*, p. 187, No. 328. His intimacy with Nerva
and Veiento is referred to by Pliny, *Ep.* 4.22.4-7:- *cenabat
Nerua cum paucis; Veiento proximus atque etiam in sinu
recumbebat...incidit sermo de Catullo Messallino...cum ipse
imperator: quid putamus passurum fuisse si uiueret? et
Mauricus: nobiscum cenaret.*
    123. Crook, 1955: p. 168, No. 176; A.R. Birley, 1981:
pp. 69-73.
    124. Devreker, 1977: p. 227. For his career and that of
his family, see Torelli, 1968: pp.170-175; Houston, 1971:
pp. 111-117; Camodeca, 1976: pp. 19-38; Vidman, 1981: pp.
377-384.
    125. Devreker, 1977: p. 227. His career is discussed by
Houston, 1971: pp. 273-279; for his role in Vespasian's
eastern policy, see Syme, 1958a: p. 31 (architect of the
entire *limes*), but Mitford, 1974: p. 173 n. 90 and Bosworth,
1976: p. 67 both express doubts.
    126. Crook, 1955: p. 148, No. 2; see also Gallivan,

1978b: pp. 621-625.
127. For Pegasus, see Crook, 1955: p. 177, No. 251 and
p. 50 n. 2. His full name and career have been established by
Champlin, 1978: pp. 269-278. It seems almost certain that he
was appointed by Vespasian - see Gallivan, 1981: p. 207 with
n. 134. The Plotius Grypus of *Hist.* 3.52; 4.39, 40 (on whom,
see Evans, 1978: p. 122) is presumably his brother. Possibly
Grypus is the L. Plotius attested as consul before 79 with a
L. Minicius (Degrassi, 1952: p. 130), though these may well be
the *cos. ord.* L. Minicius Rufus and the *cos. suff.* D. (sometimes found as L.) Plotius Grypus of 88 who were in office
together early in that year (Gallivan, 1981: p. 191). More
likely, Pegasus' brother is to be identified with the consul
of 88. For the son, see Eck, 1982: p. 305.
128. *AE* 1962, 288 (for the text and translation, see p.
145, with note 185); Alföldy, 1969: pp. 159-160.
129. For his career, see Alföldy, 1969: p. 160; Eck,
1982: p. 301 n. 76, p. 305 n. 98; his consulship during Sept.
84 is noted in *CIL* 16.30.
130. Martial, 6.76.1 - his description of Cornelius
Fuscus.
131. For Fuscus as Domitian's appointee, see Lydus, *De
Magistratibus* 2.19, and, for his career, Pflaum, 1960: pp.
77-80. For Laberius, see Pavis d'Escurac, 1976: pp. 325-326;
he was still serving in Egypt as late as 83 (Brunt, 1975a: p.
144).
132. In *P. Berl.* 8334, an unnamed emperor addresses *mi
maxime* and refers to his forthcoming promotion, connected, so
it seems, with a favour done to a certain "Julius":- *se[d cum
et] Iuliu[m Ursum suis precibus u]sum in amplissimum ordinem
transtu[lissem...*; for a discussion, see Syme, 1958a: pp.
635-636, and, more recently, Pavis d'Escurac, 1976: p. 327.
133. Brunt, 1975a: p. 144, refers to L. Julius Ursus as
"previously *pr. annonae* and later (it would seem) *pr. pr.*
perhaps on Titus' accession", but the identification is
rejected by Pavis d'Escurac, 1976: p. 327.
134. Syme, 1958a: pp. 635-636, argues that Dio's Ursus,
the (U)rsus who held a suffect consulship in 84 and the L.
Julius Ursus, *cos. II suff.* 98 should be regarded as the same
person. That senator's third consulship has recently been
discovered (Zevi, 1972: p. 438).
135. Syme, 1958a: p. 636.
136. *PIR*[1] T 208; *BJ* 6.237 (council of war); Gallivan,
1981: p. 215 (*cos. suff.* Nov./Dec. 80).
137. e.g. M. Ulpius Traianus (*leg. leg. X Fretensis* and
cos. suff. 70), T. Aurelius Fulvus (*leg. leg. III Gallicae* and
cos. suff. 71-74), L. Annius Bassus (*leg. leg. XI Claudiae* and
cos. suff. 70), Sex. Vettulenus Cerialis (*leg. leg. V Macedon-
icae, leg. leg. X Fretensis* and *cos. suff.* 72 or 73), Cn.
Pompeius Collega (*leg. leg. IV Scythicae* and *cos. suff.* before
75), C. Dillius Aponianus (*leg. leg. III Gallicae* and *cos.*

suff. 71-73), and M. Hirrius Fronto Neratius Pansa (*leg. leg.
? VI Ferratae* and *cos. suff.* 73 or 74). Equally instructive
for the present argument is the fate of the only legate of
69/70 (apart from Tittius Frugi, Roscius Coelius and Tettius
Julianus) attested as not receiving a consulship from
Vespasian, viz. M. Antonius Primus, *leg. leg.* in 69/70 - he
was "cheated of public recognition and consigned to retirement" (Syme, 1958a: p. 177). Apparently, Titus preserved
Tittius Frugi, Roscius Coelius and Tettius Julianus from a
similar fate.
    138. *PIR*[1] R 67; *Hist.* 1.60 (Britain); Gallivan, 1981:
p. 215 (*cos. suff.* March/April 81).
    139. *PIR*[1] T 239; A.R. Birley, 1967: p. 66 (Trebellius).
For the events in Britain, see Ogilvie and Richmond, 1967: p.
155.
    140. For Tettius Julianus (*PIR*[1] T 102) and his powerful
relatives, L. Funisulanus Vettonianus (*PIR*[2] F 570) and C.
Tettius Africanus Cassianus Priscus (*PIR*[1] T 100), see Evans,
1978: pp. 109 ff.
    141. For his consulship, see Gallivan, 1981: p. 215;
for his origin, Syme, 1980: p. 90; for his father, *AE* 1938,
173.
    142. Syme, 1980: p. 90. He comments that "with only one
post after the praetorship (a proconsulate), the career is
peculiar, encouraging the conjecture that Montanus owed the
consulate to especial favour from Titus" (p. 91 n. 12). The
first consul from the Greek east was probably D. Junius Novius
Priscus, *cos. ord.* 78: he seems to have been a native of
Antioch in Pisidia - see Devreker, 1982: p. 495 n. 18.
    143. His career is revealed in *AE* 1973, 500:- *T(ito)
Iunio C(ai) f(ilio) Ani(ensi) Montano, III uir a.a.a.f.f. tri.
mil. leg V Mac. q. Ponti et Bithyniae tr. pl. pr. sodali Titio
procos. prouinc. Sicilia(e) cos., patrono coloniae decreto
d(ecurionum).*
    144. Syme, 1959: p. 510.
    145. Syme, 1980: p. 57 n. 14, recalling Juvenal 4.107:-
Montani quoque uenter adest abdomine tardus.
    146. Crook, 1955: p. 175, No. 232.
    147. *amicos elegit (Titus) quibus etiam post eum
principes ut sibi et rei publicae necessariis adquieuerunt
praecipueque sunt usi: Titus* 7.5.
    148. For the details, see note 111 above.
    149. Under Vespasian, teachers of rhetoric were, for the
first time, paid a regular salary from public funds (*Vesp.*
18). Grants of money were made to encourage poets and men of
letters (*ibid.*). Saleius Bassus received five hundred thous-
and sesterces (*Dial.* 9) whilst other artists benefited
similarly (*Vesp.* 18-19). For Vespasian's advances in this
area, see Woodside, 1942: pp. 123-129; Homo, 1949: pp. 308-
309. Although Titus' brief reign does not yield such detailed
evidence for similar financial assistance, there can be little

doubt that the precedent established by his father was
followed. His interest in the arts generally is well attested - *Titus* 3.2; Pliny, *NH Praef.* 5-6; Eutropius, 7.21;
Epit. de Caes. 10.2 together with the comments of Bardon,
1967: pp. 274-280. The *subsiciua*, marginal tracts of land
often unassigned in the formation of a colony and thence
illegally occupied, were the property of the state: Hyginus,
De Gener. Controu. 133, shows that such tracts were reassigned
to the state by both Vespasian and Titus; see also note 154.
    150. Gsell, 1894: pp. 333-334, refers to the finances
"que Titus avait compromises"; similarly Weynand, *RE* 6.2725:
"In der Finanzwirtschaft scheint Titus nicht der Art des Vater
nachgefolgt zu sein". Henderson, 1927: p. 8, comments that
Titus' policies "serve the state finances but sorrily", whilst
Syme, 1930: p. 70, feels that he "can hardly have exercised a
beneficent influence on the finances of the Empire". According to Fortina, 1955a: p. 124, Titus left his brother in a
"situazione finanziaria estremamente delicata".
    151. The financial difficulties faced by Vespasian at
the beginning of his reign are set out by Homo, 1940: pp. 453-
465 and 1949: p. 140. For the damage caused by the fire of 64,
see Bishop, 1964: pp. 71 ff.; Warmington, 1969: pp. 123-124.
    152. *Vesp.* 16.3; Braithwaite, 1927: p. 61.
    153. *Vesp.* 16.1-3; Dio 66.8.3. Taxes remitted by Galba
in Spain and Gaul were promptly reimposed, whilst the exemp-
tions granted Greece by Nero were annulled (Suet., *Nero* 24.2;
Braithwaite, 1927: p. 60). The details of the new taxes are
uncertain, though it is clear that a number of free cities
including Rhodes, Samos and Byzantium, which had previously
escaped taxation, were assigned by Vespasian to provinces and
taxed accordingly. See Magie, 1950: pp. 569-570, 1427-1428 n.
9 and Rostovtzeff, 1957: p. 116, who notes that the majority
of cities now taxed were prosperous trading centres. To
Vespasian's reign should probably be assigned the *fiscus
Iudaicus*, the *fiscus Asiaticus* and the *fiscus Alexandrinus*:
for these, see Braithwaite, 1927: p. 60.
    154. For Vespasian's and Titus' policy towards these
squatters, see note 149; Domitian's more liberal attitude can
be seen in his letter of 82 to the Falerienses - McCrum and
Woodhead, 1966: p. 137, No. 462:-
    ... I, Emperor Caesar Augustus, son of the deified
    Vespasian, Domitian, employing distinguished men of each
    order as my advisers, after the case between the Faler-
    ienses and the Firmani had been heard, have pronounced
    what has been written below.
    I am moved greatly by the antiquity of the controversy,
    which after so many years is renewed by the Firmani
    against the Falerienses, since even fewer years could
    suffice for the security of those persons in possession,
    and by the letter of the deified Augustus, a most
    diligent and most indulgent prince towards his soldiers

of the fourth legion, in which he admonished them that
they should assemble and sell all their unsurveyed land.
And I do not doubt that they have obeyed so advantageous
an admonition. Wherefore, I confirm the rights of those
persons in possession. Farewell.

Given on July 22 at the Alban villa, under the super-
vision of Titus Bovius Verus, the envoys being Publius
Bovius Sabinus and Publius Petronius Achilles. By decree
of the decurions publicly. (lines 11-30)

Johnson, Coleman-Norton and Bourne, 1961: p. 153, comment as
follows:-

When preparing land for assignment, Roman surveyors laid
it out in regular rectangular tracts. In an area with an
irregular shape, this was bound to leave extra and unsurveyed parcels (*subsiciua*). These legally remained public
land, though they were used by the region's residents.
In this case, the surveyors in running their survey of
colonial land drew the boundaries in such a way that,
from one or other or both districts, land had been sub-
tracted and was unassigned to the colonials. It seems
that the survey was made on land confiscated from the
Firmans, who, when the parcels had not been assigned,
took possession of such lots as had been theirs before
confiscation.

So Domitian's policy was to confirm the squatters in their
occupancy. In a sense, this was merely following the
prescriptions of the Twelve Tables, which (6.3) provided that
uninterrupted possession of land for two years conferred
ownership of it. Vespasian and Titus, however, were far less
generous.

155. For 83, see Mooney, 1930: p. 542; Kraay, 1958:
p. 116, argues for 84.

156. For a discussion of these percentages, see Bolin,
1958: pp. 191, 207.

157. For a discussion of these activities, see Blake,
1959: pp. 99-107.

158. The freedman's dismissal is considered by Evans,
1978: p. 113.

159. For the details, see *Titus* 8.3; Dio, 66.21-23;
Pliny, *Ep.* 6.16 and the comments of Sherwin-White, 1966: pp.
372-375.

160. See, *inter alia*, Haywood, 1952: pp. 1-3; Lipscomb,
1954: p. 74; Sherwin-White, 1966: p. 372.

161. *CIL* 10.1481 = Newton, 1901: p. 52, No. 101.

162. *Digest* 22.5.9. On this, see below, note 197.

163. For the fire, see Mooney, 1930: p. 493; Fortina,
1955a: p. 113.

164. Until recently, it has been generally agreed that
Rhodes lost her freedom under Vespasian (see note 153),
regained it under Titus, then lost and subsequently regained
it under Domitian (*RE* Suppl. 5.811 ff.). A similar chronology

is accepted by Magie, 1950: pp. 569, 1427 n. 9, but rejected by Momigliano, 1951: pp. 150-153, who argues that the passages that support the accepted chronology provide little evidence for the restoration of *libertas* by Titus. On the other hand, *IGRR* 4.1129 shows that he at least promised to restore it, and the cumulative weight of the literary evidence seems convincing.

165. For Caesarea, see *Digest* 50.15.8.7 and Fortina, 1955a: p. 139 n. 120; for Aventicum, see van Berchem, 1944: pp. 45-46 and Sherwin-White, 1973: p. 370.

166. The evidence for the confiscations is provided by Rostovtzeff, 1957: pp. 669-670 n. 45; see also Fortina, 1955a: p. 124 with n. 122.

167. For some pertinent comments on the role of Vespasian's and Titus' financial adviser, see Evans, 1978: pp. 111-113.

168. Despite this, Vespasian's name only appears on the architrave (*CIL* 6.938). The completion of the temple by Domitian was recorded by the Chronographer of A.D. 354 (*Chron. Min.* 1, p. 146). For a description of the building, see Platner and Ashby, 1929: p. 556 and Blake, 1959: pp. 97-98.

169. For Titus' additions to and dedication of the amphitheatre, see *Titus* 7.3; Dio 66.25.1-5; Aurelius Victor, *De Caes.* 10.5; Eutropius, 7.21; Martial, *Spect.* 1, 7-8. *CIL* 6.2059 (= McCrum and Woodhead, 1966: No. 11) records the assignment of seats for the Arval Brethren in the amphitheatre, dating Titus' dedication to the consulship of L. Aelius Plautius Lamia and Q. Pactumeius Fronto (March/April 81: Gallivan, 1981: p. 215). On the progress of the amphitheatre under Titus, see *RE* 6.2720 and Fortina, 1955a: pp. 118-119. Precisely which sections were built in his reign is uncertain. The Chronographer of A.D. 354 (*Chron. Min.* 1, p. 146) has the following:- *Diuus Vespasianus...hic prior tribus gradibus amphitheatrum dedicauit...Diuus Titus...hic amphitheatrum a tribus gradibus patris sui duos adiecit.* It is, however, uncertain whether *tribus gradibus* includes the ground level or refers to the three tiers above; the latter is probably to be preferred in view of the contemporary numismatic evidence (Mattingly, 1930: p. 262, No. 190, showing ground level plus four tiers; cf. the similar depiction of the building on the Haterii Relief - Blake, 1959: p. 91 with Plate 1). Note also Platner and Ashby, 1929: pp. 6-11. But, however the evidence is interpreted, it is clear that, since the amphitheatre was inaugurated by Titus in 80 with *naumachiae* and games, it must have been considered finished by that date.

170. For the hasty construction of the baths, see *Titus* 7.3: *amphitheatro dedicato thermisque iuxta celeriter extructisque.* There are incidental references also in Dio, 66.25.1 and Martial, *Ep.* 3.20.15, 3.36.6; for their completion under Domitian, see the Chronographer of A.D. 354,

Chron. Min. 1, p. 146; Platner and Ashby, 1929: pp. 533-534.
171. An inscription on the arch of the Marcian aqueduct over the Via Tiburtina records the repairs:- *imp. Titus Caesar diui f. Vespasianus Aug. pontif. max. tribuniciae potestat. IX imp. XV cens. cos. VII desig. IIX p. p. riuom aquae Marciae uetustate dilapsum refecit et aquam quae in usu esse desierat reduxit* (*CIL* 6.1246 = McCrum and Woodhead, 1966: No. 409). The detailed study of the aqueduct by Deman, 1934: pp. 67-114, shows that Titus' main contribution was the encasement of a vast section of walls along the aqueduct - see also Ashby, 1935: pp. 88-158. The renovation of the *aqua Claudia* is noted on a number of inscriptions found at the Praenestine Gate (the Porta Maggiore) where the aqueduct entered the city:- *imp. T. Caesar diui f. Vespasianus Augustus...cos. VIII aquas Curtiam et Caeruleam perductas a diuo Claudio et postea a diuo Vespasiano patre suo urbi restitutas cum a capite aquarum a solo uetustate dilapsae essent noua forma reducendas sua impensa curauit* (*CIL* 6.1258 = McCrum and Woodhead, 1966: No. 408b) - see Ashby, 1935: pp. 191-192.
172. Platner and Ashby, 1929: p. 300; for the completion of the work by Domitian, see Blake, 1959: p. 101.
173. See Deman, 1912: p. 411; Platner and Ashby, 1929: p. 45; Blake, 1959: p. 98, and, for the dedicatory inscription, *CIL* 6.944.
174. See Newton, 1901: p. 52, No. 101 and Blake, 1959: p. 148 for the inscription recording Titus' activities in this area.
175. Newton, 1901: p. 53, No. 105 (Borussia Rhenana); *IGRR* 4.841 (amphitheatre), 845 (stadium). The inscriptions recording the dedication of the buildings in Phrygia show that they were presented to the community by a certain Nicostratus, probably a wealthy citizen of Laodicia: see Magie, 1950: pp. 572 and 1431 n. 17.
176. For the repairs to the aqueducts in Italy, see note 127, and for the work in Smyrna, *IGRR* 4.1411-1412; Magie, 1950: p. 584, suggests that the latter was paid for by the city itself.
177. The evidence for these various works has been gathered by Garzetti, 1974: p. 644.
178. For the inscription, see McCrum and Woodhead, 1966: No. 434, together with the comments of Buttrey, 1980: p. 26.
179. For work on the Via Flavia under Titus, see Newton, 1901: p. 59, Nos. 120 and 121 (latter half of 79), and No. 119 (A.D. 78) for the fact that it was begun under Vespasian. For the Via Aurelia, see p. 58, No. 116, and, for the Via Flaminia, p. 58 No. 118 together with Blake, 1959: p. 142. Vespasian had earlier improved the latter, building a tunnel through the rock at Intercisa (Ashby, 1912: pp. 125 ff.).
180. *AE* 1953, 179 (a milestone set up in Cyprus during the proconsulship of Pegasus' son L. Plotius P..., i.e.

81/82); for milestones from Numidia during Titus' reign, see Newton, 1901: p. 68, No. 141 (from Henschir Zaieta, dated Jan./June 80).

181. This road, constructed under the direction of the governor of Spain, C. Calpetanus Rantius Quirinalis Valerius Festus, ran from Bracara to Asturica. A number of milestones from Titus' reign attest to his work: *CIL* 2.4802, 4803, 4838, 4854, 6224; *AE* 1928, 178; 1966, 215; 1974, 401; 1975, 508.

182. Bosworth, 1976: p. 63.

183. The evidence for his activity is presented and discussed by Bosworth, 1976: pp. 72 ff.

184. His great-grandfather T. Flavius Petro had conducted a successful banking business after fleeing from Pharsalus (*Vesp*. 1.2), his grandfather Sabinus I had accumulated considerable wealth, gained equestrian rank for himself and senatorial status for his two sons, and supervised the collection of various import duties in Asia, whilst his father's *pecuniae cupiditas* (*Vesp*. 16.1) was legendary.

185. *imp. Titus Caesar Vespasianus Aug. pontif. max. trib. potest. VIII imp. XIIII cos. VII p. p. salutem dicit IIII uir. et decurionibus Muniguens. cum ideo appellaueritis, ne pecuniam quam debebatis Seruilio Pollioni, ex sententia Semproni Fusci solueretis, poenam iniustae appellationis exsigi* (sic) *a uobis oportebat; sed ego malui cum indulgentia mea quam temeritati uestra loqui et sestertia quinquaginta millia nummorum tenuitati publicae quam praetexitis remisi; scripsi autem Gallicano amico meo procos., pecuniam quae adiudicata est Pollioni, numerassetis, ex die sententiae dictae usurarum uos conputationem liberaret. reditus uectigaliorum uestrorum quae conducta habuisse Pollionem indicatis, in rationem uenire aequom* (sic) *est, nequid hoc nomine rei publicae apsit* (sic). *uale. dat. VII Idus Septembr.*: *AE* 1962, 288.

186. *CIL* 16.25.

187. *CIL* 16.24 (Sept. 8, 79: Egypt), 26 (June 13, 80: Pannonia), 27 (reign of Titus) and 158 (Jan./Feb. 80: Germany). On the grant of citizenship on discharge, see Watson, 1969: pp. 136-138. The diploma granted citizenship to the soldier and his children (but not to the wife) until the time of Antoninus Pius, when the right of *ciuitas* for the children was annulled: see Kraft, 1961: pp. 120-126; Wolff, 1974: pp. 479-510. On the laws relating to the marriage of soldiers in general, see Watson, 1969: pp. 133-142; Thomas, 1976: pp. 485-486 with n. 24; Campbell, 1978: pp. 153-166.

188. Alföldy, 1968: pp. 215-227; Mann, 1972: pp. 233-240; Holder, 1980: p. 48.

189. Mann, 1972: p. 238.

190. *CIL* 16.26.

191. *militibus liberam testamenti factionem primus quidem diuus Iulius Caesar concessit: sed ea concessio temporalis erat. postea uero primus diuus Titus dedit*: *Digest*

175

29.1.1.
192. *uulgo totis castris testamenta obsignabantur*:
Caesar, *Bellum Gallicum* 1.39.5. The form here referred to is
the *testamentum per aes et libram* (on which, see Schulz, 1951:
pp. 241-242; Jolowicz and Nicolas, 1972: p. 127) which
replaced the earlier form of military will, the *testamentum in
procinctu*, an informal declaration addressed to the testator's
comrades prior to battle. See also Lee, 1956: pp. 186-191.
193. Guarino, 1939: pp. 355-367; von Bolla, 1953: pp.
273-278.
194. *diuus Claudius duos praetores adiecit qui de
fideicommisso ius dicerent, ex quibus unum diuus Titus
detraxit*: *Digest* 1.2.2.32.
195. For the *fideicommissum*, see Schulz, 1951: pp. 395-
396. The decision of Augustus to give informal testamentary
trusts (*fideicommissa*) had required an official to control
them. Prior to Claudius' appointment of two *praetores
fideicommissarii*, the control had been exercised by the
consuls. On the function of the *praetor fideicommissarius*,
see Girard, 1924: p. 912; Schulz, 1951: p. 312; Jolowicz and
Nicolas, 1972: p. 396.
196. Garzetti, 1974: p. 262.
197. *diuus Pius Coelio Amaranto ita rescripsit,
uacantium bonorum nuntiationem quadriennio finiri, idque tempus ex die, quo certum esse coepit, neque heredem, neque
bonorum possessorem exstare, computari oportere. praescriptio
autem uiginti annorum, quae etiam circa requirendorum adnota-
torum bona obseruatur, ex constitutione diui Titi solet ex eo
numerari, ex quo quid ad fiscum pertinere potuit*: *Digest*
49.14.1.-23. The preceding section is also of some interest:-
*an bona, quae soluendo non sint, ipso iure ad fiscum
pertineant, quaesitum est. Labeo scribit, etiam ea quae
soluendo non sint, ipso iure ad fiscum pertinere. sed contra
sententiam eius edictum perpetuum scriptum est quod ita bona
ueneunt, si ex his fisco acquiri nihil possit*: *Digest* 49.14.
1.1, i.e. "Where property is not sufficient for payment, the
question arises whether it belongs to the treasury by
operation of law. Labeo says that, even if it is not
sufficient to discharge the liabilities, it will still belong
to the treasury by operation of law. The perpetual edict,
however, contradicts this opinion, because the property is
sold when none of it can be acquired by the treasury".
198. On the *praescriptio* and vacant succession, see
Buckland, 1921: p. 249; Girard, 1924: pp. 298 ff.; Schulz,
1951: p. 237; Jolowicz and Nicolas, 1972: pp. 152-153. On
the *aerarium* and the *fiscus*, see Millar, 1963: pp. 29-42;
Brunt, 1966: pp. 75-91.
199. *AE* 1954, 137; see also Leschi, 1953: pp. 189-205;
Leglay, 1968: p. 218; Buttrey, 1980: pp. 47-48.
200. Bosworth, 1976: pp. 63-78.
201. Mitford, 1974: pp. 172-173 with n. 87.

202. Notably those at Waldmössingen, Sulz, Offenburg, Rottweil, Risstissen and Günzburg, together with the auxiliary forts at Regensburg-Kumpfmühl, Straubing and the fort near Moos; see Schönberger, 1969: pp. 156-157, and, in particular, the map facing p. 176.

203. *ibid.*, p. 157 with n. 190. Syme, *CAH* 11: p. 166, comments on the establishment at Kösching:- "This fort can hardly have stood alone - it is probably a link in the chain of forts extending westwards a few miles beyond the northern bank of the Danube to Faimingen" (but see further, Schönberger, *loc. cit.*).

204. Those favouring 78 as Agricola's first year in Britain include Syme, 1958a: p. 22 with n. 6; A.R. Birley, 1967: p. 67; Frere, 1967: p. 104; Ogilvie and Richmond, 1967: p. 317; Eck, 1970: p. 125. Büchner, 1960: pp. 172 ff. and Petersen, *PIR*[2] J 126 suggest 77. More recently, however, A.R. Birley has re-examined the question and convincingly argues for the period 77-83/84 (1981: pp. 77-78); his argument has now been accepted by Eck, 1982: p. 300. Gallivan, 1981: p. 189 with n. 23 and p. 214, assigns his consulship to the last months of 77, but, as Birley, 1981: p. 77 n. 34 points out, "the known facts would not rule out 76".

205. For Agricola's movements during his third season, see *Agr.* 22 with the comments of Ogilvie and Richmond, 1967: pp. 57-59. A fort was constructed at High Rochester, smaller ones at Chew Green and Cappuck, a large one at Newstead on Tweed (Trimontium), possibly a smaller establishment at Oxton together with a terminal fort at Inveresk. In the west, forts were built at Birrens, Tassiesholm, Crawford and Castledykes.

206. *Agr.* 23 with Ogilvie and Richmond, 1967: pp. 323-328; for a map of the campaigns, see *ibid.*, p. 58 (Figure 4), where, however, the activities of the third, fourth and fifth seasons are assigned to the period 80-82 rather than 79-81.

207. On this legionary fortress, see, in particular, Ogilvie and Richmond, 1967: pp. 69-73.

208. *ignotas ad id tempus gentes crebris simul ac prosperis proeliis domuit; eamque partem Britanniae quae Hiberniam aspicit copiis instruxit*: *Agr.* 24.1.

209. Schieber, 1976: p. 140, lists such evidence as exists for the struggle.

210. There appear to have been three "false Neros" during the latter part of the first century, the first in 69 (*Hist.* 2.8.1; Dio, 63.9), the second (Terentius Maximus) in Titus' reign (Dio, 66.19) and the third ca. 88/89 (Suet., *Nero* 57.2; *Hist.* 1.2.8). Such is the view of, *inter alia*, Pappano, 1937: pp. 385-392; Gallivan, 1973: pp. 364-365; Bradley, 1978: pp. 294-295 and Chilver, 1979: p. 42. Others argue, less persuasively, for only two pretenders:- Henderson, 1909: p. 420 and 1927: p. 63; Bastomsky, 1969: pp. 321-325. Tacitus accepts at least three appearances of *falsi Nerones*, as may be inferred from his comment on the pretender of 69:-

ceterorum (i.e. "of the other pretenders") *casus conatusque in contextu operis dicemus*: *Hist*. 2.8.

211. For a discussion of the circumstances of Nero's death that gave rise to such claims, see Chilver, 1979: p. 42.

212. Debevoise, 1938: p. 214; Frye, 1963: p. 319; Colledge, 1967: p. 52, discuss the brief career of Artabanus IV; for his coins, see McDowell, 1935: pp. 190, 230 and also Sellwood, 1971: pp. 233-235.

213. Gallivan, 1973: p. 364.

214. Müller, 1841: pp. 578-579 (Vol. 4).

215. This is the view of Price, 1919: p. 83 and Gallivan, 1973: p. 364 n. 4; against, Schieber, 1976: p. 144. Titus' fifteenth salutation was probably awarded for Agricola's successful third season (79), according to A.R. Birley, 1981: p. 80.

216. For these possibilities, see Schieber, 1976: p. 144.

217. On the establishment of Aventicum, see van Berchem, 1944: pp. 45-46.

218. The arguments in favour of Doclea's foundation by Titus are discussed by Wilkes, 1969: pp. 259-261. The main evidence is the posthumous dedication to Titus - *CIL* 3.12680.

219. For Polemaeanus, see note 83, and for Montanus, notes 142, 143.

220. e.g. by Weynand, *RE* 6.2674; Scott, 1936: p. 40; Fortina, 1955a: p. 127; Hammond, 1959: p. 223; Clarke, 1966: p. 322; Blamberg, 1976: p. 216.

221. Clarke, 1966: pp. 318-321, discusses the relevant evidence for the interval between death and deification for Augustus, Claudius, Titus, Nerva, Trajan, Hadrian and Antoninus Pius.

222. *auctoritas et quasi maiestas quaedam ut scilicet inopinato et adhuc nouo principi deerat*: *Vesp*. 7.2.

223. For the evidence, see Buttrey, 1976: pp. 449-457.

224. Crook, 1951: pp. 162 ff.; Blamberg, 1976: p. 237.

225. The eruption is to be assigned to August 24 (Pliny, *Ep*. 6.16.4) in 79 (Dio, 66.21.1).

226. The ceremonial involved in the *consecratio* is described at some length by Herodian, *Hist*. 4.2.

227. Dio, 69.2.5, 69.23.3, 70.1.1-3; Aurelius Victor, 14.13-14; Eutropius, 8.7.3; HA *Hadr*. 27.3, *Anton. Pius* 5.1-2.

228. Nock, 1952: pp. 239-240.

229. Note, for instance, the provincial high priest, Raecius Gallus, who held a praetorship before the death of Vespasian (*AE* 1966, 189; Syme, 1969: p. 229). Étienne, 1974: p. 152, refers to the provincial priesthood as "ce moyen d'accès de la bourgeoisie provinciale à la carrière équestre".

230. Scott, 1936: p. 44; Blake, 1959: p. 97.

231. Mattingly, 1930: p. 269, No. 224.

232. A substantial list of municipal *flamines* is

provided by Scott, 1936: p. 45.
    233. For the coins of Domitilla, see Mattingly, 1930: p. 246, Nos. 136-138. Statius notes the deified members of Domitian's family - *fraterque, paterque et soror* (*Siluae* 1.1.97-98); if the mother (Domitilla I) had been deified, it is hard to believe that her name would have been omitted.
    234. For *Julia Augusta*, see *CIL* 6.2059 (minutes of the Arval Brethren, Jan. 3, 81) = McCrum and Woodhead, 1966: No. 11; for her coins, see Mattingly, 1930: p. 247, Nos. 139-144.
    235. On this, see Carter, 1982: p. 172.
    236. Suetonius (*Titus* 11), Dio (66.26.4) and the epitomator of the *De Caesaribus* (11.1) agree on the length of his reign, though Aurelius Victor (*De Caes.* 10.5) prefers thirty-two months and twenty days. Suetonius' statement (*Titus* 11) that he died in his forty-second year is inconsistent with his earlier (incorrect) comment (*Titus* 1) that he was born in 41; for similar chronological inaccuracies in Suetonius, see Mooney, 1930: p. 505.
    237. See note 238 for the text. The passage is discussed by Mooney, 1930: p. 503. Speculation on Titus' last words, also reported by Dio, 66.26.3, seems pointless.
    238. *spectaculis absolutis, in quorum fine populo coram ubertim fleuerat, Sabinos petit aliquanto tristior, quod sacrificanti hostia aufugerat quodque tempestate serena tonuerat. deinde ad primam statim mansionem febrim nanctus, cum inde lectica transferretur, suspexisse dicitur dimotis pallulis caelum, multumque conquestus eripi sibi uitam immerenti; neque enim exstare ullum suum factum paenitendum excepto dum taxat uno* (*Titus* 10.1) ... *excessit in eadem qua pater uilla Id. Sept. post biennium ac menses duos diesque XX quam successerat patri, altero et quadragesimo aetatis anno*: (11). Note also *Epit. de Caes.* 10.15; Orosius, 7.9, 14; Eutropius, 7.22. Suetonius could, of course, have been referring to some other *spectacula*: see McGuire, 1980: p. 166.
    239. *ueneno...interiit*: Aurelius Victor, *Caes.* 10.11.
    240. The hostility towards Domitian in the literary tradition is well known; for an assessment of its influence in this instance, see Grosso, 1956: pp. 137-162.
    241. For a full account, see Mooney, 1930: pp. 503-504.
    242. Bastomsky, 1967: pp. 22-23.
    243. *CIL* 6.2060 = McCrum and Woodhead, 1966: No. 12.
    244. *CIL* 6.2060: see Scott, 1936: p. 61; Hammond, 1959: p. 224 n. 24.
    245. As Clarke, 1966: p. 319 has pointed out, any delay would surely have been exploited by the ancient sources.
    246. Platner and Ashby, 1929: p. 556; Blake, 1959: pp. 97-98; Leon, 1971: Plate 33.
    247. Eutropius, 7.23; Chronographer of 354 A.D. (*Chron. Min.* 1, p. 146); Platner and Ashby, 1929: p. 152; Scott, 1936: pp. 62-63.

248. *ILS* 7213: see Scott, 1936: p. 63.
249. *Dom.* 1.1 (*templum*); Statius, *Siluae* 4.2.59-60, 4.3.18-19; 5.1.239-241; Martial, *Ep.* 9.1.6-10; 9.3.12; 9.20; 9.34; 9.93.6.
250. For a description of the arch, see Platner and Ashby, 1929: pp. 45-47; Scott, 1936: pp. 63-64. Gsell, 1894: p. 108 n. 2; McFayden, 1915: pp. 131-141; Magi, 1945: pp. 160-162, assign the monument to the last years of Domitian's reign or even later, but the earlier date has been convincingly defended by Toynbee, 1947: pp. 190 ff. and 1950: p. 11; Strong, 1960: p. 119 n. 3.
251. Herodian, *Hist.* 4.2, in his account of the funerary honours of Septimius Severus, states that the eagle was thought to carry the spirit of the dead emperor with him into the sky where he would be worshipped among the other gods. A detailed description of the *consecratio* in general is given by Dio, 74.4-5 (Pertinax).
252. On the *sodales*, see Newton, 1901: pp. 95 ff.; Momigliano, 1935: pp. 165-171; Scott, 1936: pp. 79-81.
253. The *flamines* of Titus are discussed by Newton, 1901: pp. 98-99; Scott, 1936: pp. 61-62; Fortina, 1955a: pp. 143, 149 n. 22. They are attested in Gallia Transpadana (*CIL* 5.5239, 5667), Latium (14.400, 4142, 4622), Hispania Tarraconensis (2.4212), Liguria (5.6995), Carthage (8.14364), Dougga (8.26470) and Novaria (3.12692, 12695).

BIBLIOGRAPHY

ABAECHERLI, A.L. 1935. "Imperial Symbols on certain Flavian
    Coins", *CPh* 10: pp. 131-140
ABEL, F.M. 1949. "Topographie du siège de Jérusalem en 70",
    RBi 56: pp. 238-258
ABEL, F.M. 1952. *Histoire de la Palestine depuis la conquête
    d'Alexandre jusqu'à l'invasion arabe* (Gabalda, Paris)
ABEL, F.M. 1967. *Géographie de la Palestine* (Lecoffre, Paris:
    3rd edn.)
ABRAHAMS, I. 1927. *Campaigns in Palestine from Alexander the
    Great* (Oxford University Press, London).
ALBRIGHT, W.F. 1941. "New Light on the Walls of Jerusalem in
    the New Testament Age", *Bulletin of Am. Schools of
    Oriental Research in Jerusalem and Baghdad* 81: pp. 6-10
ALFÖLDY, G. 1967. "Die Legionslegaten der römischen
    Rheinarmeen". *ES* 3
ALFÖLDY, G. 1968. "Zur Beurteilung der Militärdiplome der
    Auxiliarsoldaten", *Historia* 17: pp. 215-227
ALFÖLDY, G. 1969. *Fasti Hispanienses. Senatorische Reichs-
    beamte und Offiziere in der Spanischen Provinzen der
    römisches Reiches von Augustus bis Diokletian* (F. Steiner,
    Wiesbaden)
ALFÖLDY, G. and HALFMANN, H. 1973. "M. Cornelius Nigrinus
    Curiatius Maternus, General Domitians und Rivale Trajans",
    Chiron 3: pp. 331-373
AMIRAN, R. 1971. "The First and Second Walls of Jerusalem
    reconsidered in the Light of the New Wall", *IEJ* 21:
    pp. 166-167
ANDERSON, J.G.C. 1922. *Cornelii Taciti de Vita Agricolae*
    (Clarendon Press, Oxford)
APPELBAUM, Sh. 1971. "The Zealots: The Case for Revaluation",
    JRS 61: pp. 155-170
ARIAS, P.E. 1945. *Domiziano* (G. Crisafulli, Catania)
ARNIM, H. 1898. *Leben und Werke des Dio von Prusa* (Weidmann,
    Berlin)
ARNOLD, E.V. 1911. *Roman Stoicism* (Cambridge University Press,
    Cambridge)

ASHBY, T. 1921. "The Via Flaminia", *JRS* 11: pp. 125-190
ASHBY, T. 1935. *The Aqueducts of Ancient Rome* (Clarendon Press, Oxford)
ASSA, J. 1962. "Aulus Bucius Lappius Maximus", *Akten des IV. internationalen Kongresses für griechische und lateinische Epigraphik*: pp. 31-39
AVI-YONAH, M. 1936. "Map of Roman Palestine", *QAP* 5: pp. 139-183
AVI-YONAH, M. 1953. "The Missing Fortress of Flavius Josephus", *IEJ* 3: pp. 94-98
AVI-YONAH, M. 1957. "The Archaeological Survey of Masada, 1955-1956", *IEJ* 7: pp. 1-60
AVI-YONAH, M. 1968. "The Third and Second Walls of Jerusalem", *IEJ* 18: pp. 98-125
AVI-YONAH, M. 1975. *The World History of the Jewish People: Vol. 7: The Herodian Period* (Rutgers University Press, New Brunswick)
BALDWIN, B. 1975. "Vespasian and Freedom", *RFIC* 103: pp. 306-308
BALLANTI, A. 1954. "Documenti sull' opposizione degli intellettuali a Domiziano", *AFLN* 4: pp. 75-95
BALSDON, J.P.V.D. 1934a. *The Emperor Gaius* (Clarendon Press, Oxford)
BALSDON, J.P.V.D. 1934b. "Notes Concerning the Principate of Gaius", *JRS* 24: pp. 13-24
BALTY, J. and J. 1977. "Apamée de Syrie I", *ANRW* II 8, pp. 122-123
BARAG, D. 1978. "The Palestinian Judaea Capta coins of Vespasian and Titus and the Era on the Coins of Agrippa II minted under the Flavians", *NC* 18: pp. 14-23
BARDON, H. 1962. "Le Goût à l'époque des Flaviens", *Latomus* 21: pp. 732-748
BARDON, H. 1968. *Les Empereurs et les Lettres Latines d'Auguste à Hadrien* (Les Belles Lettres, Paris)
BARINI, C. 1952. *Triumphalia: imprese ed onori militari durante l'impero romano* (Società Editrice Internazionale, Turin)
BARNES, T.D. 1971. "The First African Consul", *CR* 21: p. 332
BARNES, T.D. 1977. "The Fragments of Tacitus' *Histories*", *CPh* 72: pp. 224-231
BARON, S.W. 1952-1973. *A Social and Religious History of the Jews* (Columbia University Press, New York and London)
BARRETT, A.A. 1977. "Sohaemus, King of Emesa and Sophene", *AJPh* 98: pp. 153-159
BASTIANINI, G. 1975. "Lista dei prefetti d'Egitto dal 30^a al 299^p", *ZPE* 17: pp. 263-328
BASTIANINI, G. 1980. "Lista dei prefetti d'Egitto dal 30^a al 299^p: Aggiunte e correzioni", *ZPE* 38: pp. 75-89
BASTOMSKY, S.J. 1967. "The Death of the Emperor Titus: A Tentative Suggestion", *Apeiron* 1: pp. 22-23
BASTOMSKY, S.J. 1969. "The Emperor Nero in Talmudic Legend",

JQR 59: pp. 321-325

BAUMANN, R.A. 1974. *Impietas in Principem* (C.H. Beck, Munich)

BAXTER, T.F. 1973. Review of Urban. *Phoenix* 27: pp. 207-208

BENGSTON, H. 1979. *Die Flavier. Vespasian, Titus und Domitian. Geschichte eines römischen Kaiserhauses* (C.H. Beck, Munich)

BÉRANGER, J. 1939. "L'Hérédité du Principat", *REL* 17: pp. 171-187

BÉRANGER, J. 1953. *Recherches sur l'aspect idéologique du Principat* (Reinhardt, Basle)

BÉRANGER, J. 1955. Review of Briessmann. *REL* 33: pp. 412-416

BÉRANGER, J. 1973. Review of Urban. *REL* 51: pp. 420-422

BERCHEM, D. van. 1944. "Les Colons d'Aventicum". *Mélanges Ch. Gilliard* (Fac. De Lettres de Lausanne, Lausanne)

BERNAYS, J. 1885. "Über die Chronik des Sulpicius Severus". *Gesammelte Abhandlungen*, Vol. II (W. Hertz, Berlin)

BERNSTEIN, L. 1938. *Flavius Josephus, his Times and His Critics* (Liverbright, New York)

BIANCO, E. 1968. "Indirizzi programmatici e propagandistici nella monetazione di Vespasiano", *RIN* 70: pp. 145-224

BICKNELL, P. 1968. "The Emperor Gaius' Military Activities in A.D. 40", *Historia* 17: pp. 502-504.

BIETENHARD, H. 1977. "Die Syrische Dekapolis von Pompeius bis Trajan", *ANRW* II, pp. 220-261

BIRK, G. 1967. *Der Wandel der römischen Führungschicht unter Vespasian* (Diss., Tübingen)

BIRLEY, A.R. 1962. "The Oath not to put Senators to Death", *CR* 12: pp. 197-199

BIRLEY, A.R. 1967. "The Roman Governors of Britain", *ES* 4: pp. 63-102

BIRLEY, A.R. 1973. "Petillius Cerialis and the Conquest of Brigantia", *Britannia* 4: pp. 179-190

BIRLEY, A.R. 1975. "Agricola, the Flavian Dynasty and Tacitus", *The Ancient Historian and his materials; Essays in honour of C.E. Stevens:* pp. 139-154

BIRLEY, A.R. 1981. *The Fasti of Roman Britain* (Clarendon Press, Oxford)

BIRLEY, E. 1946. "Britain under the Flavians: Agricola and his Predecessors", *DUJ* 7: pp. 79-84

BIRLEY, E. 1953. "Senators in the Emperors' Service", *PBA* 39: pp. 197-214

BIRLEY, E. 1978. "The Adherence of Britain to Vespasian", *Britannia* 9: pp. 243-245

BISHOP, J. 1964. *Nero: The Man and the Legend* (Robert Hale, London)

BLAKE, M.E. 1959. *Roman Construction in Italy from Tiberius through the Flavians* (Carnegie Institute of Washington, Washington)

BLAMBERG, J.E. 1976. *The Public Image Projected by the Roman Emperors (A.D. 69-117) as Reflected in Contemporary Imperial Coinage* (Diss., Indiana)

BOER, W. den. 1973. *Les Culte des Souverains dans l'empire romain* (Fondation Hardt, Entretiens 19: Geneva)

BOISSEVAIN, V.P. 1901. *Cassii Dionis Historiarum quae Supersunt*, Vol. III (Weidmann, Berlin)

BOLIN, S. 1958. *State and Currency in the Roman Empire to 300 A.D.* (Almqvist and Wiksell, Stockholm)

BOLLA, S. von. 1953. "Zum römischen Militärtestament", *St. Arango-Ruiz* 1: pp. 273-278

BOMSTEAD, R.G. 1979. *Governing Ideas of the Jewish War of Flavius Josephus* (Diss., Yale)

BORZSAK, E. 1973. Review of Urban. *Latomus* 32: pp. 643-644

BOSCH, C. 1935. *De kleinasiatischen Munzen der römischen Kaiserzeit* (Kohlhammer, Stuttgart)

BOSWORTH, A.B. 1973. "Vespasian and the Provinces: Some Problems of the Early 70's A.D.", *Athenaeum* 51: pp. 49-78

BOSWORTH, A.B. 1976. "Vespasian's Reorganisation of the North-East Frontier", *Antichthon* 10: pp. 63-78

BOSWORTH, A.B. 1980. "Firmus of Arretium", *ZPE* 39: pp. 267-277

BOULVERT, G. 1981. "La Carrière de Tiberius Claudius Augusti Libertus Classicus (*AE* 1972, 574)", *ZPE* 43: pp. 31-41

BOURNE, F.C. 1941. *The Public Works of the Julio-Claudians and the Flavians* (Diss., Princeton)

BOWERSOCK, G.W. 1973. "Syria under Vespasian", *JRS* 63: pp. 133-140

BOWERSOCK, G.W. 1976. Review of Schürer. *JRS* 65: pp. 180-185

BOWMAN, A. 1976. "Papyri and Roman History", *JRS* 66: pp. 153-173

BRADLEY, K.R. 1978. *Suetonius' Life of Nero: an Historical Commentary* (Collection Latomus 157: Brussels)

BRADLEY, K.R. 1979. "Nero's Retinue in Greece, A.D. 66-67", *ICS* 4: pp. 152-157

BRAITHWAITE, A.W. 1927. *C. Suetonii Tranquilli Divus Vespasianus with an Introduction and a Commentary* (Clarendon Press, Oxford)

BRANDON, S.G.F. 1957. *The Fall of Jerusalem and the Christian Church: A Study of the Effect of the Jewish Overthrow of A.D. 70 on Christianity* (SPCK, London)

BRANDON, S.G.F. 1958. "Josephus, Renegade or Patriot", *HT* 8: pp. 830-836

BRANDON, S.G.F. 1965. "The Zealots. The Jewish Resistance against Rome, A.D. 66-73", *HT* 15: pp. 632-641

BRANDON, S.G.F. 1970. "The Defeat of Cestius Gallus", *HT* 20: pp. 38-46

BRASSLOFF, S. 1904. "Patriciat und Quästor in der römischen

Kaiserzeit", *Hermes* 39: pp. 618-629
BRASSLOFF, S. 1905. "Die Grundsätze bei der Commendation der Plebejer", *JÖAI* 8: pp. 60-70
BRASSLOFF, S. 1910. "Sevirat und Vigintivirat", *WS* 32: pp. 117-121
BRIESSMANN, A. 1955. *Tacitus und das flavische Geschichtsbild* (Hermes Einzelschriften 10: F. Steiner, Wiesbaden)
BRUNT, P.A. 1966. "The 'Fiscus' and its Development", *JRS* 56: pp. 75-91
BRUNT, P.A. 1975a. "The Administrators of Roman Egypt", *JRS* 65: pp. 124-147
BRUNT, P.A. 1975b. "Stoicism and the Principate", *PBSR* 43: pp. 6-35
BRUNT, P.A. 1977a. "The Lex de Imperio Vespasiani", *JRS* 67: pp. 95-116
BRUNT, P.A. 1977b. "Josephus on Social Conflicts in Roman Judaea", *Klio* 59: pp. 149-153
BÜCHNER, K. 1960. "Reicht die Statthalterschaft des Agricola von 77-82 oder von 78-83 n. Chr.?", *RhM* 103: pp. 172-178
BÜCHNER, K. 1964. "Die Riese des Titus", *Studien zur römischen Literatur IV* (Wiesbaden)
BUCKLAND, W. 1921. *A Textbook of Roman Law from Augustus to Diocletian* (Cambridge University Press, Cambridge)
BUREN, V.W. van. 1969. "Some Roman Reminiscences of Titus' Conquest of Jerusalem". *Hommages à M. Renard* (Collection Latomus 103: Brussels), pp. 610-612
BURN, A.R. 1965. *Agricola and Roman Britain* (English Universities Press, London: 2nd edn.)
BURR, V. 1955. *Tiberius Julius Alexander* (Habelt, Bonn)
BURTON, G.P. 1972. Review of Eck, 1970. *JRS* 62: p. 183
BURTON, G.P. 1977. Review of Boulvert, 1970. *JRS* 67: pp. 162-166
BUTTREY, T.V. 1972. "Vespasian as Moneyer", *NC* 12: pp. 89-109
BUTTREY, T.V. 1976. "Vespasian's *Consecratio* and the Numismatic Evidence", *Historia* 25: pp. 449-457
BUTTREY, T.V. 1980. *Documentary Evidence for the Chronology of the Flavian Titulature* (Beiträge zur Klassischen Philologie 112: A. Hain, Meisenheim)
CAGNAT, M.R. 1891. "L'Armée romaine au siège de Jérusalem", *REJ* 22: pp. 28-58
CALDERINI, A. 1940/1941. "Teoria e pratica politica nella *Vita di Appollonio* di Tiana", *RIL* 74: pp. 213-241
CAMODECA, G. 1976. "La carriera del giurista L. Neratius Priscus", *AAN* 97: pp. 19-38
CAMPBELL, B. 1978. "The Marriage of Soldiers under the Empire", *JRS* 68: pp. 153-166
CARCOPINO, J. 1949. "L'Hérédité dynastique chez les Antonins", *REA* 51: pp. 262-321
CARTER, J.M. 1982. *Suetonius, Diuus Augustus* (Bristol Classical Press, Bristol)

CASSON, L. 1951. "Speed under Sail of Ancient Ships", *TAPhA* 82: pp. 136-148

CASSON, L. 1959. *The Ancient Mariners* (Gollancz, London)

CASTRITIUS, H. 1969. "Zu den Frauen der Flavier", *Historia* 18: pp. 492-502

CÉBEILLAC, M. 1972. *Les "Quaestores Principis et Candidati" aux 1er et 11ème Siècles de l'Empire* (Cisalpino-Goliardica, Milan)

CHAMBALU, A. 1882. *De Magistratibus Flaviorum* (Strauss, Bonn).

CHAMBALU, A. 1885. "Flaviana", *Philologus* 44: pp. 106-131, 502-517

CHAMPLIN, E. 1978. "Pegasus", *ZPE* 32: pp. 269-278

CHARLESWORTH, M.P. 1926. "Fear of the Orient in the Roman Empire", *Cambridge Historical Journal* 2: pp. 1-16

CHARLESWORTH, M.P. 1937. "Flaviana", *JRS* 27: pp. 54-62

CHASTAGNOL, A. 1973. "La Naissance de l'ordo senatorius", *MEFR* 85: pp. 581-607

CHASTAGNOL, A. 1975. *"Latus clavus* et *Adlectio*. L'accès des hommes nouveaux au sénat romain sous le haut empire", *RD* 53: pp. 375-394

CHASTAGNOL, A. 1976. "Le Laticlave de Vespasien", *Historia* 25: pp. 253-256

CHAUMONT, L. 1976. "L'Arménie entre Rome et l'Iran. I, De l'avènement d'Auguste a l'avènement de Dioclétien", *ANRW* II.9: pp. 71-194

CHILVER, G.E.F. 1950. "Augustus and the Roman Constitution", *Historia* 1: pp. 408-435

CHILVER, G.E.F. 1956. Review of Briessmann. *JRS* 46: pp. 203-205

CHILVER, G.E.F. 1957. "The Army in Politics A.D. 68-70", *JRS* 47: pp. 29-35

CHILVER, G.E.F. 1979. *A Historical Commentary on Tacitus' Histories I and II* (Clarendon Press, Oxford)

CIZEK, E. 1977. *Structures et Idéologie dans "Les Vies des douze Césars" de Suétone* (Editura Academiei, Bucharest and Paris)

CLARKE, G.W. 1966. "The Date of the *Consecratio* of Vespasian", *Historia* 15: pp. 318-327

COLLEDGE, M.A.R. 1967. *The Parthians* (Thames and Hudson, London)

COMBÈS, R. 1966. *Imperator: Recherches sur l'emploi et la Signification du titre d'imperator dans la Rome républicaine* (Presses Universitaires, Paris)

CONRAD, E. 1974. "The *Iudaea Navalis* Brass of Titus", *NCirc* 82: p. 331

CONTI, L. 1975. "Sul Ritratto Monetale di Tito", *NAC* 4: pp. 209-214

CORBETT, P.E. 1969. *The Roman Law of Marriage* (Clarendon Press, Oxford: 2nd edn.)

CORTE, F. della. 1967. *Suetonio, eques romanus* (La Nuova

Italia, Florence: 2nd edn.)
COTTON, H.M. 1981. "Military Tribunates and the Exercise of Patronage", *Chiron* 11: pp. 229-238
CROOK, J. 1951. "Titus and Berenice", *AJPh* 72: pp. 162-175
CROOK, J. 1955. *Consilium Principis: Imperial Councils and Counsellors from Augustus to Diocletian* (Cambridge University Press, Cambridge)
CUST, L. 1924. *Jerusalem: A Historical Sketch* (A. and C. Black, London)
DABROWA, E. 1980. "Le Limes anatolien et la frontière caucasienne au temps des Flaviens", *Klio* 62: pp. 379-388
DACK, E. van T'. 1972. Review of Eck. *RBPh* 50: pp. 626-627
DALTROP, G. et al. 1966. *De Flavier, Vespasian, Titus, Domitian, Nerva, Julia Titi, Domitilla, Domitia* (Mann, Berlin)
DAUBE, D. 1976. "Father of Three", *AJAH* 1: pp. 145-147
DEBEVOISE, N.C. 1938. *A Political History of Parthia* (University of Chicago Press, Chicago)
DEGRASSI, A. 1947. "Un nuovo diploma militare e i consoli dell'anno 80 d.C.", *PP* 2: pp. 349-356
DEGRASSI, A. 1952. *I Fasti Consolari dell' Impero romano dal 30 av. C. al 613 d.C.* (Edizioni di Storia e Letteratura, Rome)
DE LAET, S.J. 1949. *Portorium: Étude sur l'organisation douanière chez les Romains, surtout à l'époque du haut-empire* (De Tempel, Brugge: repr. Arno Press Inc., 1975)
DEMAN, E.B. Van. 1912. "The Methods of determining the date of ancient Roman concrete construction", *AJA* 16: pp. 230-241; 387-432
DEMAN, E.B. Van. 1934. *The Building of the Roman Aqueducts* (Carnegie Institute of Washington, Washington)
DERCHAIN, P. 1953. "La visite de Vespasien au Sérapéum d'Alexandrie", *CE* 28: pp. 261-271
DERCHAIN, P., and HUBAUX, J. 1953. "Vespasien au Sérapéum", 12: pp. 38-52
DESSAU, H. 1924-1930. *Geschichte der römischen Kaiserzeit* (Weidmann, Berlin)
DE VAUX, R. 1958. "An Archaeologist and the Dead Sea Scrolls", *Listener* 68: pp. 1007-1008
DE VAUX, R. 1959. "Les Manuscrits de Qumrân et l'Archéologie", *RBi* 66: pp. 87-100
DEVREKER, J. 1976a. "C. Messalla Vipstanus Gallus ou l'histoire d'un nom", *ZPE* 22: pp. 203-206
DEVREKER, J. 1976b. Review of Kreiler. *Epigraphica* 38: pp. 179-188
DEVREKER, J. 1977. "La Continuité dans le *Consilium Principis* sous les Flaviens", *Ancient Society* 8: pp. 223-243
DEVREKER, J. 1980. "L'*Adlectio in senatum* de Vespasien", *Latomus* 39: pp. 70-87
DEVREKER, J. 1982. "Les Orientaux au Sénat romain d'Auguste

à Trajan", *Latomus* 41: pp. 492-516
DOBÓ, A. 1968. *Die Verwaltung der römischen Provinz Pannonien von Augustus bis Diocletianus* (A. Hakkert, Amsterdam)
DOREY, T.A. 1958. "Tacitus and the Treatment of Antonius Primus", *CPh* 53: p. 244
DREXLER, H. 1956. Review of Briessmann. *Gnomon* 28: pp. 519-527
DRIVER, G.R. 1965. *The Judaean Scrolls: The Problem and the Solution* (Blackwell, Oxford)
DUNKLE, J.R. 1971. "The Rhetorical Tyrant in Roman Historiography: Sallust, Livy and Tacitus", *CW* 64: pp. 12-20
DURRY, M. 1938. *Pline le Jeune: Panégyrique de Trajan* (Les Belles Lettres, Paris)
DURRY, M. 1964. "Sur Trajan Père". *Les Empereurs romains d'Espagne: Colloques internationaux du Centre national de la recherche scientifique* (Ed. du CRNS, Paris): pp. 45-54
DURRY, M. 1968. *Les Cohortes Prétoriennes* (repr.: De Boccard, Paris)
DUSANIC, S. 1968. "On the *Consules suffecti* of A.D. 74-76", *Epigraphica* 30: pp. 59-74
DUSANIC, S. and VASIC, M. 1977. "An Upper Moesian Diploma of A.D. 96", *Chiron* 7: pp. 291-304
ECK, W. 1970. *Senatoren von Vespasian bis Hadrian* (Vestigia 13: C.H. Beck, Munich)
ECK, W. 1971. Review of Dobó. *Bonner Jahrb.* 171: pp. 743-750
ECK, W. 1972a. Review of Kneissl. *Gnomon* 44: pp. 171-176
ECK, W. 1972b. "M. Pompeius Silvanus, consul designatus tertium - ein Vertrauter Vespasians und Domitians", *ZPE* 9: pp. 259-276
ECK, W. 1973. "Sozialstruktur des römischen Senatorenstandes der hohen Kaiserzeit und statistische methode", *Chiron* 3: pp. 375-394
ECK, W. 1974. "Beförderungskriterien innerhalb der senatorischen Laufbahn, dargestelt an der Zeit von 69 bis 138 n. Chr.", *ANRW* II.1: pp. 158-228
ECK, W. 1980. "Epigraphische Untersuchungen zu Konsuln und Senatoren des 1.-3. Jh. n. Chr.", *ZPE* 37: pp. 31-68
ECK, W. 1982. "Jahres- und Provinzialfasten der senatorischen Statthalter von 69/70 bis 138/139", *Chiron* 12: pp. 281-362
EICHHOLZ, D.E. 1972. "How long did Vespasian serve in Britain?", *Britannia* 3: pp. 149-163
EQUINI, E. 1967. "Un frammento inedito dei Fasti ostiensi del 74", *Epigraphica* 29: pp. 11-17
ETIENNE, R. 1974. *Le culte impérial dans la péninsule ibérique d'Auguste à Dioclétien* (De Boccard, Paris)
EVANS, J.K. 1975. "The Dating of Domitian's War Against the Chatti Again", *Historia* 24: pp. 121-124
EVANS, J.K. 1978. "The Role of *suffragium* in Imperial

Political Decision-Making: A Flavian Example", *Historia* 27: pp. 102-128

EVANS, J.K. 1979. "The Trial of P. Egnatius Celer", *CQ* 29: pp. 198-202

FABIA, P. 1982. "Pline l'ancien a-t-il assisté au siège de Jérusalem par Titus?", *R.Ph.Lit. et Hist.Anc.* 16: pp. 149-155

FISHWICK, D. 1965. "Vae puto deus fio", *CQ* 15: pp. 155-157

FISHWICK, D. 1970. "Flamen Augustorum", *HSPh* 74: pp. 299-312

FORTINA, M. 1955a. *L'Imperatore Tito* (Società Editrice Internazionale, Turin)

FORTINA, M. 1955b. *Un generale romano del I secolo dell' impero, C. Licinio Muciano* (Mora, Novara)

FRANK, T. 1936ff. *An Economic Survey of Ancient Rome* (Johns Hopkins University Press, Baltimore)

FRANKFORT, Th. 1957. Review of Fortina. *Latomus* 16: p. 179

FRANKFORT, Th. 1962. "Le Royaume d'Agrippa II et son Annexion par Domitien" (Collection Latomus 58: Brussels) pp. 659-672

FRERE, S.S. 1967. *Britannia: A History of Roman Britain* (Routledge and Kegan Paul, London)

FRÉZOULS, E. 1977. "Cyrrus and la Cyrrhestique I", *ANRW* II.8: pp. 184-185

FRIEDLÄNDER, L. 1921-1923. *Darstellungen aus der Sittengeschichte Roms in der Zeit von Augustus bis zum Untergang der Antonine* (Hirzel, Leipzig: 9./10. Aufl.)

FRYE, R.N. 1963. *The Heritage of Persia* (Weidenfeld and Nicolson, London)

FUKS, I.A. 1948/1949. "Marcus Julius Alexander", *Zion* 13/14: pp. 15-17

FUKS, I.A. 1957-64. *Corpus Papyrorum Judaicorum*, Vol. II (Cambridge, Mass.)

FURNEAUX, R. 1973. *The Roman Siege of Jerusalem* (Hart-Davis MacGibbon, London)

GAGÉ, J. 1931. "Divus Augustus", *RA* 34: pp. 11-41

GAGE, J. 1952. "Vespasien et la mémoire de Galba", *REA* 54: pp. 290-315

GAGÉ, J. 1959. "La propagande sérapiste et la lutte des empereurs flaviens avec les philosophes (stoiciens et cyniques)", *RPh* 149: pp. 73-100

GALLIVAN, P.A. 1973. "The False Neros: a Re-examination", *Historia* 22: pp. 364-365

GALLIVAN, P.A. 1974. "Some Comments on the *Fasti* for the Reign of Nero", *CQ* 24: pp. 290-311

GALLIVAN, P.A. 1978a. "The *Fasti* for the Reign of Claudius", *CQ* 28: pp. 407-426

GALLIVAN, P.A. 1978b. "Who was Acilius?", *Historia* 27: pp. 621-625

GALLIVAN, P.A. 1981. "The Fasti for A.D. 70-96", *CQ* 31: pp. 186-220

GALLOTTA, B. 1978. "Cn. Domizio Corbulone", *RIL* 112: pp. 305-317

GARZETTI, A. 1966. "L. Cesennio Peto e la rivalutazione flaviana di personaggi neroniani", *Mélanges Piganiol*: pp. 777-790

GARZETTI, A. 1973. Review of Urban. *RSA* 3: pp. 201-204

GARZETTI, A. 1974. *From Tiberius to the Antonines: A History of the Roman Empire, A.D. 14-192* (tr. J.R. Foster: Methuen, London)

GEPHARDT, R.F.C. 1922. *C. Suetonii Tranquilli Vita Domitiani: Suetonius' Life of Domitian with Notes and Parallel Passages* (Diss., Pennsylvania)

GIET, S. 1952a. "La *Guerre des Juifs* de Flavius Josèphe et quelques énigmes de l'Apocalypse", *RSR* 26: pp. 1-29

GIET, S. 1952b. "Les épisodes de la guerre juive et l'Apocalypse", *RSR* 26: pp. 325-362

GILLIAM, J.F. 1967. "Titus in Julian's *Caesares*", *AJPh* 88: pp. 203-208

GILMARTIN, K. 1973. "Corbulo's Campaigns in the East. An Analysis of Tacitus' Acçount", *Historia* 22: pp. 583-626

GIRARD, P.F. 1924. *Manuel Élémentaire de Droit Romain* (Rousseau, Paris: 7th edn.)

GOETZE, H. 1954. "Ein Triumphalbildnis des Titus", *Festschrift Schweitzer*: pp. 354-357

GORDON, A.E. 1955. "Vespasian and Titus as Consuls A.D. 70", *CPh* 50: pp. 194-195

GRAF, H.R. 1937. *Kaiser Vespasian: Untersuchungen zu Suetons Vita Divi Vespasiani* (Kohlhammer, Stuttgart)

GRANT, M. 1946. *From Imperium to Auctoritas* (Cambridge University Press, Cambridge)

GRENADE, P. 1961. *Essai sur les origines du principat: investiture et renouvellement des pouvoires impériaux* (De Boccard, Paris)

GRENZHEUSER, B. 1964. *Kaiser und Senat in der Zeit von Nero bis Nerva* (Diss., Münster)

GRIFFIN, M. 1976. *Seneca: A Philosopher in Politics* (Clarendon Press, Oxford)

GRIFFITH, J.G. 1969. "Juvenal, Statius and the Flavian Establishment", *G&R* 16: pp. 134-150

GRIFFITH, J.G. 1970. "Tacitus, *Hist.* 5.13.2 and the Dead Sea Scrolls", *RhM* 113: pp. 363-368

GRIFFITH, J.G. 1979. "Tacitus and the HODAYOT in the Dead Sea Scrolls", *RhM* 122: pp. 99-100

GROAG, E. 1896. "Patricier und III viri monetales", *Arch.-Epigr. Mitt.* 19: pp. 145-146

GROAG, E. 1929. "Zum Konsulat in der Kaiserzeit", *WS* 47: pp. 143-146

GROSSO, F. 1954a. "La *Vita di Apollonio di Tiana* come fonte storica", *Acme* 7: pp. 333-532

GROSSO, F. 1954b. "Tendenziosità dell' *Agricola* : *In Mem. A. Beltrami Miscell. Phil.*: pp. 94-145

GROSSO, F. 1954c. "Aspetti della politicà orientale di
    Domiziano, I", *Epigraphica* 16: pp. 117-179
GROSSO, F. 1955. "Aspetti della politicà orientale di
    Domiziano, II", *Epigraphica* 17: pp. 33-78
GROSSO, F. 1956. "La morte di Tito", *Antidoron U.E. Paoli*:
    pp. 137-162
GROSSO, F. 1957. "M. Ulpio Traiano, Governatore di Siria",
    RIL 91: pp. 318-342
GRY, L. 1948. "La ruine du temple par Titus. Quelques
    traditions juives plus anciennes et primitives à la base
    de *Pesikta Rabbathi XXVI*", *RBi* 55: pp. 215-226
GSELL, S. 1894. *Essai sur le règne de l'empereur Domitien*
    (Thorin, Paris)
GUARDUCCI, M. 1971/1972. "Una moneta di Tito nella villa
    pontificia di Castelgandolfo", *RPAA* 44: pp. 167-172
GUARINO, A. 1939. "Sull' origine del testamento dei militari
    nel diritto romano", *RIL* 72: pp. 355-367
HALFMANN, H. 1979. *Die Senatoren aus dem östlichen Teil des
    Imperium Romanum bis zum Ende des 2. Jh. n. Chr.* (Vanden-
    hoeck and Ruprecht, Göttingen)
HAMILTON, C.C. 1969. "The *Tresuiri monetales* and the
    Republican *cursus honorum*", *TAPhA* 100: pp. 181-199
HAMMOND, M. 1933. *The Augustan Principate* (Harvard University
    Press, Harvard)
HAMMOND, M. 1938. "The Tribunician Day during the Early
    Empire", *MAAR* 15: pp. 23-61
HAMMOND, M. 1956. "The Transmission of the Imperial Powers
    of the Roman Emperor from the Death of Nero in A.D. 68 to
    that of Alexander Severus in A.D. 235", *MAAR* 24: pp. 63-
    133
HAMMOND, M. 1957a. "Composition of the Senate in A.D. 68-
    235", *JRS* 47: pp. 74-81
HAMMOND, M. 1957b. "Imperial Elements in the Formula of the
    Roman Emperors during the First Two and a Half Centuries
    of the Empire", *MAAR* 25: pp. 17-64
HAMMOND, M. 1959. *The Antonine Monarchy* (American Academy in
    Rome, Rome)
HAMMOND, M. 1963. *"Res olim dissociabiles: principatus ac
    libertas.* Liberty under the Early Roman Empire", *HSPh*
    67: pp. 93-113
HART, H.S.J. 1952. "Judaea and Rome: The Official Comment-
    ary", *JThS* 3: pp. 172-198
HAUSMANN, U. 1975. "Zu den Bildnissen der Domitia Longina
    und der Julia Titi", *MDAI(R)* 82: pp. 315-328
HAYWOOD, R.M. 1952. "The Strange Death of the Elder Pliny",
    CW 46: pp. 1-3
HEILMEYER, W.D. 1975. "Titus vor Jerusalem", *MDAI(R)* 82:
    pp. 299-314
HENDERSON, B.W. 1905. *The Life and Principate of the Emperor
    Nero* (Methuen, London)
HENDERSON, B.W. 1927. *Five Roman Emperors, A.D. 69-117*

(Cambridge University Press, Cambridge)
HENRICHS, A. 1968. "Vespasian's Visit to Alexandria", *ZPE* 3: pp. 51-80
HERKERT, C.H. 1956. *Historical Commentary drawn from the Natural History for the Years 54-76 A.D.* (Diss., Pennsylvania)
HERRMANN, L. 1953. "Basilides", *Latomus* 12: pp. 312-315
HERRMANN, L. 1979. "Babrius et Titus", *REG* 92: pp. 113-119
HEURGON, J. 1970. "Pline le Jeune tenté par l'histoire", *REL* 47 bis: pp. 345-354
HILL, P.V. 1970. "An unpublished Denarius of Titus", *NCirc* 78: pp. 49-50
HILL, P.V. 1975. "An unpublished Denarius of Titus", *NCirc* 83: p. 380
HOFFMAN, O.A. 1883. *De imperatoribus Titi temporibus recte definiendis* (Elwirt, Marburg)
HOFFMAN, F. 1883. *Quomodo quando Titus imperator factus sit* (Diss., Bonn)
HOFFMANN-LEWIS, M.W. 1955. *The Official Priests of Rome under the Julio-Claudians. A Study of the Nobility from 44 B.C. to A.D. 68* (American Academy in Rome, Rome)
HOLDER, P.A. 1980. *Studies in the Auxilia of the Roman Army from Augustus to Trajan* (B.A.R., Oxford)
HOMO, L. 1940. "Une leçon d'outre - tombe: Vespasien financier", *REA* 42: pp. 453-465
HOMO, L. 1949. *Vespasien, l'empereur du bon sens* (A. Michel, Paris)
HOUSTON, G.W. 1971. *Roman Imperial Administrative Personnel during the Principates of Vespasian and Titus* (Diss., North Carolina)
HOUSTON, G.W. 1972. "M. Plancius Varus and the Events of A.D. 69-70", *TAPhA* 103: pp. 167-180
HOUSTON, G.W. 1975. "P. Marius P.f.cos.ord. A.D. 62", *ZPE* 16: pp. 33-35
HOUSTON, G.W. 1976a. "The Duration of the Censorship of Vespasian and Titus", *Emerita* 44: pp. 397-402
HOUSTON, G.W. 1976b. "Notes on Some Documents Pertaining to Flavian Administrative Personnel", *ZPE* 20: pp. 25-34
HOUSTON, G.W. 1977. "Vespasian's Adlection of Men *in Senatum*", *AJPh* 98: pp. 35-63
HUBBARD, P.S. 1966. "The Topography of Ancient Jerusalem", *PEQ* 98: pp. 130-154
HÜBNER, H.S. 1963. *Cornelius Tacitus: Die Historien*, Vol. II (Winter, Heidelberg)
HUNT, T.J. 1964. "Tacitus and the Jews", *Pegasus* 2: pp. 17-19
INSTINSKY, H.U. 1948. "Der Ruhm des Titus", *Philologus* 97: pp. 370-371
ISAAC, B.H. and ROLL, I. 1976. "A Milestone of A.D. 69 from Judaea: The Elder Trajan and Vespasian", *JRS* 66: pp. 15-19

ISAGER, J. 1976. "Vespasiano e Augusto", *Studia Romana in honorem P. Krarup, septuagenarii*: pp. 64-71
JAGENTEUFEL, A. 1958. *Die Statthalter der römischen Provinz Dalmatia von Augustus bis Diokletian* (Rohrer, Vienna)
JOHNSON, A.C., COLEMAN, P. and BOURNE, F.C. 1961. *Ancient Roman Statutes* (University of Texas Press, Austin)
JOLOWICZ, H.F. and NICOLAS, B. 1972. *Historical Introduction to the Study of Roman Law* (Cambridge University Press, Cambridge: 3rd edn)
JONES, A.H.M. 1938. *The Herods of Judaea* (Clarendon Press, Oxford)
JONES, A.H.M. 1939. *The Greek City from Alexander to Justinian* (Clarendon Press, Oxford)
JONES, A.H.M. 1971. *The Cities of the Eastern Roman Provinces* (Clarendon Press, Oxford)
JONES, B.W. 1971. "Preparation for the Principate", *PP* 139: pp. 264-270
JONES, B.W. 1972. "Designation to the Consulship under the Flavians", *Latomus* 31: pp. 849-853
JONES, B.W. 1973a. "Domitian's Attitude to the Senate", *AJPh* 94: pp. 79-91
JONES, B.W. 1973b. "The Dating of Domitian's War against the Chatti", *Historia* 22: pp. 79-90
JONES, B.W. 1975a. "Titus and Some Flavian *Amici*", *Historia* 24: pp. 453-462
JONES, B.W. 1975b. "Praetorian Proconsuls under Domitian", *Historia* 24: pp. 631-632
JONES, B.W. 1976a. "The Consuls of A.D. 90", *Historia* 25: pp. 499-501
JONES, B.W. 1976b. "Dalmatia Again", *CP* 71: pp. 256-257
JONES, B.W. and DEVELIN, R. 1976. "M. Arrecinus Clemens", *Antichthon* 10: pp. 79-83
JONES, C.P. 1968. "A New Commentary on the Letters of Pliny", *Phoenix* 22: pp. 111-142
JONES, C.P. 1973. Review of Eck. *Gnomon* 45: pp. 688-691
JONES, J.R. 1966. "Vespasian Junior", *NC* 6: pp. 61-63
JONES, J.R. 1970. "Mint Magistrates in the Early Roman Empire", *BICS* 17: pp. 70-78
JORDAN, R. 1974. *Berenice* (Barnes and Noble, New York)
JOUGUET, P. 1941/42. "L'arrivée de Vespasien à Alexandrie", *BLE* 24: pp. 21-32
KELLER, E. 1967. "Studien zu den Cancelleria Reliefs", *Klio* 49: pp. 193-217
KINDSTRAND, J.F. 1978. "The Date of Dio of Prusa's Alexandrian Oration - a Reply", *Historia* 27: pp. 378-383
KINGDON, H.P. 1970. "Who were the Zealots and their Leaders in A.D. 66?", *NTS* 17: pp. 68-72
KLEINER, G. 1962. "Der Triumph des Titus", *Festschrift Max Wegner*: pp. 42-43
KNEISSL, P. 1969. *Die Siegestitulatur der römischen Kaiser* (Hubert, Göttingen)

KOEPPEL, G. 1969. "Profectio und Adventus", *Bonner Jahrb.*
169: pp. 130-194

KORNEMANN, E. 1930. *Doppelprinzipat und Reichsteilung in
Imperium Romanum* (Teubner, Leipzig and Berlin)

KORTENBEUTEL, H. 1940. "Ein Kodizill eines römischen
Kaisers", *APAW* 13: pp. 3-16

KOUMANOUDIS, S.N. 1970. "Q. Vibius Crispus", *AAA* 3: pp. 403-
406

KRAAY, C.M. 1954. "The Titulature of Titus and Domitian on
Sestertii of Vespasian", *NC* 62: p. 395

KRAAY, C.M. 1958. "Two New Sestertii of Domitian", *ANSMusN*
8: pp. 109-116

KRAFT, K. 1951. *Zur Rekrutierung der Alen und Kohorten an
Rhein und Donau* (Dissertationes Bernenses 1.3: Francke,
Berlin)

KRAFT, K. 1961. "Zum Bürgerrecht der Soldatenkinder",
Historia 10: pp. 120-126

KREILER, B. 1974. "P. Valerius Patruinus, Statthalter in
Galatien-Kappadokien 83-87 n. Chr.", *Chiron* 4: pp. 451-
452

KREILER, B. 1975. *Die Statthalter Kleinasiens unter den
Flaviern* (Diss., Augsburg)

LACEY, W.K. 1979. "*Summi Fastigii Vocabulum*: The Story of a
Title", *JRS* 69: pp. 28-38

LAPERROUSAZ, E.M. 1979. "A propos du premier mur et du
deuxième mur de Jérusalem ainsi que du rempart de
Jérusalem à l'époque de Néhémie", *REJ* 138: pp. 1-16

LAST, H. 1948. "On the Flavian Reliefs from the Palazzo
della Cancelleria", *JRS* 38: pp. 9-14

LATTIMORE, R. 1934. "Portents and Prophesies in connection
with the Emperor Vespasian", *CJ* 29: pp. 441-449

LEE, R.W. 1956. *The Elements of Roman Law* (Sweet and
Maxwell)

LEGLAY, M. 1968. "Les Flaviens et l'Afrique", *MEFR* 80: pp.
201-246

LEGLAY, M. 1981. "Les Censitores Provinciae Thraciae", *ZPE*
43: pp. 175-184

LEHMANN-HARTLEBEN, K. 1934. "L'Arco di Tito", *BCAR* 62: pp.
89-112

LEO, F. 1901. *Die griechisch - römische Biographie nach
ihrer literarischen Form* (G. Olms, Hildesheim: repr.)

LEON, C.F. 1971. *Die Bauornamentik des Trajansforums und
ihre Stellung in der früh - und mittelkaiserzeitlichen
Architekturdekoration Roms* (Böhlau, Berlin)

LESCHI, L. 1953. "Inscriptions latines de Lambèse et de
Zama, I. Un nouveau camp de Titus à Lambèse (81 ap. J.
C.)", *Libyca* 1: pp. 189-197

LESUISSE, L. 1961. "La nomination de l'empereur et le titre
d'*Imperator*", *AC* 30: pp. 415-428

LEVI, M.A. 1954. "La clemenza di Tito", *PP* 9: pp. 288-293

LEVICK, B. 1967. *Roman Colonies in Southern Asia Minor*

(Clarendon Press, Oxford)
LIFSHITZ, B. 1977a. "Scythopolis", *ANRW* II.8, pp. 262-294
LIFSHITZ, B. 1977b. "Jérusalem sous la Domination romaine", *ANRW* II.8, pp. 444-489
LIFSHITZ, B. 1977c. "Césarée de Palestine", *ANRW* II.8, pp. 490-518
LIPSCOMB, H.C. 1954. "The Strange Death of the Elder Pliny", *CW* 47: p. 74
LUCK, G. 1964. "Über Suetons Divus Titus", *RhM* 107: pp. 63-75
LUTZ, C.E. 1947. "Musonius Rufus: The Roman Socrates", *YCS* 10: pp. 3-147
MACÉ, A. 1900. *Essai sur Suétone* (Thorin, Paris)
MACMULLEN, R. 1967. *Enemies of the Roman Order: Treason, Unrest and Alienation in the Empire* (Harvard University Press, Harvard)
MACURDY, G.H. 1935. "Julia Berenice", *AJPh* 56: pp. 246-253
MACURDY, G.H. 1937. *Vassal Queens and Some Contemporary Women in the Roman Empire* (Johns Hopkins University Press, Baltimore)
MADDEN, F.W. 1881. *Coins of the Jews* (G. Olms, Hildesheim: repr. 1976)
MAGI, F. 1945. *I Rilievi flavi dal Palazzo della Cancelleria* (Bardi, Rome)
MAGIE, D. 1950. *Roman Rule in Asia Minor to the End of the Third Century after Christ* (Princeton University Press, Princeton)
MAKIN, E. 1922. "The Triumphal Route with particular reference to the Flavian Triumph", *JRS* 12: pp. 25-36
MANN, J.C. 1972. "The Development of Auxiliary and Fleet Diplomas", *ES* 9: pp. 233-241
MARSDEN, E.W. 1969. *Greek and Roman Artillery* (Clarendon Press, Oxford)
MARTIN, R. 1974. Review of Urban. *CR* 24: pp. 154-155
MARTINET, H. 1981. *C. Suetonius Tranquillus: Divus Titus. Kommentar* (Beiträge zur Klassischen Philologie 123: A. Hain, Meisenheim)
MATTINGLY, H. 1920. "The 'restored' coins of Titus, Domitian and Nerva", *NC* 20: pp. 177-207
MATTINGLY, H. 1923. *Coins of the Roman Empire in the British Museum, I: Augustus to Vitellius* (Trustees of the B.M., London)
MATTINGLY, H. 1930. *Coins of the Roman Empire in the British Museum, II: Vespasian to Domitian* (Trustees of the B.M., London)
MATTINGLY, H. and SYDENHAM, E.A. 1926. *Roman Imperial Coinage, II* (Spink and Sons, London)
MAYER, G. 1900. *Kaiser Titus* (Diss., Egger)
McALINDON, D. 1956. "Senatorial Opposition to Claudius and Nero", *AJPh* 77: pp. 113-132
McALINDON, D. 1957a. "Entry to the Senate in the Early

Empire", *JRS* 47: pp. 191-195
McALINDON, D. 1957b. "Claudius and the Senators", *AJPh* 78: pp. 279-286
McALINDON, D. 1957c. "Senatorial Advancement in the Age of Claudius", *Latomus* 16: pp. 252-262
McCRUM, M. and WOODHEAD, A.G. 1966. *Select Documents of the Principates of the Flavian Emperors including the Year of Revolution* (Cambridge University Press, Cambridge)
McDERMOTT, W.C. 1969. "Pliniana", *AJPh* 90: pp. 329-332
McDERMOTT, W.C. 1970. "Fabricius Veiento", *AJPh* 91: pp. 124-148
McDERMOTT, W.C. 1973. "Flavius Silva and Salvius Liberalis", *CW* 66: pp. 335-351
McDERMOTT, W. and ORENTZEL, A.E. *Roman Portraits: The Flavian-Trajanic Period* (University of Missouri Press, Columbia and London)
McDOWELL, R.H. 1935. *Coins from Seleucia on the Tigris* (University of Michigan Studies 37: Ann Arbor University Press, Ann Arbor)
McELDERRY, R. Knox. 1913. "Some Conjectures on the Reign of Vespasian", *JRS* 3: pp. 116-126
McFAYDEN, D. 1915. "The Date of the Arch of Titus", *CJ* 11: pp. 131-141
McFAYDEN, D. 1920. *The History of the Title "Imperator" under the Roman Empire* (University of Chicago Press, Chicago)
McGUIRE, M.E. 1980. *A Historical Commentary on Suetonius' "Life of Titus"* (University Microfilms Int., Ann Arbor and London)
MERKELBACH, R. 1979. "Ephesische Parerga (26). Warum Domitians Siegername "Germanicus" eradiert worden ist", *ZPE* 34: pp. 62-64
MEYSHAM, J. 1961. "A New Coin Type of Agrippa II and its Meaning", *IEJ* 9: pp. 181-183
MICHEL, O. 1968. "Studien zu Josephus. Simon bar Giora", *NTS* 14: pp. 402-408
MICHEL, O. and BAUERNFEIND, O. 1964. *Flavius Josephus, De Bello Judaico* (Kösel, Munich)
MILLAR, F. 1963. "The Fiscus in the First Two Centuries", *JRS* 53: pp. 29-42
MILLAR, F. 1964. *A Study of Cassius Dio* (Clarendon Press, Oxford)
MILLAR, F. 1967. "Emperors at Work", *JRS* 57: pp. 9-19
MILLAR, F. 1968. Review of Sherwin-White, *JRS* 58: pp. 218-224
MILLAR, F. 1977. *The Emperor in the Roman World* (Duckworth, London)
MILLER, M.C.J. 1978. "A New Record of Titus' Return to Alexandria after the Sack of Jerusalem (April 25, A.D. 71)", *AncW* 1: pp. 137-140
MILNS, R.D. 1973. "The Career of M. Aponius Saturninus", *Historia* 22: pp. 284-294

MIREAUX, E. 1950. *La Reine Bérénice* (A. Michel, Paris)
MIRKOVIC, M. 1967. "Die Auxiliareinheiten in Moesien unter
  den Flaviern", *ES* 5: pp. 177-183
MITFORD, T.B. 1974. "Some Inscriptions from the Cappadocian
  Limes", *JRS* 64: pp. 160-175
MITFORD, T.B. 1980. "Cappadocia and Armenia Minor", *ANRW*
  II.7.2, pp. 1169-1228
MODUGNO, S., PANCIERA, S., and ZEVI, F. 1973. "Osservazioni
  sui consoli dell' 85 d.C.", *RSA* 3: pp. 87-108
MOMIGLIANO, A. 1934. *Claudius: The Emperor and his Achieve-*
  ment (Clarendon Press, Oxford)
MOMIGLIANO, A. 1951. Review of Wirszubski. *JRS* 41: pp.
  146-153
MOMMSEN, Th. 1871. "Imperatortitel des Titus", *Numismatische*
  Zeitschrift 3: pp. 458-478
MOMMSEN, Th. 1885. *The Provinces of the Roman Empire from*
  Caesar to Diocletian, II (tr. W.P. Dickson: Ares
  Publishers Inc., 1974, repr.)
MOMMSEN, Th. 1887. "Zu den Münzen des Titus", *Zeitschrift*
  für Numismatik 14: pp. 31-35
MOMMSEN, Th. 1887-1888. *Römisches Staatsrecht* (Hirzel,
  Leipzig)
MONTEFIORE, H. 1962. "Sulpicius Severus and Titus' Council
  of War", *Historia* 11: pp. 156-170
MOONEY, G.W. 1930. *C. Suetoni Tranquilli de Vita Caesarum.*
  Libri VII-VIII. (Longmans, Green and Co., London;
  Hodges, Figgis and Co., Dublin)
MORFORD, M.P.O. 1968. "The Training of Three Roman
  Emperors", *Phoenix* 22: pp. 57-72
MORRIS, J. 1953. "The Consulate of the Elder Trajan", *JRS*
  43: pp. 79-80
MORRIS, J. 1964. "Leges Annales under the Principate, I",
  LF 87: pp. 316-337
MORRIS, J. 1965. "Leges Annales under the Principate, II",
  LF 88: pp. 22-31
MÜLLER, C. 1841ff. *Fragmenta Historicorum Graecorum* (Didot,
  Paris)
MÜNZER, F. 1899. "Die Quelle des Tacitus für die Germanen-
  kriege", *Bonner Jahrb.* 104: pp. 67-111
MUSURILLO, H.A. 1954. *The Acts of the Pagan Martyrs: Acta*
  Alexandrinorum (Clarendon Press, Oxford)
NESSELHAUF, H. 1952. "Tacitus und Domitian", *Hermes* 80:
  pp. 222-245
NESSELHAUF, H. 1954. Review of Degrassi. *Gnomon* 26: pp.
  265-271
NEWTON, H.C. 1901. *The Epigraphical Evidence for the Reigns*
  of Vespasian and Titus (Cornell Studies in Classical
  Philology 16: Macmillan, New York)
NICHOLAS, B. 1962. *An Introduction to Roman Law* (Clarendon
  Press, Oxford)
NICOLS, J. 1978. *Vespasian and the Partes Flavianae*

(Historia Einzelschriften 28: F. Steiner, Wiesbaden)
NIESE, B. 1895. *Flavii Josephi Opera* (Weidmann, Berlin)
NOCK, A.D. 1928. "Religious Development from Vespasian to Trajan", *Theology* 31: pp. 152-160
NOCK, A.D. 1952. "The Roman Army and the Religious Year", *HThR* 45: pp. 239-240
OGILVIE, R.M. and RICHMOND, I. 1967. *Cornelii Taciti de Vita Agricolae* (Clarendon Press, Oxford)
OLIVER, J.H. 1947. "The Descendants of Asinius Pollio", *AJPh* 68: pp. 147-160
OLIVER, J.H. 1963. "Domitian's Freedman Antiochus", *Hesperia* 32: p. 87
OLIVER, R.P. 1977. "The *Praenomen* of Tacitus", *AJPh* 98: pp. 64-70
OLIVER, R.P. 1979. "Tacitus, Librarian?", *CQ* 29: pp. 223-224
OOTEGHEM, J. van. 1968. "Verginius and Vindex", *LEC* 36: pp. 18-27
PALADINI, M.L. 1962. "Divinizzazione di Traiano padre", (Collection Latomus 58: Brussels) pp. 1194-1206
PAPPANO, E. 1937. "The False Neros", *CJ* 32: pp. 385-392
PARATORE, E. 1962. *Tacito* (Edizioni dell' Ateneo, Rome: 2nd edn.)
PARETI, L. 1960. *Storia di Roma e del mondo romano, V* (Utet, Turin)
PARKER, E.R. 1946. "Education of Heirs in the Julio-Claudian Family", *AJPh* 67: pp. 29-50
PARKER, H.M.D. 1928. *The Roman Legions* (Clarendon Press, Oxford)
PASOLI, A. 1950. *Acta Fratrum Arvalium* (Zuffi, Bologna)
PASSERINI, A. 1939. *Le Coorti Pretorie* (A. Signorelli, Rome)
PASSERINI, A. 1940. "M. Arrecino Clemente", *Athenaeum* 18: pp. 145-163
PAVIS D'ESCURAC, H. 1976. *La Préfecture de l'Annone: Service Administratif Impérial d'Auguste à Constantin* (BEFAR 226: Rome)
PÉKARY, Th. 1968. "Goldene Statuen der Kaiserzeit", *Röm. Mitteilungen* 75: pp. 144-148
PEROWNE, S. 1958. *The Later Herods* (Hodder and Stoughton, London)
PETERSEN, H. 1962. "The Legionary Command of Salvius Liberalis", *CPh* 57: pp. 32-33
PFLAUM, H.G. 1950. *Les Procurateurs Équestres sous le Haut-Empire Romain* (A. Maisonneuve, Paris)
PFLAUM, H.G. 1951. "A propos des préfets d'Égypte d'Arthur Stein", *Latomus* 10: pp. 471-477
PFLAUM, H.G. 1960. *Les Carrières Procuratoriennes Équestres sous le Haut-Empire Romain* (P. Geuthner, Paris)
PFLAUM, H.G. 1961. "Une tessera nummularia inédite. Deux nouveaux consuls", *BSFN* 1961: pp. 72 ff., 86 ff.
PFLAUM, H.G. 1962. "Légats impériaux à l'intérieur de

provinces sénatoriales" (Collection Latomus 57: Brussels) pp. 1232-1242

PFLAUM, H.G. 1964. "Les Correspondents de l'orateur M. Cornelius Fronto de Certa", *Hommages à J. Bayet*: pp. 544-560

PFLAUM, H.G. 1969. "Remarques sur le changement de statut administratif de la province de Judée: à propos d'une inscription récemment découverte à Sidé de Pamphylie", *IEJ* 19: pp. 225-233

PICK, B. 1885a. "Zur Titulatur der Flavier: Der Imperatortitel des Titus", *Zeitschrift für Numismatik* 13: pp. 190-238

PICK, B. 1885b. "Zur Titulatur der Flavier: Die Consulats Domitians als Caesar", *Zeitschrift für Numismatik* 13: pp. 356-383

PICK, B. 1887. "Zur Titulatur der Flavier: Die griechischen Münzen", *Zeitschrift für Numismatik* 14: pp. 294-374

PISTOR, H.H. 1965. *Prinzeps und Patriziat in der Zeit von Augustus bis Commodus* (Diss., Freiburg)

PLATNER, S.B. and ASHBY, B. 1929. *A Topographical Dictionary of Ancient Rome* (Oxford University Press, Oxford and London)

PLEKET, H.W. 1961. "Domitian, the Senate and the Provinces", *Mnemosyne* 14: pp. 296-315

POOLE, R.S. 1892. *A Catalogue of the Greek Coins in the British Museum: Alexandria and the Nomes* (Forni, Bologna: repr. 1976)

PRICE, H. 1919. *C. Suetonii Tranquilli de Vita Caesarum, liber VIII: Divus Titus* (Diss., Pennsylvania)

PRICE, H. 1945/1946. "Titus, *Amor ac Deliciae Generis Humani*", *CW* 39: pp. 58-61

RADICE, B. 1962. "A Fresh Approach to Pliny's Letters", *G&R* 9: pp. 160-168

RADICE, B. 1968. "Pliny and the *Panegyricus*", *G&R* 14: pp. 166-172

RADIN, M. 1915. *The Jews among the Greeks and the Romans* (Jewish Publishing Company of America, Philadelphia)

RADIN, M. 1929. "The Pedigree of Josephus", *CPh* 24: pp. 193-196

RAEPSAET-CHARLIER, M.T. 1973. "Germania Inferior and Germania Superior", *Latomus* 32: pp. 158-161

RAJAK, T. 1979. Review of Smallwood, 1976. *JRS* 69: pp. 192-194

RAOSS, M. 1960. "La rivolta di Vindice ed il successo di Galba", *Epigraphica* 22: pp. 37-123

RAT, M. and BAYET, J. 1914. "Les *curatores uiarum*", *Revue Epigraphique* 2: pp. 46-47, 237-247

REAGAN, C.J. 1969. *A Study of the Roman Civil Service in the Time of Pliny the Younger* (Diss., Cornell)

REAGAN, C.J. 1970. "Laterculum prosopographicum Plinianum", *RIL* 104: pp. 414-436

REED, N. 1976. "Some Neglected Evidence on the Early Career of Tacitus", *CQ* 26: pp. 304-314

REIDINGER, W. 1956. *Die Statthalter des ungeteilten Pannonien und Oberpannoniens von Augustus bis Diokletian* (Antiquitas 11: Habelt, Bonn)

REINMUTH, O.W. 1934. "The Edict of Tiberius Julius Alexander", *TAPhA* 69: pp. 248-259

RICHMOND, I.A. 1962. "Gnaeus Julius Agricola", *JRS* 34: pp. 34-35

RICHMOND, I.A. 1944. "The Roman Siege Works of Masada, Israel", *JRS* 52: pp. 142-155

RIES, W. 1969. *Gerücht, Gerede, öffentliche Meinung: Interpretationen zur Psychologie und Darstellungskunst des Tacitus* (Diss., Heidelberg)

RITTER, H.W. 1972. "Zur Lebensgeschichte der Flavia Domitilla, der Frau Vespasians", *Historia* 21: pp. 759-761

ROBERTS, C.H. 1949. "Titus and Alexandria. A New Document", *JRS* 39: pp. 79-80

RODGERS, R.H. 1982. "Curatores Aquarum", *HSPh* 86: pp. 171-180

ROGERS, P.M. 1980. "Titus, Berenice and Mucianus", *Historia* 29: pp. 86-95

ROGERS, R.S. 1949. "A Criminal Trial of A.D. 70: *Hist.* 4.44", *TAPhA* 80: pp. 347-350

ROGERS, R.S. 1952. "A Tacitean Pattern in Narrating Treason Trials", *TAPhA* 83: pp. 279-311

ROGERS, R.S. 1960. "A Group of Domitianic Treason Trials", *CPh* 55: pp. 19-23

ROMANELLI, P. 1951. "Iscrizione inedita di Leptis Magna con nuovi contributi ai fasti della provincia d'Africa", *QAL* 2: pp. 71-79

ROSTOVTZEFF, M. 1957. *The Social and Economic History of the Roman Empire* (Rev. by P.M. Fraser: Clarendon Press, Oxford: 2nd edn.)

ROTH, C. 1959a. "The Zealots: A Jewish Religious Sect", *Judaism* 8: pp. 33-40

ROTH, C. 1959b. "The Zealots in the War of 66-73", *JSS* 4: pp. 332-355

ROTH, C. 1964. "The Constitution of the Jewish Republic 66-70", *JSS* 9: pp. 295-319

ROUGÉ, J. 1952. "La navigation hivernale sous l'empire romain", *REA* 54: pp. 316-325

ROUGÉ, J. 1953. "Voyages officiels en Méditerranée orientale à la fin de la république et au premier siècle de l'empire", *REA* 55: pp. 294-300

ROXAN, M.M. 1978. *Roman Military Diplomas, 1954-1977* (Occasional Papers 2: Institute of Archaeology, London)

RUFFILLI, P. 1971. "Nota à IG II/III^2, 3229", *Epigraphica* 33: pp. 147-150

RÜGER, C.B. 1979. "Ein Siegesdenkmal der Legio VI Victrix",

Bonner Jahrb. 179: pp. 187-200

SAINT-DENIS, E. de 1947. "Mare Clausum", *REL* 25: pp. 196-214

SANFORD, E.M. 1935. "Propagation and Censorship in the Transmission of Josephus", *TAPhA* 66: pp. 127-145

SAUTER, F. 1934. *Der römische Kaiserkult bei Martial und Statius* (Kohlhammer, Stuttgart and Berlin)

SCHALIT, A. 1974. "Die Erhebung Vespasians nach Flavius Josephus, Talmud und Midrasch. Zur Geschichte einer messianischen Prophetie", *ANRW* II.2: pp. 208-327

SCHIEBER, A.S. 1976. *The Flavian Eastern Policy* (Diss., New York)

SCHMITT, G. 1973-1975. "Zur Chronologie des jüdischen Krieges", *Theokratia* 3: pp. 224-231

SCHNEIDER, K.Th. 1942. *Zusammensetzung des römisches Senates von Tiberius bis Nero* (Diss., Zurich)

SCHÖNBERGER, H. 1969. "The Roman Frontier in Germany: an Archaeological Survey", *JRS* 59: pp. 144-197

SCHULZ, F. 1951. *Classical Roman Law* (Clarendon Press, Oxford)

SCHÜRER, E. 1973. *The History of the Jewish People in the Age of Jesus Christ (175 B.C. - A.D. 135)* (Rev. and ed. by G. Vermes and F. Millar: T. and T. Clark, Edinburgh)

SCOTT, K. 1931. "The Significance of Statues in Precious Metals in Emperor Worship", *TAPhA* 62: pp. 101-123

SCOTT, K. 1932a. "The Elder and Younger Pliny on Emperor Worship", *TAPhA* 63: pp. 156-165

SCOTT, K. 1932b. "On Suetonius' *Life of Vespasian* 12", *CPh* 27: pp. 82-84

SCOTT, K. 1934. "The Role of Basilides in the Events of A.D. 69", *JRS* 24: pp. 138-140

SCOTT, K. 1936. *The Imperial Cult under the Flavians* (Kohlhammer, Stuttgart and Berlin)

SCRAMUZZA, V.M. 1940. *The Emperor Claudius* (Harvard University Press, Harvard)

SELLWOOD, D. 1971. *An Introduction to the Coinage of Parthia* (Spink and Sons, London)

SHERK, R.K. 1951. *The Legates of Galatia from Augustus to Diocletian* (Johns Hopkins University Press, Baltimore)

SHERK, R.K. 1957. "Roman Imperial Troops in Macedonia and Achaea", *AJPh* 78: pp. 52-62

SHERK, R.K. 1971. "Specialization in the Provinces of Germany", *Historia* 20: pp. 110-121

SHERK, R.K. 1980. "Roman Galatia", *ANRW* II.7.2: pp. 954-1052

SHERWIN-WHITE, A.N. 1966. *The Letters of Pliny* (Clarendon Press, Oxford)

SHERWIN-WHITE, A.N. 1973. *The Roman Citizenship* (Clarendon Press, Oxford: 2nd edn.)

SHOTTER, D.C.A. 1967. "Tacitus and Verginius Rufus", *CQ* 17: pp. 370-381

SHOTTER, D.C.A.   1969.   "Irregular Legionary Commands", *CQ*   19: pp. 371-373
SHOTTER, D.C.A.   1975.   "A Time-table for the *Bellum Neronis*", *Historia* 24: pp. 59-74
SIMON, E.   1960.   "Zu den flavischen Reliefs von der Cancelleria", *JDAI* 75: pp. 134-156
SMALLWOOD, E.M.   1967.   *Documents Illustrating the Principates of Gaius, Claudius and Nero* (Cambridge University Press, Cambridge)
SMALLWOOD, E.M.   1976.   *The Jews under Roman Rule from Pompey to Diocletian* (E.J. Brill, Leiden)
SNYDER, W.F.   1940.   "On Chronology in the Imperial Books of Cassius Dio's Roman History", *Klio* 33: pp. 39-56
STAVRIDIS, A.   1978.   "Zwei Porträts des Kaisers Titus in Nationalmuseum zu Athen", *MDAI(R)* 85: pp. 477-478
STECH, B.   1912.   *Senatores Romani qui fuerint inde a Vespasiano usque ad Traiani exitum* (Klio, Beiheft 10: Dieterich, Leipzig)
STEIDLE, W.   1951.   *Sueton und die antike Biographie* (C.H. Beck, Munich)
STEIN, A.   1940a.   *Die Legaten Von Moesien* (Dissertationes Pannonicae 1,11: Instit. de Num. et Archéol., Budapest)
STEIN, A.   1940b.   "Zu den kaiserlichen Ernennungsschreiben in P. Berol. 8334", *Aegyptus* 20: pp. 51-60
STEIN, A.   1950.   *Die Präfekten von Agypten in der römischen Kaiserzeit* (Dissertationes Bernenses 1,1: Francke, Berne)
STRONG, D.E.   1960.   "Examples of the Composite Capital", *JRS* 50: pp. 119-128
STUCCHI, S.   1956/57.   "Il ritratto di Traianus pater", *Studi in onore di A. Calderini e R. Paribeni* 3: pp. 527-540
SULLIVAN, P.B.   1953.   "A Note on the Flavian Accession", *CJ* 49: pp. 67-70
SULLIVAN, R.D.   1977a.   "The Dynasty of Emesa", *ANRW* II.8, pp. 198-219
Sullivan, R.D.   1977b.   "The Dynasty of Judaea in the First Century", *ANRW* II.8, pp. 296-354
SULLIVAN, R.D.   1977c.   "The Dynasty of Commagene", *ANRW* II. 8: pp. 732-798
SULLIVAN, R.D.   1977d.   "Papyri Reflecting the Eastern Dynastic Network", *ANRW* II.8, pp. 908-939
SUOLAHTI, J.   1963.   *The Roman Censors: A Study on Social Structure* (Annales Academiae Fennicae B 117, Helsinki)
SUTHERLAND, C.H.V.   1935.   "The State of the Imperial Treasury at the Death of Domitian", *JRS* 25: pp. 150-162
SWAN, M.   1970.   "Josephus, *AJ* XIX 251-252:   Opposition to Gaius and Claudius", *AJPh* 91: pp. 149-164
SYME, R.   1928.   "Rhine and Danubian Legions under Domitian", *JRS* 18: pp. 41-55
SYME, R.   1930.   "The Imperial Finances under Domitian, Nerva and Trajan", *JRS* 20: pp. 55-70
SYME, R.   1936.   "A Governor of Syria under Nerva", *Philologus*

91: pp. 238-245
SYME, R. 1939. *The Roman Revolution* (Clarendon Press, Oxford)
SYME, R. 1956. "Some Friends of the Caesars", *AJPh* 77: pp. 264-273
SYME, R. 1957. "Antonine Relatives: Ceionii and Vettuleni", *Athenaeum* 35: pp. 306-315
SYME, R. 1958a. *Tacitus* (Clarendon Press, Oxford)
SYME, R. 1958b. "Consulates in Absence", *JRS* 48: pp. 1-9
SYME, R. 1958c. "Imperator Caesar: A Study in Nomenclature", *Historia* 7: pp. 172-188
SYME, R. 1959. Review of Jagenteufel. *Gnomon* 31: pp. 510-517
SYME, R. 1969. "Pliny the Procurator", *HSPh* 73: pp. 201-236
SYME, R. 1970. "Domitius Corbulo", *JRS* 60: pp. 27-39
SYME, R. 1971. *Danubian Papers* (AIESEE, Bucharest)
SYME, R. 1977. "The Enigmatic Sospes", *JRS* 67: pp. 38-49
SYME, R. 1978. "Antonius Saturninus", *JRS* 68: pp. 12-21
SYME, R. 1980. *Some Arval Brethren* (Clarendon Press, Oxford)
SYME, R. 1981. "Governors Dying in Syria", *ZPE* 41: pp. 125-144
TAYLOR, L.R. 1931. *The Divinity of the Roman Emperor* (American Philological Association, Middleton)
TAYLOR, L.R. 1956. "Trebula Suffenas and the Plautii Silvani", *MAAR* 24: pp. 9-30
THACKERAY, H.St.J. 1929. *Josephus, the Man and the Historian* (Jewish Institute of Religion Press, New York)
THOMAS, J.A.C. 1976. *Textbook of Roman Law* (North-Holland, Amsterdam)
THOMASSON, B.E. 1960. *Die Statthalter der römischen Provinzen Nordafrikas von Augustus bis Diocletianus* (C.W.K. Gleerup, Lund)
TORELLI, M. 1968. "The *cursus honorum* of M. Hirrius Fronto Neratius Pansa", *JRS* 58: pp. 170-175
TORRENT, A. 1968. "Para una interpreta̧cion de la *potestas censoria* en los emperadores Flavios", *Emerita* 36: pp. 213-229
TOWNEND, G.B. 1959. "The Date of Composition of Suetonius' *Caesares*", *CQ* 9: pp. 285-293
TOWNEND, G.B. 1961. "Some Flavian Connections", *JRS* 51: pp. 54-62
TOWNEND, G.B. 1962. "The Consuls of A.D. 69-70", *AJPh* 83: pp. 113-129
TOWNEND, G.B. 1972. "The Earliest Scholiast on Juvenal", *CQ* 22: pp. 376-387
TOWNEND, G.B. 1973. "The Literary Substrata to Juvenal's Satires", *JRS* 63: pp. 148-160
TOYNBEE, J.M.C. 1944. "Dictators and Philosophers in the First Century A.D.", *G&R* 13: pp. 43-58
TOYNBEE, J.M.C. 1947. Review of Magi, 1945. *JRS* 37: pp. 187-191
TOYNBEE, J.M.C. 1957. *The Flavian Reliefs from the Palazzo*

della Cancelleria in Rome (Oxford University Press, London)

TRAUB, H.W. 1955. "Pliny's Treatment of History in Epistolary Form", *TAPhA* 86: pp. 213-232

TREU, M. 1948. "M. Antonius Primus in der taciteischen Darstellung", *Würzburger Jahrbücher für die Altertumswiss.* 3: pp. 241-262

TURNER, E.G. 1954. "Tiberius Julius Alexander", *JRS* 44: pp. 54-64

URBAN, R. 1971. *Historische Untersuchungen zum Domitianbild des Tacitus* (Diss., Munich)

VALETON, I.M.J. 1899. "De Bedoeling van Keizer Vespasianus om trent Jeruzalem en den temple tijdens het beleg", *Verslagen en Mededeelingen d. K. Akad. van Wetenschappen* (Afdeeling Letterkunde)

VANELLA, G. 1965. *L'Adventus di Vespasiano nei suoi aspetti mistico-religiosi e giuridico-costitutuzionali* (Cultura e Vita, Naples)

VAUX, R.de. 1958. "An Archaeologist and the Dead Sea Scrolls", *Listener* 59: pp. 1007-1008

VAUX, R.de 1959. "Les manuscrits de Qumrân et l'archéologie", *RBi* 66: pp. 87-110

VELKOV, V. 1965. "Eine neue Inschrift über Laberius Maximus", *Epigraphica* 27: pp. 90-109

VEYNE, P. 1962. "Les honneurs posthumes de Flavia Domitilla et les dédicaces grecques et latines", *Latomus* 21: pp. 49-98

VIDMAN, L. 1975. "Traianus der Ältere in der Fasti Ostienses", *LF* 98: pp. 66-71

VIDMAN, L. 1981. "Die Familie des L. Neratius Marcellus", *ZPE* 43: pp. 377-384

VISCUSI, P.L. 1973. *Studies on Domitian* (Diss., Delaware)

VITTINGHOFF, F. 1936. *Der Staatsfeind in der römischen Kaiserzeit: Untersuchungen zur Damnatio Memoriae* (Diss., Bonn)

VITUCCI, G. 1956. *Ricerche sulla praefectura urbi in età imperiale* (Bretschneider, Rome)

VOGEL-WEIDEMANN, U. 1979. "The Opposition under the Early Caesars: Some Remarks on its Nature and Aims", *Acta Classica* 22: pp. 91-107

WARDMANN, A.E. 1967. "Description of Personal Appearance in Plutarch and Suetonius: the Use of Statues as Evidence", *CQ* 17: pp. 414-420

WARMINGTON, B.H. 1969. *Nero: Reality and Legend* (Chatto and Windus, London)

WATERS, K.H. 1963. "The Second Dynasty of Rome", *Phoenix* 17: pp. 198-218

WATERS, K.H. 1964. "The Character of Domitian", *Phoenix* 18: pp. 49-77

WATERS, K.H. 1969. "Traianus Domitiani Continuator", *AJPh* 90: pp. 385-405

WATERS, K.H.   1972.   Review of Urban. *JRS* 62: pp. 225-226
WATSON, G.R.   1969.   *The Roman Soldier* (Thames and Hudson,
London)
WEAVER, P.R.C.   1965.   "The Father of Claudius Etruscus:
Statius, *Silvae* 3.3", *CQ* 15: pp. 145-154
WEAVER, P.R.C.   1972.   *Familia Caesaris* (Cambridge University
Press, Cambridge)
WEAVER, P.R.C.   1980.   "Two Freedman Careers", *Antichthon*   14:
pp. 143-156
WEBER, W.   1921.   *Josephus und Vespasian: Untersuchungen zu
dem jüdischen Krieg des Flavius Josephus* (Kohlhammer,
Berlin, Stuttgart and Leipzig)
WEILER, I.   1968.   "Titus und die Zerstörung des Tempels von
Jerusalem - Absicht oder Zufall?", *Klio* 50: pp. 139-158
WELLESLEY, K.   1972.   *The Histories, Book III* (Sydney Univer-
sity Press, Sydney)
WELLESLEY, K.   1975.   *The Long Year* (P. Elek, London)
WHITE, P.   1974.   "Ecce Iterum Crispinus", *AJPh* 95: pp. 377-
382
WIEGELS, R.   1974.   Review of Alföldy, 1969. *Gnomon* 46: pp.
188-198
WILKES, J.J.   1967.   "A New Governor of Dalmatia", *ES* 4: pp.
119-121
WILKES, J.J.   1969.   *Dalmatia* (Routledge and Kegan Paul,
London)
WILSON, E.   1969.   *The Dead Sea Scrolls 1947-1969* (W.H. Allen
and Co., London: 3rd edn.)
WIRSZUBSKI, C.   1950.   *Libertas as a Political Idea at Rome
during the Late Republic and Early Principate* (Cambridge
University Press, Cambridge)
WOLFF, H.   1974.   "Zu den Bürgerrechtsverleihungen an Kinder
von Auxiliaren und Legionaren", *Chiron* 4: pp. 479-510
WOLFF-BECKH, B.   1905.   *Kaiser Titus und der Jüdische Krieg*
(Diss., Berlin)
WOODSIDE, M.S.   1942.   "Vespasian's Patronage of Education and
the Arts", *TAPhA* 73: pp. 123-129
YADIN, Y.   1962.   *The Scroll of War of the Sons of Light
against the Sons of Darkness* (tr. B. and Ch. Rabin:
Oxford University Press, London)
YAVETZ, Z.   1975.   "Reflections on Titus and Josephus", *GRBS*
16: pp. 411-432
ZEVI, F.   1972.   "Nuovi Frammenti dei Fasti Ostienses", *Akten
des VI. internationalen Kongresses für griechische und
lateinische Epigraphik*: pp. 438-439

CHRONOLOGICAL TABLE

3   ?Birth of Sabinus II

9   Birth of Vespasian

14   Death of Augustus (Aug. 19), accession of Tiberius

16   Pomponius Graecinus *cos. suff.*

17   Pomponius Flaccus *cos. ord.*

18   Germanicus *cos. II ord.*; ?birth of L. Caesennius Paetus

19   P. Petronius *cos. suff.*; death of Germanicus (Oct. 10)

25   C. Petronius *cos. suff.*

28   Birth of Berenice; ?? Vespasian's vigintivirate

29   A. Plautius *cos. suff.*

30   ?Birth of Sabinus III and Q. Petillius Cerialis Caesius
     Rufus; Vespasian *trib. mil.* (of ?*IV Scythica*) in Thrace

33   ?Sabinus II praetor; ?birth of M. Arrecinus Clemens

34   Q. Marcius Barea *cos. suff.*

35   ?Vespasian quaestor in Crete-Cyrene; ?birth of
     (Arrecina)

37   C. Petronius Pontius Nigrinus *cos. ord.*; death of
     Tiberius (March 16), accession of Gaius

38   ?Vespasian aedile

39   BIRTH OF TITUS (Dec. 30)

40 ?Vespasian praetor; ?birth of Arrecina Tertulla

41 Q. Pomponius Secundus *cos. suff.*; assassination of Gaius
(Jan. 24), accession of Claudius; birth of Britannicus
(Feb. 12); Q. Marcius Barea *procos. Africae*

42 ?Sabinus II in Britain

43 L. Vitellius *cos. II ord.*; Vespasian *leg. leg. II Aug.*
in Britain; ?birth of L. Junius Caesennius Paetus;
?Berenice marries M. Julius Alexander

44 P. Pomponius Secundus *cos. suff.*; Sabinus II *cos. suff.*;
?Vespasian receives *ornamenta triumphalia*

45 Ti. Plautius Silvanus *cos. suff.*

46 Berenice marries Herod of Chalcis

47 L. Vitellius *cos. III ord.*; ?Vespasian returns from
Britain; ??Vespasian (and Sabinus II) adlected *inter
patricios*; ?TITUS' EDUCATION AT COURT

48 A. Vitellius *cos. ord.*; L. Vitellius *cos. suff.*; death
of Messallina; death of Herod of Chalcis

49 Claudius marries Agrippina

50 L. Domitius Ahenobarbus adopted by Claudius; ?Sabinus
II consular legate of Moesia

51 Vespasian *cos. suff.*; death of L. Vitellius; birth of
Domitian (Oct. 24); TITUS' 12th BIRTHDAY (Dec. 30)

52 Barea Soranus *cos. suff.*; ??birth of Domitilla II

53 ?Birth of Domitia Longina; ?birth of Sabinus IV

54 Death of Claudius (Oct. 13), accession of Nero

55 Death of Britannicus; TITUS' 16th BIRTHDAY (Dec. 30)

56 ?Sabinus II *praefectus urbi*

59 Death of Agrippina (March) and of A. Plautius (P 345);
TITUS' 20th BIRTHDAY (Dec. 30)

60 ?TITUS' VIGINTIVIRATE; ?birth of T. Flavius Clemens

61 L. Caesennius Paetus *cos. ord.* with P. Petronius
Turpilianus; ?TITUS' MILITARY TRIBUNATE; ?Plautius

Silvanus consular legate of Moesia; ?Q. Petillius
Cerialis Caesius Rufus *leg. leg. IX Hisp.* in Britain; P.
Petronius Turpilianus consular legate of Britain; ?Barea
Soranus *procos. Asiae*

62 L. Caesennius Paetus consular legate in east

63 ?Vespasian *procos. Africae*; P. Petronius Turpilianus
curator aquarum; ?TITUS MARRIES ARRECINA TERTULLA; Ti.
Julius Alexander with Corbulo in the east

64 ?TITUS QUAESTOR; birth of Julia; death of Arrecina
Tertulla; ?TITUS MARRIES MARCIA FURNILLA; ?birth of
Domitilla III

65 ?TITUS DIVORCES MARCIA FURNILLA; Pisonian conspiracy
revealed; ?Berenice marries Polemo of Cilicia; death of
Q. Plautius Lateranus

66 Outbreak of Jewish revolt (May); Ti. Julius Alexander
prefect of Egypt; Berenice leaves Polemo; death of
Barea Soranus, Thrasea Paetus and (ca. Oct.) Corbulo;
defeat of Cestius Gallus (Nov.); ?Vespasian appointed to
suppress revolt (Dec.)

67 Vespasian reaches Antioch (Feb.); campaign of 67 (see
Table 8); TITUS MEETS BERENICE (July) and WELCOMES
MUCIANUS (Sept./Oct.)

68 Campaign of 68 (see Table 8); Vespasian hears of Vindex's
revolt (ca. March 11); ?TITUS IN REGULAR CONTACT WITH
MUCIANUS; death of Nero (June 9); accession of Galba;
Vespasian, in Caesarea, hears of Nero's death (end June);
dismissal of Sabinus II (Nov.); ?confirmation by Galba
of Vespasian's Judaean command (Dec.); John of Gischala
enters Jerusalem (? Dec.); TITUS LEAVES TO VISIT GALBA
IN ROME

69 Vitellius hailed as *imperator* by Lower German Legions
(Jan. 2); death of Galba (Jan. 15) and accession of
Otho; TITUS AT CORINTH (Jan./Feb.), AT PAPHOS, ?VISITS
MUCIANUS IN SYRIA (Feb.); Flavians plan to usurp power
(Feb.); TITUS' NEGOTIATIONS WITH TI. JULIUS ALEXANDER,
MUCIANUS, BERENICE AND AGRIPPA (Feb./June); Sabinus II
reappointed *praefectus urbi* (March); Vespasian commences
69 campaign (?March/April); death of Otho (April 16),
Vitellius recognized by senate; Simon, son of Giora,
enters Jerusalem (April); death of Ananus; Mt Carmel
Conference (May/June); proclamation of Vespasian by
Egyptian legions (July 1); Berytus Conference; depart-
ure of Mucianus (mid-August); Vespasian and TITUS IN

SYRIA AND PALESTINE (?until Sept.); battle of Cremona (Oct.); Vespasian and TITUS IN ALEXANDRIA (Oct./Dec.); death of Vitellius (Dec. 20) and of Sabinus II; TITUS' ALLEGED COMPLAINT AGAINST MUCIANUS

70 TITUS *COS. ORD.*; Tettius Julianus loses and regains his praetorship (by Jan. 3); *Lex de Imperio Vespasiani* (by Jan. 9); CAPTURE OF AGRIPPA'S WALL (May 5), OF SECOND WALL (May 14) AND OF ANTONIA (July 17); DESTRUCTION OF TEMPLE (Aug. 10); TITUS HAILED IMPERATOR BY LEGIONS IN JERUSALEM; Vespasian leaves Alexandria for Rome (Aug./ Sept.); UPPER CITY BURNED (Sept. 8); TITUS AT MARITIME CAESAREA (Oct. 24), AT BERYTUS (Nov. 17) AND AT ZEUGMA (?Dec.); L. Caesennius Paetus reaches Syria (Dec.); TITUS OFFICIALLY IMPERATOR

71 TITUS VISITS ANTIOCH, JERUSALEM, MEMPHIS, ALEXANDRIA (April 25); REACHES ROME (June); JOINT TRIUMPH (June); TRIB. POT. I (July 1); Domitian *cos. suff.*; TITUS IMP. II (by Dec.)

72 TITUS COS. II ORD; Mucianus *cos. III suff.*; TITUS PRAETORIAN PREFECT (?March) and IMP. IV (by Dec.)

73 Domitian *cos. II ord.*; TITUS CENSOR (April) and IMP. V (by Dec.)

74 TITUS COS. III ORD.; Petillius Cerialis, Plautius Silvanus, Vibius Crispus and Eprius Marcellus *cos. II suff.*; TITUS IMP. VIII (by Dec.)

75 TITUS COS. IV ORD.; Domitian *cos. III suff.*; arrival of Berenice in Rome

76 TITUS COS. V ORD.; Domitian *cos. IV suff.*; ?Tampius Flavianus and Pompeius Silvanus *cos. II suff.*; TITUS IMP. XII (by Dec.)

77 TITUS COS. VI ORD.; Domitian *cos. V suff.*; ?Agricola consular legate in Britain

78 ?Heras beheaded, Diogenes flogged; Agricola's second season in Britain; TITUS IMP. XIV (by Dec.)

79 TITUS COS. VII ORD.; Domitian *cos. VI suff.*; death of Eprius Marcellus, of Caecina Alienus and of Julius Sabinus and his wife; dismissal of Berenice; death of Vespasian (June 24) and ACCESSION OF TITUS; death of elder Pliny (Aug. 24); Agricola's third season in Britain

80 TITUS COS. VIII ORD.; Domitian *cos. VII ord.*; *consecratio* of Vespasian; Agricola's fourth season; L. Funisulanus Vettonianus in Dalmatia, L. Tettius Julianus in Numidia, C. Tettius Africanus in Egypt and Ti. Julius, Aug. lib., *a rationibus* in Rome; Berenice returns and departs; TITUS IMP. XV (by Dec.)

81 L. Flavius Silva Nonius Bassus and L. ?Asinius Pollio Verrucosus *cos. ord.*; opening of Flavian Amphitheatre (March/April); Agricola's fifth season; Sabinus III designated *cos. ord.* for 82; TITUS IMP. XVII, DEATH OF TITUS (Sept. 13)

INDEXES

1　INDEX OF PERSONS

Roman emperors and members of their families are entered under their conventional or most familiar names; most other Romans are catalogued according to their *gentilicia*. Consular dates and *PIR* numbers, when available,are given in brackets, and, unless otherwise stated, the letters A - L are to be interpreted as *PIR²* A - L, and M - V as *PIR¹* M - V.

INDEXES

2   INDEX OF TOPICS

Reference should also be made to the Table of Contents; items listed there are not repeated in this index.

221

APPENDICES

1 LITERARY PASSAGES CITED

Passages merely cited without further comment are not included.

Augustine, *De Ciuitate Dei*
5.21   26 n.40

Aurelius Victor, *Caesares*
10.6   26 n.40
10.11   179 n.239

Caesar, *Bellum Gallicum*
1.39.5   176 n.192

Censorinus, *De Die Natali*
18.14   104 n.33

Digesta
1.2.2.32   176 n.194
49.14.1.1-3   176 n.197

Dio Cassius
49.7.6   78
61.30.1   16
61.32.5   27 n.59
66.18.1   158 n.6
66.18.5   26 n.40
66.19.1-2   115
66.19.3   141,146
67.1.2   139
79.18.1-3   150-151

Epitome de Caesaribus
10.4   108 n.81

Eutropius, *Breuiarum ab Urbe Condita*
7.21   26 n.40

Frontinus, *Strategemata*
4.2.3   110 n.94

Josephus, *Bellum Iudaicum*
3.7   35
3.65   36
3.236-239   17
3.298   36
3.397   65 n.20
3.401   65 n.21
4.35   112-113 n.123
4.87-88   66 n.23
5.45-46   50
6.133   70 n.63
7.121   100 n.5
7.157   78

Juvenal, *Satires*
1.131-134   106-107 n.55
4.89-90   108 n.75,
                    112 n.122
4.107   170 n.145
6.156-158   75 n.103

Orosius, *Historiae Aduersum Paganos*
7.9.5-6   70 n.65

223

2.2	158 n.5
2.5	66 n.33, 110 n.92
2.8	178 n.210
2.77	30 n.92, 107 n.65
2.79	76 n.112
2.81	74 n.97
2.82	106 n.48
2.84	132
2.85	97, 110 n.110
2.97	31 n.119
3.8	166 n.102
3.48	166 n.103
3.66	31 n.115
4.7	32 n.132, 167 n.110
4.39	97, 111 n.111
4.40	97, 112 n.113
4.52	88, 89, 107 nn.63, 67

Valerius Flaccus, *Argonautica*

1.13-14	70 n.65

APPENDICES

2   COINS, INSCRIPTIONS AND PAPYRI CITED

Documents merely cited without further comment are not included.

Mattingly, 1923		5.4312	105 n.36
p.360, No. 261	163 n.50	6.944	68 n.50
		6.1246	174 n.171
Mattingly, 1930		6.1258	174 n.171
p.121, Nos.565,566	162 n.42	6.1984	104 n.14
p.128, No.590	163 n.50	6.2059	173 n.169
p.140, No.634	162 n.44	6.31766	32 n.131
p.147, No.652	162 n.44	8.875	104 n.36
p.215, Nos.870-872	66 n.28	14.354	24 n.8
p.258, No.177	162 n.44		
p.259, Nos.178-181	162 n.43	*IGRR*	
p.260, No.188	162 n.41	3.223	159 n.13, 161 n.34
pp.269 ff.,Nos.221-	163 n.51	3.1244	60
225			
p.281, No.261	163 n.48	*ILS*	
pp.281 ff.,Nos.261-		157	159 n.21
280	162 n.47	254	79
p.292, No.305#	163 n.49	258	104 nn.29, 30
		260	105 n.36
AE		264	102 n.19
1928, 82	75 n.102	986	122, 163 n.52
1953, 179	174-175 n.180	988	69 n.55
1962, 288	146, 175 n.185	992	109 n.86
1972, 574	167 n.108	995	23 n.6
1973, 141	23 n.6	1015	165 n.87
1973, 500	170 n.143	1839	35 n.136
		8903	73 n.80
CIL		8904	73 n.80
2.3250	105 n.36	9485	163 n.86
2.5217	105 n.36		
3.318	161 n.33		

Coins, Inscriptions and Papyri Cited

McCrum and Woodhead, 1966

11	173 n.169
53	68 n.50
87	79
102	104 nn.29, 30
152	101 n.14
261	122, 163 n.52
309	165 n.87
315	165 n.86
408b	174 n.171
409	174 n.171
462	171-172 n.154

P. Berl.

8334	106 n.53, 137-138, 169 nn.132-135

P. Oxy.

2725	72 n.76

.

To most students of the Roman Empire, Titus is known mainly for his capture of Jerusalem (depicted vividly on the Arch of Titus in Rome) and for his liaison with Berenice. As successor to Vespasian, his reign encapsulates much that is distinctive about the Flavian principate as it developed after the critical year of the Four Emperors. Overshadowed by his own successor, Domitian, Titus repays attention as his own man, not only for himself but for what he can show us of the *cursus honorum* of a successful general and, eventually, ruler.

The book covers his early career to 66 AD, with stress on the family's background, their patrons and the implications of his two marriages; the Judaean campaigns of 67 and 68 AD, his part in the siege of Jerusalem, his voyage in the east and the significance of Agrippa II and Berenice. It also examines Titus' position in Vespasian's reign and an attempt is made to assess the alleged conflict with Mucianus. Finally various aspects of his reign are considered in detail — economic policy, conflict with Domitian, administrative and foreign policy, his *amici* and senior officials, public works and the imperial cult.